Timetabling

Keith Johnson

First published 1980
Reprinted 1980, 1981 (twice), 1982, 1983, 1985, 1993, 1995

© Keith Johnson 1980

Set in 10/12 Times Roman

Printed and bound in Great Britain by
TJI Digital, Padstow, Cornwall

British Library Cataloguing in Publication Data

Johnson, Keith
  Timetabling.
  1. Schedules, School
  I. Title
  371.2'42   LB1038

ISBN 0 7487 1077 9

Foreword

John Tomlinson, Chairman of the Schools Council

We are in the thick of discussing the school curriculum. Political and professional attention has swung from the structure of the schools to the content and process. What should be taught? In what mix? How should it be taught? Who should decide all this, and how much or which aspects should be decided nationally, by the LEA or by the school? This is a healthy and necessary development and will, no doubt, take some years to reach any coherence.

Meanwhile, and indeed after any kind of agreement is reached, schools will have to make timetables. The timetable is the practical embodiment of the curriculum. All the fine talk about skills, knowledge, concepts, areas of human experience, the interrelationship of subjects and the totality of the curriculum is set at naught if the school does not have an efficient engine for changing the theory into practice. At the end of the day, the teachers (as individuals and teams) have to be allocated to spend time (in differing spans) with the children (divided into groups appropriate for the purpose in hand), and it all has to be done with the constraints imposed by the building (or buildings) and the balance of practical and general accommodation available. If the translation is done well, the intentions for an integrated curriculum, the sum of whose parts adds up to the intended whole is achieved. Done badly, the timetable actually inhibits the intentions of those who planned the curriculum and committed themselves to its value system. As in all human organizations, therefore, the most mechanical-seeming process needs as much care and thought as the more obviously profound. Those who neglect the detailed and the arduous (or, even worse, regard as beneath their concern) find their grand designs frustrated.

I welcome this book because it approaches its task in what seems to be exactly the right spirit. Get your philosophy of the curriculum and teaching method clear first. Then take pains and devise the best timetable circumstances allow. This practical and sometimes humorous guide will help and sustain those who use it and indirectly benefit generations of pupils.

Contents

Acknowledgements

1 Timetabling

1.1	Introduction	9
1.2	The flow chart	10
1.3	A timetable of timetabling	13

2 Option schemes

2.1	Introduction	14
2.2	Types of option pools — 'Free choice', 'Faculty', 'Courses'	15
2.3	Methods of determining the option pools	20
2.4	Obtaining the pupils' choices — Option Booklets and Option Forms	22
2.5	Using microcomputers in schools	25
2.6	Analysing the pupils' choices — part 1: the Clash Table	26
2.7	Deciding the subjects in the pools — worked example.	27
2.8	Part 2: comparing the option pools with the pupils' choices	30
2.9	Part 3: unfitted pupils	32
2.10	Part 4: option group lists	33
2.11	Sixth Year options	33
2.12	Other computer programs	33
2.13	Summary	34

3 Staff deployment analysis

3.1	Introduction	35
3.2	Worked example — 4th Year	36
3.3	Worked example — 1st Year	39
3.4	Short cuts	41
3.5	The Sixth Form	41
3.6	The contact ratio	42
3.7	The Curriculum Equation	43
3.8	Relative bonus	43
3.9	Worked example	44
3.10	The nomogram	45
3.11	Sixth Forms	45
3.12	Summary	48

4 Collecting the Data

4.1	Introduction	49
4.2	Matching the departments to the curriculum	50
4.3	The Curriculum Plan	51
4.4	The Staffing Forms	53
4.5	Checking the Staffing Forms	55
4.6	The Staff Loading Chart	55

5 Timetabling Test 1 — The Combing Chart

5.1	Introduction	58
5.2	Teacher teams	59
5.3	The principle of compatibility	62
5.4	Choosing teacher teams — worked example	64
5.5	The Combing Chart — worked example	65
5.6	The Combing Chart for more than one department — worked example	67
5.7	Schematic diagrams	71
5.8	The principle of compatibility and time	72
5.9	The principle of compatability and class-combinations	73
5.10	The principle of compatability and room-combinations	75
5.11	Summary	75

6 Timetabling Test 2 — The Conflict Matrix

6.1	Introduction	76
6.2	The Conflict Matrix — worked example	77
6.3	Conflict Matrices for more than two year-groups	80
6.4	Including the effect of period-breakdown — worked example	81
6.5	Including the effect of other resources — rooms, equipment, part-time teachers	84
6.6	Using a microcomputer	84
6.7	Summary	85

7 Timetable Test 3 — Accommodation

7.1	Introduction	86
7.2	The rooming fraction	87
7.3	Priorities — worked example	89
7.4	The Rooming Equation	90
7.5	The nomogram	91
7.6	Johnson's Rule	92
7.7	Worked example	92
7.8	Summary	94

8 Other timetable checks

8.1	Introduction	95
8.2	Zarraga's Rule	96
8.3	Balancing the teaching power for lower school classes	97
8.4	Option pools for the Lower Sixth and the Upper Sixth	98
8.5	Minority subjects in the Sixth Form	99
8.6	Deciding priorities — fixed points, part-time teachers, split-site schools etc.	101
8.7	Summary	104

9 Scheduling

9.1	Introduction	105
9.2	Six timetable models	106
9.3	Ten rules for scheduling	114
9.4	Worked example	119
9.5	Nine tactics and moves	120
9.6	Fitting a difficult item	126
9.7	Allowing for different period-breakdowns	127
9.8	Improving the quality	128
9.9	Rooming	129
9.10	Checking the timetable	130
9.11	Distributing the timetable	131
9.12	Assessing your timetable	132
9.13	Alternative timetable cycles	133
9.14	Block timetabling	133
9.15	Summary	134

10 Computer Timetabling

10.1	Introduction	135
10.2	The Nor-Data system	137
10.3	The SPL system	138
10.4	The Oxford school timetabling system	139
10.5	The future	139

Appendices

1	A complete flow chart of curriculum planning	140
2	21 curriculum formulae	144
3	Using the computer program	148

The following are complete listings of the programs with full explanation.

4	OPT1 — Drawing a Clash Table and writing a data tape	150
5	OPT2 — Fitting the pupils' choices to the option pools	155
6	OPT3 — Editing the data tape	161
7	OPT4 — Printing option group lists	165
8	OPT5 — Printing option group lists	169
9	OPT6 — Printing pupils' option timetables	172
10	TT1 — Staff deployment analysis	175
11	TT2 — Combing Chart	188
12	TT3 — The Conflict Matrix	192
13	TT4 — Zarraga's Rule	197
14	TT5 — Timetable memory	201
15	TT6 — Printing individual timetables	203

Bibliography 212

Index 214

Acknowledgements

It is impossible to acknowledge all the people who have contributed to my knowledge of timetabling in many discussions over many years, but among those whose particular contribution I can remember are: Mike Zarraga, formerly of the School Timetabling Applications Group; Peter Thompson, formerly Senior Secondary Inspector in Manchester; Donald Moore, formerly Head of Wilbraham High School; I.B. Butterworth, HMI and Fred Tye, Director of the North-West Educational Management Centre; Paul Murphy and Steve Bates, members of the Manchester Schools Timetabling Group.

1 Timetabling

1.1 Introduction
1.2 The flow chart
1.3 A timetable of timetabling

Timetabling is probably the most important single event in the school year. The completed timetable may well rule the lives of a thousand pupils and seventy staff for the 200 days in the school year, period by period, bell by bell. Such a powerful tool may easily make or break teachers and teaching situations, may easily distort or destroy the curricular philosophy of the school.

Timetabling has been called the art of compromise. From a given set of data there are likely to be many possible solutions, each involving compromises which detract from the ideal. Clearly we wish to obtain the solution with the fewest, least important compromises. This solution will give a timetable with the best quality — a timetable which is *enabling,* not restrictive, so that the teaching staff may develop to the full the curricular aims of the school.

The aim of this book is to describe ways of achieving a quality timetable by methods which are as logical and painless as possible. If you are already a timetabler yourself, I hope you will find it of interest to compare my methods with your own. If you have yet to try your first timetable, I hope this book will help to launch you gently, at the shallow end. Even if you intend never to do any timetabling at all, I hope you will find these pages helpful in reducing the mystique surrounding timetabling — the mystique which too often allows a timetabler to end a discussion by saying, without reasons, 'It can't be done'. I feel sure schools can only benefit by a more widespread understanding of the language and the problems of timetabling, so that discussions — whether in the Head's Room, the Staff Room or in Staff Meetings — can take place within a framework of informed opinion.

10   *Timetabling*

Flow chart

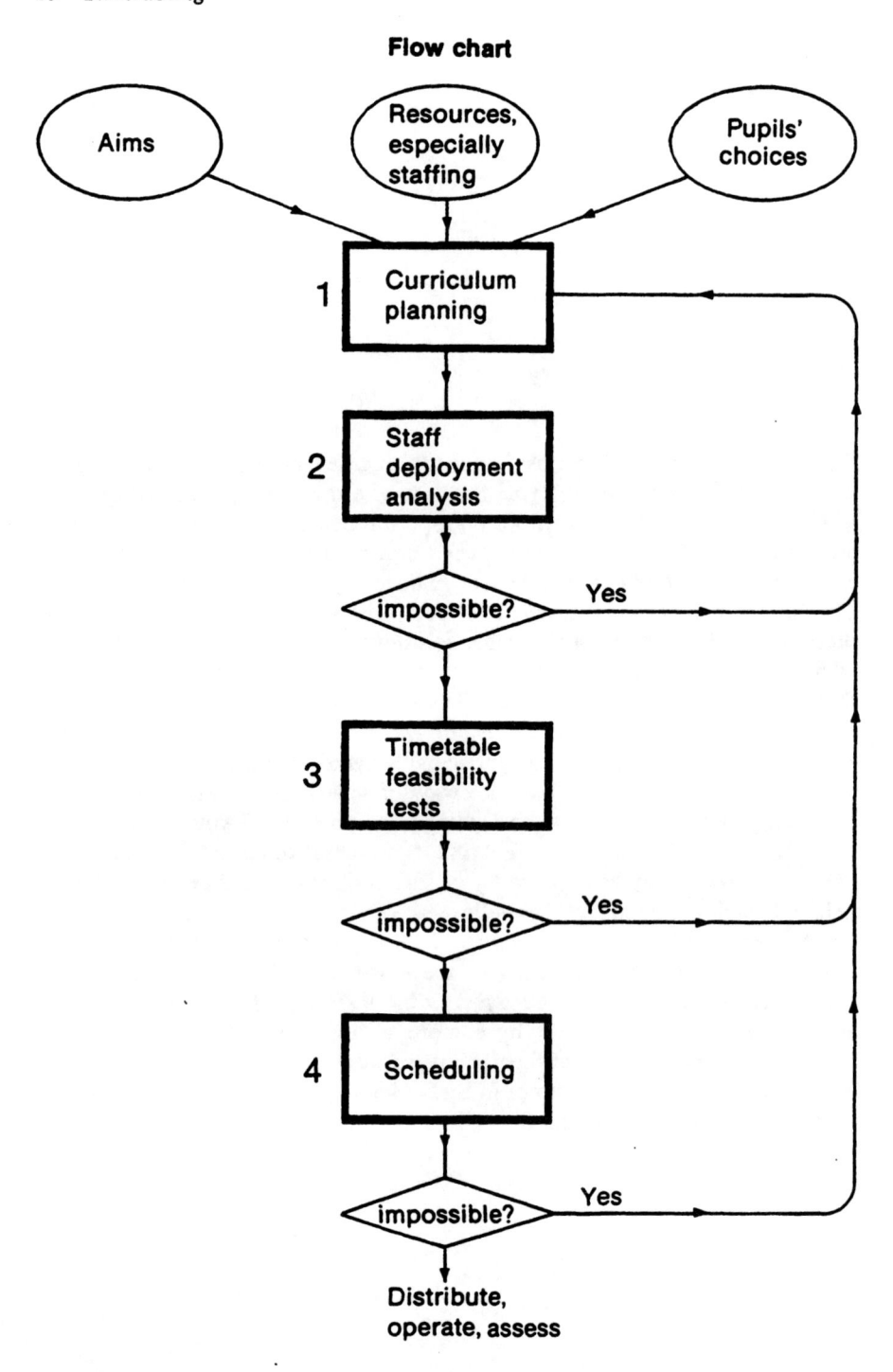

Figure 1   A more detailed flow chart is shown in Appendix 1.

1.2 The flow chart

The activity which is usually called 'timetabling' (the fitting of classes, teachers, rooms into particular times of the week) should more properly be called scheduling. It is only a part of the overall process, as the flow chart shows. The flow chart has four main parts:

1 Curriculum

By considering the aims of the school (preferably laid down in writing for all members of staff) and the available resources (particularly staffing and accommodation) a *curriculum plan* is produced. This will show the subjects and the numbers of periods to be provided for each group of pupils throughout the school. The greatest attention is likely to be given to the 3rd Year or 4th Year where pupils are given some choice in the subjects that they will study. Most schools take some account of their pupils' preferences when deciding the groups or 'pools' of options. This is discussed in more detail in chapter 2.

2 Analysis

In order to see whether this curriculum plan is feasible, some analysis of staffing should take place. This may be done by counting the number of periods required. Another method is that originated by T.I. Davies and often called 'curriculum analysis' or more properly, *staff deployment analysis*. This method allows us to compare classes and year-groups in order to see the distribution throughout the school of our most important resource, staffing. In some cases (for example, when newly joining a school or when the size of the intake is changing) it may be more useful to consider this analysis as the first step in the flow chart, to be completed before deciding the curriculum plan. The method is discussed in chapter 3.

The events covered by steps 1 and 2 normally take place during the Autumn and Spring terms.

3 Timetable tests

Later, during the scheduling stage, problems will arise and the assigning of a class or a teacher will appear to be impossible. But is it really impossible? Is there a mathematical impossibility in the data or is it merely the timetabler's inability to see the solution? Clearly, it helps if most or all of the mathematical impossibilities have been removed earlier — the timetabler is then more likely to persevere in the hope of finding a solution with little or no compromise.

There is no known test for showing whether a given set of data will produce a timetable. However there are tests for showing whether a timetable is *im*possible. These feasibility tests are described in chapters 5–8. Despite the temptation to rush to the final stage, it is essential to apply some or all of the tests if you are to achieve a timetable of the highest quality. These tests will normally be completed in May or June.

4 Scheduling

This is the integration of the 5 variables — teachers, subjects, classes, rooms, time — into a viable pattern. It is a kind of 5-dimensional jigsaw, built up with the aid of a timetable 'model' by following certain rules. These are discussed in chapters 9 and 10. The scheduling is normally completed in July.

The list on page 13 outlines the sequence of events during the school year. A detailed flow chart is given in Appendix 1.

A timetable of timetabling

Autumn Term
- Evaluation
    - Distribute timetables and details of option groups to pupils
    - Interview pupils who now wish to change options
    - Discuss and evaluate the new timetable, via Heads of Departments and Staff Room
    - Staff deployment analysis?
    - Review of curriculum policy by Management Team
    - Curriculum Study Group reports?

Spring Term
- Options
    - Careers advice to 3rd Year
    - Options Booklet — Options Form
    - 3rd Year examinations and reports?
    - Parents' Evening, Careers Convention?
    - Option Forms vetted
    - Choices analysed
    - Option pools determined

Summer Term
- Data
    - Staffing checks — staff deployment analysis?
    - Curriculum plan
    - Staffing Forms to Heads of Departments
    - Staffing Forms vetted
    - Staff Loading Chart
- Tests
    - Timetable test 1 — Combing Chart
    - Timetable test 2 — Conflict Matrix
    - Timetable test 3 — rooming
    - Other timetable tests
    - Consultation with staff as necessary
- Scheduling
    - Scheduling; compromise and consultation as necessary
    - Staff and class timetables; homework timetables

Figure 2

2 Option schemes

2.1 Introduction
2.2 Types of option pools — 'Free choice', 'Faculty', 'Courses'
2.3 Methods of determining the option pools
2.4 Obtaining the pupils' choices — Options Booklets and Options Forms
2.5 Using microcomputers in schools
2.6 Analysing the pupils' choices — part 1: the Clash Table
2.7 Deciding the subjects in the pools — worked example
2.8 Part 2: comparing the option pools with the pupils' choices
2.9 Part 3: unfitted pupils
2.10 Part 4: option group lists
2.11 Sixth Year options
2.12 Other computer programs
2.13 Summary

In most British secondary schools, the pupils are allowed some choice in their curriculum for the last two years of compulsory schooling. There may be some element of choice earlier (for example in the introduction of a second foreign language), but this chapter is concerned with the option pools offered to pupils at the age of thirteen or fourteen. An option pool is defined as a set of subjects or teaching groups which are timetabled to occur simultaneously and from which a pupil must choose one subject.

In some schools, option pools may account for 70% of the school week. In recent years there has been a move towards a larger common core and a reduced number of option pools. However few schools are likely to remove options entirely and so the problems associated with option pools and their timetabling remain with us.

Option pool structures

A 'Free choice' structure (heterogeneous pools)

pool 1	Astron	or	Lit	or	Comm	or	Mwk
2	Phys	or	Hist	or	Fre	or	Nwk
3	Germ	or	Art	or	Chem	or	TD
4	Biol	or	Wwk	or	Typ	or	Geog
5	Phys	or	Hist	or	DSc	or	Mus

B 'Faculty' structure (homogeneous pools)

pool 1	Hist	or	Hist	or	Geog	or	Geog			Humanities
2	Fre	or	Fre	or	Eur St	or	Eur St			Languages
3	Phys	or	Chem	or	Biol	or	Gen Sc			Science
4	Art	or	Wwk	or	Mwk	or	Dsc	or	Nwk	Creative/Practical

C 'Courses' structure

A	B	C	D
Academic	Technical	Commercial	General
Hist	TD	Comm	Art
Geog	Mwk	Typ	Craft
Fre	Wwk	Off Pr	DSc
Phys	Eng Sc	Sh-hd	Typ
Chem	Phys	Biol	Gen Sc

Figure 3

16 *Timetabling*

2.2 Types of option pools

Option pool structures may be classified into three types. These are shown in the tables in Figure 3. The examples are based on real schools. They do not show the compulsory part of the curriculum (English, Mathematics, Physical Education, Religious Education, General Studies etc.)

A *'Free choice' structure (heterogeneous pools)*

In this type of structure, the subjects are arranged so as to try to accommodate all the pupils' requests — the school is trying to provide 'customer satisfaction'.

In the example shown, the numbers of groups imply that the scheme is being offered to a 'band' of about 90 pupils (perhaps a half-year group or one-third of a year-group). However the pools could easily be extended in width to be applied to a whole year-group, because none of the pools is likely to demand all the school's resources. (For example, none of the pools shown needs more than one science laboratory or more than one craft room.)

However there are some disadvantages with this type of option pool. Philosophically, it looks rather odd. For example, pool 1:

Astronomy *or* English Literature *or* Commerce *or* Metalwork

presents a strange choice to the pupil. In conjunction with the other pools, it allows pupils to select an unbalanced curriculum (for example: Astronomy, Needlework, Art, Typing and Domestic Science). The school must then devise rules, sometimes quite complicated, to ensure that pupils select a balanced curriculum (for example, at least one science, at least one of the 'humanities'). All the choices will need to be checked (by the Director of Studies, Careers Tutor, Year-Tutor, House-Tutor or Form-Tutor).

When it comes to timetabling these heterogeneous pools, difficulties will arise. You may wish to timetable some science 'sets' in the 3rd Year (i.e. two or more science groups timetabled to occur 'in parallel', at the same time). This means that a group of science teachers must be free to teach the 3rd Year as a team. This is less likely to happen with a heterogeneous structure because the science groups are dispersed throughout the option pools and so the science teachers are neither teaching nor free as a team. Similarly with the Languages Department.

If the option pools are changed from year to year to satisfy the pupils' choices then the number of timetable clashes is likely to increase and prohibit any setting in the lower school (unless several members of staff teach lower school classes only). The heterogeneous nature of the pools almost certainly prevents the timetabling of departmental conference periods and precludes the possibility of attempting 'block' timetabling.

In this context it is important to remember that it is *teachers* who cause clashes on the timetable, not subjects. Until the curriculum plan shows staffing as well as subjects, one cannot be sure about where the clashes will occur (this is particularly difficult when some staff teach more than one subject in the pools).

A further disadvantage of heterogeneous pools arises in the teaching groups. In the example shown, there are two groups for Physics but the groups are in different pools. This implies that each Physics group will include the full range of ability of the band. This may lead to a difficult teaching situation. A tactic sometimes adopted is to pair subjects in the way shown by Physics and History in Figure 3A (pools 2 and 5). The aim is to have a better Physics group paired with a poorer History group and vice versa. Such tactics do not work well in practice because of the poor correlation between abilities in the subjects concerned. Of course, each Physics group shown in the diagram could really be two teaching groups or 'sets', but this is a move towards the second type of option pool.

Summary of heterogeneous pools

Advantages
1   Pupils' satisfaction rate is high.
2   Pools can be applied across a whole year-group (but see disadvantage 3).

Disadvantages
1   Rules and vetting are needed to ensure a balanced curriculum for each pupil (this may affect advantage 1).
2   Timetabling difficulties: setting in lower school, departmental meetings, block timetabling are limited or impossible.
3   Pools may enforce mixed-ability teaching in most or all subjects.

B   'Faculty' structure (homogeneous pools)
The word 'faculty' is not meant to imply that the school must be staffed, administered or accommodated in true faculties; only that similar subjects are grouped together in the curriculum (and thus on the timetable).

Figure 3B (page 15) shows a humanities pool, a languages pool, a science pool and a creative/practical pool.

In this type of structure, the educational philosophy is explicit: subjects within a pool have a similar methodology, content or skill. Physics *or* Chemistry is a valid option and is allowed: Physics *or* Art is not. The curriculum plan forces pupils to make a balanced choice and no extra rules are needed (although the pupils' choices still may need to be vetted with a view to career prospects).

With the pools shown in the diagram, there is no opportunity for a pupil to take two languages, two sciences or two humanities. However we shall see later how these can be accommodated with a 'bias' pool.

A disadvantage of homogeneous pools is that the satisfaction rate for fitting the pupils' choices is unlikely to be as high as with heterogeneous pools.

A further disadvantage may arise: most schools will not have sufficient resources to timetable homogeneous option pools across a full year-group (schools are unlikely to have the necessary number of science laboratories or craft rooms).

If homogeneous option pools are timetabled across half-year groups, then within each pool or 'faculty' most schools can offer a range of courses, aimed at different examination levels and thus reducing the spread of ability within each group. For example, the science department may offer a range of courses from O-level to CSE in one half-year and courses from CSE to non-examination in the other half-year. If it is argued that the 'hump' of the normal distribution curve is the wrong place at which to divide a population, then the pools and the courses for the two half-years may be identical. Alternatively, in a large school, the year-group may be divided into three ability-bands (and of course some bands may be more homogeneous, some more heterogeneous in structure).

The more homogeneous the option pools, the more likely that the timetable will benefit. If the languages teachers are scheduled *as a team* to teach a languages pool in the 4th Year, then it is likely that at other times they will be free *as a team* to teach languages sets in the 3rd Year. Similarly with other departments. In the same way, there is a greater likelihood that departmental conference periods can be timetabled and that 'block' timetabling can be used.

Summary of homogeneous pools

Advantages
1 The pools force a balanced curriculum.
2 Timetabling of sets and departmental periods is made easier.
3 A range of courses within each 'faculty' reduces the spread of ability within a group.

Disadvantages
1 The pupils' satisfaction rate is likely to be lower than with heterogeneous pools.
2 Homogeneous pools normally cannot be timetabled across a full year-group.

C 'Courses' structure
Figure 3C (page 15) shows a simple 'courses' structure. Such schemes are less common than previously, mostly because of the increased recognition of the need for a balanced curriculum.

This structure is fairly easy to timetable because each group in course A is independent of each group in courses B, C, and D (unless the same teacher or room is involved).

There are disadvantages: the satisfaction rate may be low (because a pupil choosing course A must study *all* of course A). Moreover a pupil choosing course A may have to take GCE examinations in every subject; a pupil in course B may have to take CSE examinations in every subject. As a variation, within each course there may be some option pools of either the homogeneous or heterogeneous type.

Summary of 'courses' structure

Advantages
1 Timetabling is easier.
2 They can be applied across a full year-group.

Disadvantages
1 The pupils' satisfaction rate is likely to be lower than with heterogeneous pools.
2 The curriculum is less likely to be balanced.
3 There may be a wide range of ability within a group unless pupils are persuaded into certain courses.
4 Examination targets for some pupils may be more restricted than in other structures.

So far we have looked at the three types of structure in their 'pure' form. In practice they are usually combined in ways which reduce their individual disadvantages. Examples of actual pools may be found in other books (see the bibliography.

D Combinations of homogeneous and heterogeneous pools

At the time of writing there is a growing recognition of the need for a more balanced curriculum. One way of achieving this is to give less choice to the pupils: increase the compulsory common core of the curriculum to 80% (or more) of the school week and allow only two (or fewer) option pools, probably of the heterogeneous type.

An alternative which is likely to be more acceptable in most schools, is to adopt a homogeneous pool structure with one addition: since the 'pure' homogeneous pools do not allow a pupil to follow his special interests by taking two sciences or two languages, we may add one (or two) heterogeneous 'bias' pools (Figure 4).

pool 1	Hist or Hist or Geog or Geog	Humanities
2	Fre or Fre or Eur St or Eur St	Languages
3	Phys or Chem or Biol or Gen Sc	Science
4	Art or Wwk or Mwk or Dsc or Nwk	Creative/Practical
5	Span or Hist or Phys or Biol	Bias

Figure 4

This example would allow pupils to study two humanities, two languages or two sciences depending on each pupil's personal bias. Obviously the pupils' satisfaction rate will depend upon the care with which the bias pool is determined.

For a band of less academic pupils, two bias pools may be more appropriate (for example, pools 4 and 5 in Figure 4 may be mixed up).

With care in choosing the number of groups and the contents of the bias pool (as detailed later in this chapter), a combination like this can preserve the advantages of both the homogeneous and heterogeneous types.

2.3 Methods of determining the option pools

Once the *type* of pool structure is decided by a school, the precise contents of each pool have to be determined. The method varies from school to school. For example:

School A
1. The Head or the Management Team decides the number of teaching groups for each subject and the arrangement of those groups in the pools on a philosophical basis (but with due regard to the limitations of staffing and accommodation).
2. The pupils (and their parents) are given information on the courses and relevant careers and then asked to choose one subject from each pool (possibly with a second choice as reserve).

School B
1. The pupils (with or without their parents) are asked in a preliminary survey to indicate five choices from a full list of subjects (with a warning that this is only a survey).
2. Using this information, the school (the Head or the Management Team) decides the number of groups for each subject (for example, 'one more Chemistry group this year, one less Biology group')
3. The school decides the arrangement of these groups within the pools without directly consulting the pupils' individual choices.
4. The pupils and their parents are given information about the courses and careers and then asked to choose one subject from each pool.
5. The Director of Studies, the Careers Tutor or Heads of Departments vet the replies for suitability.

School C
1. The pupils (and their parents) are given information about the examination courses and relevant careers.
2. If the pools are to be heterogeneous, pupils are given advice about a balanced curriculum.
3. The pupils are asked to choose five subjects, in order of preference, from a full list (with two other subjects as reserves) with a warning that the school cannot guarantee to offer the pupil all of his choices.
4. The replies are vetted for balance and, for some subjects, ability to take the course.
5. Using the pupils' replies, the school decides the number of groups for each subject.
6. The school uses the pupils' choices (and their order of preference) to decide the subjects in the bias pool (or all the pools in a heterogeneous structure).
7. Pupils who do not fit into the final arrangement of pools are interviewed and reassigned (preferably using their second-choice subjects).

Other permutations of events are possible, but of the three given here School C would seem to offer the best approach, in that it tries to respond as the needs of the school's population change from year to year.

It may be difficult to make a response that requires much less Needlework and much more Computer Studies, but it is relatively easy to make small changes in the grouping of subjects so as to increase the satisfaction of the pupils. Even a small increase in the motivation of the pupils and a consequent decrease in disruptive behaviour ought to make the effort worthwhile. To illustrate the sort of simple change I am suggesting, consider the two examples in Figure 5 of parts of 'homogeneous + bias' structures.

Scheme 1

| pool 3 | Phys | or | *Chem* | or | Chem | or | Biol | Science |
| pool 5 | Span | or | Hist | or | *Phys* | or | Biol | Bias |

Scheme 2

| pool 3 | Phys | or | *Phys* | or | Chem | or | Biol | Science |
| pool 5 | Span | or | Hist | or | *Chem* | or | Biol | Bias |

Figure 5

The numbers of groups, teachers and rooms are the same in each case; simply a Physics and a Chemistry group are interchanged. There is no clear preference on a philosophical basis. The better scheme cannot be determined until the choices of this particular group of children have been inspected to determine the satisfaction rates and the sizes of the teaching groups in each case. One scheme should give a better motivation and a better teaching atmosphere than the other.

There are two disadvantages to the procedure outlined under School C above. One is that pupils and parents may be upset, despite the warning in step 3, if they do not receive all of their first choices and have to be re-assigned (step 7). Explaining the reasons for the procedure helps to solve this problem. The second disadvantage is the length of time involved in analysing the pupils' choices. However this is mostly a routine task, ideally suited to the small microcomputers which are becoming increasingly common in our schools. Later in this chapter I shall show how such microcomputers can help us to analyse our pupils' requests in order to provide the best possible option scheme.

The remainder of this chapter follows the steps listed earlier under School C.

2.4 Obtaining the pupils' choices

Whether they are asked to choose a few subjects from a full list or one subject from each option pool, the pupils and their parents can expect to receive more than a single sheet of notes from the school. The decisions to be made are so important that parents can surely expect to receive comprehensive details in the form of an *Options Booklet*. An outline of such an Options Booklet is given in Figure 6.

Outline of an Options Booklet
(perhaps 30 pages long in A5 format)

Pupils' questions and answers

Why choose? Why choose now? Can I change my mind later? Can I take any subject? Which subjects are compulsory? How many do I choose? How should I choose? — do's and don't's. What is a good balance? How can I get careers advice? Will I definitely get the subjects I ask for?

Careers advice

Availability of Careers Teacher, reference to "Your Choice at 13+" (CRAC) Details of Parents' Evening or Careers Convention (if provided)

Assessment

Details of assessments made during the next two years — times of reports and examinations, relevance of 'mock' examinations, the times expected for homework etc.

At the end of the fifth year

The alternatives, including arrangements for entering the Sixth Form and the courses offered at present
Possibly a sample ideal Leaving Certificate, if you provide them

Examinations

The distinctions between GCE O-level, CSE, GCSE 16+, RSA etc.
The letters and numbers used in the grades and their meanings

The subjects offered

Perhaps 200 words on each, including:
— the aims, relevance and importance of the subject
— an outline of the course to be followed
— any special facilities available
— the style of the examination (continuous assessment etc.) perhaps including the proportion of marks to each part

Final questions

How do I fill in the Options Form?
What do I do if I need help?

Figure 6

24 *Timetabling*

Provided with the Options Booklet will be the *Options Form,* detailing either the option pools (as in Schools A and B) or the list of subjects from which a few are to be chosen (as in School C). In the latter case, it helps if the subjects are grouped into humanities, languages, sciences, creative/practical so that a balanced curriculum can be first chosen and later vetted more easily. Since large numbers of Options Forms will have to be inspected later, it helps (for right-handed people) if the subjects are shown in a vertical list to the right of the page with the spaces for the pupil to indicate his choices near the right hand edge. The instructions for the pupils (and their parents) should be clear and concise — it helps to have a practice in school before the Options Forms go home. The instructions should explain how to mark a '1' next to their first choice, a '2' for their second choice and so on. They should be told how to mark their reserve subjects (perhaps with a '6' and a '7'). If you are going to use the OPT1 computer program to analyse the pupils' choices, it helps to include a one-letter subject code next to each subject to save time and obviate mistakes later (see Appendix 4). The Options Form might appear like this:

```
          Laura Norder High School
                Options Form

How to complete                Geography (G)    ..........
The Option Form                   History (H)   ....1....
..................            English literature (L)  ....5....
(detailed step-by-step)
instructions)
.....................             French (F)   ....3....
.....................             German (D)   ..........
.....................
.....................
.....................             Biology (B)   ....6....
                                  Chemistry (C) ..........
                              General Science (S) ....4....
                                  Physics (P)  ..........

If you have a                       Art (A)    ....2....
particular career           Computer Studies (X) ..........
in mind, write                  Fashion (N)    ..........
it here ..............      Home Economics (E) ..........
                                  Music (M)    ....7....
                                     etc.
```

Figure 7

The distribution of the Options Booklet and the Options Form will normally take place during the Spring Term — the earlier the better, although some schools may be limited by the wish to hold 3rd Year examinations either before the choices are made or before the choices are vetted. A Parents' Evening (perhaps with a Careers Convention) ought to occur before the Options Forms are returned to school.

When all the Forms are received, they ought to be vetted (by the Director of Studies, Careers Tutor, Year-Tutor, House-Tutor, Form-Tutor or Heads of Departments) to check the following points:

1 Does each Option Form have different numbers clearly written against the correct number of subjects?
2 Has the pupil followed your rules in choosing a balanced curriculum and is the choice of subjects a sensible one?
3 If the pupil has a particular career in mind, do the chosen subjects allow for that career?
4 In each of his chosen subjects, does the pupil have sufficient ability to cope with the work? To assist in this, the Director of Studies might request Heads of Departments or Subject Teachers to provide class lists with two groups of pupils marked as follows:
   (a) The top quarter of the class or those with a particular aptitude for that subject marked with a + sign.
   (b) The bottom quarter of the class or those with a distinct weakness in that subject marked with a − sign.

Having received the pupils' information and vetted it, how can we analyse it in the most convenient way? Since this can be done either manually or by computer, a word here about microcomputers.

2.5 Using microcomputers in schools

Increasingly, computers are likely to be used in performing many of the tedious administrative tasks in our schools (as well as being used in Computer Studies courses). Already computers are being used to update class lists (either monthly or yearly), sort lists of pupils by alphabetical order, ages or addresses, address envelopes to parents, write letters containing standard paragraphs, provide a weighted listing of staff names to cover for absent colleagues, compute the age-group numbers needed for Form 7 and compute marks and positions from examination papers.

Some of the programs on the market require large computers, but the programs I have included in the appendices of this book were written for a minimal system — in fact for a Commodore PET-8 microcomputer which cost less than £500 and was needed for a Computer Studies course. A printer is a very useful addition, but not absolutely necessary as information can be copied by hand from the TV screen.

No doubt microcomputers seem very strange for the first hour or so, but in

26 *Timetabling*

fact they are slightly easier to use than a typewriter (in that typing mistakes are easier to correct than on a typewriter).

The programs in this book have been designed to be as idiot-proof, as 'goof-proof', as possible and they all contain many prompts so that the machine appears to 'talk' you through the program.

The listings given in the appendices can be typed directly on to a PET computer and then saved on tape for the next time. Alternatively, ready-to-run tapes of the programs can be obtained from the address given at the back of the book (page 148).

Schools possessing Research 380Z, Tandy TRS80 or Apple machines should find that most of each program can be used directly as I have tried to write the programs in a 'portable' BASIC. However some of the print statements will have to be changed in order to get the correct display on the screen or a printer.

2.6 Analysing the pupils' choices — part 1: The Clash Table

In order to see the number of pupils requesting each subject (and hence the number of groups for each subject) and to see the ways in which these subjects might fit together into option pools, we need a *Clash Table*. This consists of a list of the subjects along two sides of a square, with the number of clashes at each intersection of a row and a column.

Consider this example of a Clash Table:

M	5	3	3	4	2	1	2	2	8	**10**
A	20	10	10	—	4	5	8	10	**25**	8
S	15	10	5	1	11	3	3	**20**	10	2
P	30	25	20	2	10	20	**40**	3	8	2
C	25	15	10	1	10	**30**	20	3	5	1
B	35	20	25	3	**40**	10	10	11	4	2
D	15	7	12	**15**	3	1	2	1	—	4
F	50	30	**55**	12	25	10	20	5	10	3
G	30	**50**	30	7	20	15	25	10	10	3
H	**75**	30	50	15	35	25	30	15	20	5
	H	G	F	D	B	C	P	S	A	M

Figure 8

The table shows the results of 10 subjects offered to an 'academic' band of three forms (90 pupils). The pupils were asked to choose 4 subjects each, with a view to providing 4 option pools.

The figures along the diagonal show the total numbers of pupils choosing each subject. For example, 75 have chosen History (H), 50 have chosen Geography (G), 55 French etc.

The two triangles forming the two halves on either side of the diagonal are mirror images of each other (reflected in the diagonal). The number of pupils requesting both History *and* French is 50 (as shown at the intersection of the H column and the F row, *or* the H row and the F column). The number of pupils requesting both Geography *and* German (D) is 7, etc.

The Clash Table can be obtained manually in the following way:
(i) Choose one subject, preferably one that is popular, let us say History (H). Flick through all the pupils' Options Forms and take out all the Forms that show H as one of the main choices (do not include those that show H only as a reserve).
(ii) Count these H Option Forms to get the number on the diagonal at the intersection of the H row/H column (75 in the example)
(iii) Now flick through these H Option Forms to count the number that also have Geography (G) chosen as one of the main choices (as before, do not include reserves). This number, 30 in the example, is marked at the intersection of the G row/H column and at the intersection of the H row/G column.
(iv) Then go through the H Option Forms counting the number that also have French (F), then German (D) etc. until all the H column and the H row are completed.
(v) Then, from the whole of the Option Forms (not just the H Option Forms) take out all the G Option Forms and repeat steps (ii) (iii) and (iv) to complete the remainder of the G row and the G column.
(vi) Continuing in this way, the number of steps to be repeated shrinks as you move towards the upper right hand corner of the Clash Table.

If you have a microcomputer, this tedious business can be much reduced by using the OPT1 program described in Appendix 4. This program also produces a tape copy of the pupils' choices to save time in later stages.

Having got the Clash Table, how then do we use it to decide the option pools? To illustrate this, we can use the Clash Table shown above to obtain one possible solution.

2.7 Deciding the subjects in the pools

First let me emphasize that this is a simplified example using only 4 option pools and the numbers shown in the Clash Table. Your real situation will be both larger (perhaps 20 subjects) and more particular to your own school.

(a) The first step is to decide the number of groups to be provided in each subject, using the numbers along the diagonal of the Clash Table.

With 75 pupils, History (H) is clearly popular enough for 3 groups; 2 groups would seem right for Geography (G); 2 for French (F); 1 for German (D): 2 for Biology (B); 1 rather large group for Chemistry (C); 2 for Physics (P); 1 for General Science (S); 1 for Art (A); and 1 rather small group for Music (M). This would give 16 groups for 4 option pools and so 4 groups per pool.

If you have a borderline case (e.g. Chemistry has 30 pupils requesting it) then you can investigate the effect of the pupils' reserve choices. This is done by looking at all the Chemistry Option Forms to count how many pupils (say 9) have put Chemistry as their *last* main choice. Subtracting this number from 30 gives 21 as a lower limit. Then look through all the other Option Forms to see how many pupils (say 2) have put Chemistry as their first reserve. Adding this to 30 gives 32 as an upper limit. We can write this as:

    Chemistry 21-**30**-32

This shows that Chemistry is much more likely to shrink and remain as one group than grow to 2 groups. Considering other subjects in the same way can sometimes make a dramatic difference to a subject's claim for a place in the pools. For example:

    Music 2-**10**-10

This suggests that we shall have to be rather careful in the placing of Music in the pools in order to preserve it as a viable group.

(b) Having looked at the desirable numbers of groups for each subject, reality must decide how many can be afforded (see also section 4.2). Perhaps the first way to view this is by comparing these desirable numbers with the numbers of groups in the present 5th Year curriculum which is about to disappear.

You may have to try 'musical chairs' moves. For example, if one more Physics group is needed but one less Chemistry group, then this can usually be achieved by adjustments in the lower school Science staffing. It often helps to ask different members of staff to take Games lessons in the coming year. Alternatively you might ask all members of staff to tell you which other subjects they are able to teach.

The solutions will vary from school to school. Let us assume for this example that a solution can be found, so that we have the 16 groups decided in part (a).

(c) Let us now suppose that the school's policy is to have at least two homogeneous groups. A Science pool will ensure that all pupils take at least one science. The popularity of History suggests a humanities pool. Thus:

    pool 1 P C B S
    pool 2 H H H G

The Languages department would prefer the two French groups to be in parallel for setting purposes; German must be in a different pool from French to allow two languages to be studied.
Hence:

    pool 1   P C B S
        2   H H H G
        3   F F — —
        4   D — — —

There are 5 groups (A, M, P, B, G) yet to be fitted. If there is no clear philosophical preference for their arrangement then the Clash Table will help us.

Consider the subjects that have only one group (A and M). The Clash Table shows that *no one* wants to do German and Art, so clearly Art can go into pool 4. Such blanks (or low numbers) on the Clash Table always indicate possible pairings of subjects in the pools.

Putting Music (M) also into pool 4 would cause difficulties because 8 of the 10 musicians want to do Art. Thus:

```
P  C  B  S
H  H  H  G
F  F  M  —
D  A  —  —
```

At this point it often helps to have the subjects marked on coloured cards or magnetic plastic (as described in chapter 9) so that they can be moved easily to try new arrangements.

Throughout these stages it is important to remember three constraints that apply:
1 Subjects in the same pool must have the same 'period-breakdown'. That is, if one subject is taught in two double periods, *all* the subjects in that pool must be taught in two double periods. If one subject demands four single periods, all subjects in the pool must be timetabled as four singles. In the example, it looks as if German will have to accept two doubles per week.
2 Subjects taken in specialist craft rooms must not have more than 20 pupils in the group. This does not apply in our example; if craft subjects had been included it might have meant one pool of 5 groups.
3 In mixed schools, despite encouragement for boys and girls to cross traditional barriers in crafts and some sciences, there remains some bias. Subjects with such a bias should be balanced in each pool.

Returning to our example, there are three groups unfitted (P, B, G), leading to three possible solutions. One possibility is to put P and B together in pool 4. Alternatively, P and B can be placed in different pools (this will permit pupils to take three sciences, although whether this should be allowed is a matter for school policy).

In this way we arrive at three possible schemes:

```
(1) P  C  B  S    (2) P  C  B  S    (3) P  C  B  S
    H  H  H  G        H  H  H  G        H  H  H  G
    F  F  M  G        F  F  M  P        F  F  M  B
    D  A  P  B        D  A  B  G        D  A  G  P
```

There are two methods which might help us to decide between these three alternatives. The first method is to add the numbers of pupils expected in each pool, assuming for the moment that each Physics groups contains one-half of 40 because there are two Physics groups. (Similarly for B, G.)

30 *Timetabling*

Adding the numbers for each pool gives:

(1) PCBS = 85	(2) PCBS = 85	(3) PCBS = 85
HHHG = 105	HHHG = 105	HHHG = 105
FFMG = 90	FFMP = 85	FFMB = 85
DAPB = 80	DABG = 85	DAGP = 85

The greater imbalance of numbers in (1) suggests that it might be the least preferable on this basis, but the differences in this example are not clear-cut.

The second method which might help in deciding between alternative schemes, involves first simplifying the pools by deleting all subjects which appear in more than one pool. Then the total number of clashes in each pool can be found (by looking at each pair of subjects in the Clash Table). In our example, each of the three alternatives reduces to:

  CS = 3 clashes
  H   = 0 clashes
  FM = 3 clashes
  DA = 0 clashes

So this method will not distinguish between our three alternative schemes. However, to illustrate the method, if we had put Music into pool 4 with Art, then we would have found:

  CS = 3 clashes
  H   = 0 clashes
  F   = 0 clashes
  DAM = 0 + 8 + 4 = 12 clashes

At the end of this stage of our example, we are still left with three possibilities. The Clash Table, dealing with the pupils in bulk, cannot help further. To decide on the best of the three schemes we should look at the choices of each individual pupil.

2.8 Part 2: comparing the option pools with the pupils' choices

To see which option scheme will be best for this particular population of pupils, we should try each pupil's choice of subjects against the proposed option pools to see which pupils will not fit. The choices for these 'unfitted' pupils can then be inspected by considering some or all of the following points:

1. Has the pupil lost a subject which he/she thought was of high priority, or is the lost subject his/her last choice (i.e. the least-wanted subject)?
2. Did the pupil choose the lost subject for valid reasons or perhaps because his/her friends intended to take that subject?
3. Is the lost subject necessary either for a balanced curriculum or for a particular careers intention?
4. Is this particular pupil (and his/her parents) well motivated?
5. Is this pupil likely to be particularly upset by losing this subject?

6 Will the pupil be able to take his/her first reserve subject instead?
7 Can the situation be improved by changing one of the other subjects originally chosen by the pupil?

As a first step towards comparing the pupils' choices with the proposed pools, it helps to simplify the pools so that a subject does not appear more than once on a line. For example, the third of the three alternative schemes from the last section would be simplified to:

(3) PCBS
    HG
    FMB
    DAGP

Taking each pupil's choices and comparing them with each of the proposed schemes can take a long time. It is possible to ask the pupils to do it, but even the more able pupils (and their parents) are not very reliable when given three alternative schemes, even after a practice session. However, this routine task is ideal for a microcomputer and the OPT2 program given in Appendix 5 will do all this for you. The program allows you to type in a proposed options scheme and then switch on the tape recorder to play a tape of the pupils' choices (the tape is obtained automatically from the previous OPT1 program). You can then leave it running for a double period while it compares each pupil's choices against your proposed options scheme and prints out the results.

Whether you do it manually or by computer, the results should look something like this:

Pool 1
P 16(− 2)   C 26(− 4)   B 22(− 3)   S 18(− 1)   (82)

Pool 2
H 72(− 3)   G 18(− 4)   (90)

Pool 3
F 52(− 3)   M 8(− 2)   B 17(− 1)   (77)

Pool 4
D 14(− 1)   A 22(− 3)   G 28(− 4)   P 22(− 2)   (86)

73 pupils fitted out of 90 (81%)

Figure 9

This corresponds to the third of three possible option schemes developed earlier (in section 2.7). It shows, for example, that of the 30 pupils requesting Chemistry (see the Clash Table), 26 pupils have fitted into the group in pool 1 (bearing in mind the order of preference of the choices of each pupil), but that 4 pupils could not fit (perhaps they had put S as a higher priority or they wished to study a combination like HGPC). It also shows that, of the 40 pupils requesting Physics, 16 will fit into pool 1 and 22 into pool 4, but 2 pupils will not fit.

32 *Timetabling*

The table also shows, at the end of each pool, the total number fitted to that pool (ideally all these numbers would balance out at 90 since there are 90 pupils). At the end it shows the number and percentage of pupils fitted (the total of the negative numbers in the brackets and this final number do not correspond because some pupils lost two of their subjects).

In addition, the computer will give a display to show which pupils are fitted or not fitted. For example:

Johnson Keith 3A

Choices: 1 2 3 4   Pools: 1 2 3 4
          P H F C   C H F P

This shows that Keith Johnson in form 3A had chosen, in order, PHFC. He would be able to study all of these subjects by taking C in pool 1, H in pool 2, F in pool 3 and P in pool 4.

If the pupil's choices do not fit into the pools, the display is slightly different:

Johnson Chris 3A

Choices: 1 2 3 4   Pools: 1 2 3 4
          H C D A̲   C H __ D

This shows that the pupil chose, in order, HCDA. The underlining shows that he would not get his last choice, A. He was fitted to C in pool 1, H in pool 2, and D in pool 4. The underlining shows he could only get A if an Art group was added to pool 3.

Using all this information, the Head, the Management Team or a meeting of Heads of Departments can decide on the best option scheme for this particular group of pupils.

2.9 Part 3: unfitted pupils

The next step ought to be the interviewing of individual 'unfitted' pupils, either by the Director of Studies, the Careers Tutor or perhaps by someone who knows the pupil better. Consideration can be given to the seven points listed at the beginning of section 2.8 (page 30). When the pupil has modified his choices to fit the option pools, the parents should be informed (and invited to discuss the situation if necessary). The pupil's Option Form (or the computer printout sheet) can be updated.

If a computer is to be used to print the option group lists then the tape of the pupils' choices (produced by OPT1) should be updated, using the OPT3 program (see Appendix 6). An alternative to interviewing all the unfitted pupils, if a computer is available, is to update the tape (with OPT3) using each unfitted pupil's first reserve choice; then re-running OPT2 will show if there is a better fit.

2.10 Part 4: option group lists

The lists of pupils in each option group will need to be ready for September, preferably earlier. Ideally all the groups in one option pool will fit on to one sheet of paper. The groups should be headed by the name of the subject and the teacher's name. The groups should be in alphabetical order. Schools usually prefer to keep the sexes separate. It helps if the lists for different bands of pupils are printed on different colours of paper. Individual sheets can be given to the staff teaching the groups; booklets of complete sets should be provided to the Head, Deputies, Year-Tutors, Office Staff, Staff noticeboard etc.

A printer attached to a microcomputer can be used 'secretarially' to produce these lists; then the lists can be photocopied and duplicated. If the number of pupils is not too large then the OPT4 program can be used. If the number of pupils is too large for the memory of the computer then, less conveniently, the OPT5 program can be used, providing the pupils were entered into the OPT1 program in alphabetical order (and boys/girls separated if necessary). More details are given in Appendix 7 and Appendix 8. If a computer and printer are used it is important that the pupils' names are spelled correctly when entered into OPT1 (particularly names like Ann/Anne, Tracy/Tracey, Steven/Stephen) because staff are likely to use these group lists when writing pupils' names on reports to send to parents.

2.11 Sixth Year options

If you have a Sixth Form you may decide to take a survey of Fifth-Formers before they leave, in order to see how many are likely to return and which subjects they might be considering. Such surveys are not very reliable.

If you do take such a survey then, of course, you can analyse it in the same way as for the 4th Year options, drawing up a Clash Table and seeing how the pupils fit the proposed options (either manually or using OPT1 and OPT2). The problem is likely to be much simpler than with the 4th Year options (because of the number of pupils and the number of subjects).

How valid the results will be when the students return in September may be decided by experience, but the individual attention you give your pupils in this way may well help to keep them from drifting away to the local technical college.

2.12 Other computer programs

There are some programs available from other sources but they need full-size computers such as are found in the Town Hall or the local polytechnic.

For example there is an 'options' suite of programs developed at Sheffield City Polytechnic, Pond Street, Sheffield. The program costs about £150. It will do all that the OPT1-5 programs will do, with the advantage that the information is entered only once and then held in the computer's large memory. A disadvantage is that when fewer than 6 option pools are used, one or more 'dummy' subjects have to be entered every time. When running the OPT2 part of the program, several additional features are available. The most useful of these will list the names, choices and pools for all the pupils who have not been fitted to any subject specified by the user. Similar programs have been developed in Hertfordshire and East Sussex (see bibliography for more details).

Other programs have been developed to take the pupils' choices and from them construct a heterogeneous option scheme which satisfies all the pupils. It is then left to the school to decide which groups are uneconomic in size and to calculate whether the remaining groups can be provided with staff and rooms. Such a program is available from the National Computing Centre at a cost of £1200 for a four-year lease. Not only is this expensive, but the system is not interactive, just 'take-it-or-leave-it'. Similar programs have been developed in Dundee and Cleveland.

The Birmingham Educational Computing Centre, Hope Street, Birmingham 5, has developed several programs to assist in school administration, including one to help with 'Form 7'.

My expectation for computers in school administration is not so much that they will reduce the time spent in curriculum planning, but rather that they will free us to apply our professional judgement more wisely and to greater effect, in producing timetables of better quality.

2.13 Summary

Of the different types of option schemes, the one with the most advantages appears to be a combination of several homogeneous pools with one heterogeneous bias pool. Whatever type of option scheme is chosen by a school, information must be given to the pupils (Options Booklet) and information must be obtained from the pupils (Options Form).

The exact contents of each option pool can be decided by looking at a Clash Table and at the pupils' individual choices. Easy-to-use programs for a school's microcomputer can save a great deal of time and allow staff to spend more time advising and motivating individual pupils.

3 Staff deployment analysis

3.1　Introduction
3.2　Worked example — 4th Year
3.3　Worked example — 1st Year
3.4　Short cuts
3.5　The Sixth Form
3.6　The contact ratio
3.7　The Curriculum Equation
3.8　Relative bonus
3.9　Worked example
3.10　The nomogram
3.11　Sixth Forms
3.12　Summary

Once a new curriculum is decided, it ought to be analysed carefully. In particular, it ought to be analysed to see the disposition of the most valuable of our resources, the teaching staff. One can do this simply by counting teaching periods, but there are two disadvantages — the large numbers are unwieldy and the method will not allow you to compare your school with others.

These disadvantages are overcome by a method developed by T.I. Davies (see the bibliography). This method will emphasize the deployment of staff in your curriculum, express this deployment in terms of small, manageable numbers, and allow you to compare your school with others, nationally. Sometimes called *Curriculum Analysis,* the method is more properly called *Staff Deployment Analysis.*

36 *Timetabling*

3.2 Worked example — 4th Year

Consider the following example of a 4th Year curriculum:

```
4A                    4B                    4C
(60)                  (60)                  (69)
PE/PE₃                PE/PE₃                PE/PE/PE₃
X/X₄                  X/X₄                  X/X/X₄
F/F/F₅                F/B/G₅                H/H/G₄
H/H/G₄                H/H/G₄                B/B/S/S₄
P/C/B₄                P/C/B/S₄              A/W/E/E₄
A/T/G₄                A/Y/P/K₄              N/T/Y/Y₄
M/D/P₄                W/T/N/E₄              M/N/K/K₄
                                            M/M/M₆
          M/M/M/M₆                          E/E/E₇
          E/E/E/E₆
```

Figure 10

The diagram shows a hypothetical curricular layout for a school operating a 40-period week, with the 4th Year organized in three bands, 4A, 4B, 4C. The numbers of pupils in the three bands are shown as 60, 60, 69 respectively. The groups marked X are agglomerates of minority-time subjects like RE, Music, Careers, General Studies, Form Time. The brackets indicate that Mathematics and English are setted across two bands. The number of periods for each pool of subjects is shown as a suffix.

The names of the subjects need not trouble us here, as we are not concerned with the quality of this curriculum, only with the number of staff involved. In fact, we can dispense with the subject names and write only the numbers of periods:

```
4A              4B              4C
(60)            (60)            (69)
3/3             3/3             3/3/3
4/4             4/4             4/4/4
5/5/5           5/5/5           4/4/4
4/4/4           4/4/4           4/4/4/4
4/4/4           4/4/4/4         4/4/4/4
4/4/4           4/4/4/4         4/4/4/4
4/4/4           4/4/4/4         4/4/4/4
                                6/6/6
          6/6/6/6                7/7/7
          6/6/6/6
```

Figure 11

We can go a step further and add up the number of periods expended in each band, bearing in mind that 4A's 'share' of the Maths sets is 2 groups (and similarly with English sets).
We get:

	4A	4B	4C
pupils	(60)	(60)	(69)
periods	101	113	136

Looking at these figures we can easily see that 4B is more favoured than 4A, in that the same number of pupils (60) has more periods allocated (113 instead of 101). What we cannot see clearly is the position of 4C. There are more periods allocated, but also more pupils. Has the greater number of periods compensated for the greater number of pupils or not?

Part of the solution to this problem lies in the concept of a *curriculum unit*. A curriculum unit is defined as exactly *one-ninth* of the teaching week. This seems a very strange concept at first but its advantage lies in the fact that it allows us to overcome variations from school to school caused by 40-period, 35-period or other variations on the teaching week. (Davies could have chosen one-tenth or any other number; he chose one-ninth because British curricula are often divided into nine blocks – see section 3.4).

If you work to a 40-period week then:
1 curriculum unit (1cu) = $\frac{40}{9}$ = 4.44 periods.

If you work to a 35-period week then:
1 curriculum unit (1cu) = $\frac{35}{9}$ = 3.88 periods.

If you work to a 20-period week then:
1 curriculum unit (1cu) = $\frac{20}{9}$ = 2.22 periods.

Most of your option pools are likely to have a teaching time of about 1 cu.

Our example is based on a 40-period week, and so to convert from teaching periods to curriculum units we must *divide by 4.44*.

Thus 4A has been provided with $\frac{101}{4.44}$ = 22.7, say 23 curriculum units. Similarly 4B has $\frac{113}{4.44}$ = 25 curriculum units. 4C has $\frac{136}{4.44}$ = 31 cu's.
The 4th Year can now be summarized as:

	4A	4B	4C
pupils	(60)	(60)	(69)
cu's	23	25	31

Again we can see that the provision for 4B is better than the provision for 4A (more curriculum units for the same number of pupils). However the position of 4C is still obscure.

Davies solved this problem by introducing the idea of a *basic provision* of curriculum units. He proposed that the size of this basic provision should be:

$$\text{basic provision of curriculum units} = \frac{\text{number of pupils}}{3}$$

38 *Timetabling*

There is nothing absolute about this value: Davies chose it as a convenient datum-line and we have kept to it ever since. It is a reasonable value because 1st-Year classes of 30 pupils are often provided with $\frac{30}{3} = 10$ curriculum units (with a basic provision for full class sizes except when split into two groups for craft).

Returning to 4A and its 60 pupils, we can say that the basic provision would be $\frac{60}{3} = 20$ curriculum units. But we saw that the actual provision for 4A was 23 cu's. Hence there is a *bonus* of +3 cu's for 4A. The bonus is defined by:

bonus = actual provision − basic provision.

For 4B, also 60 pupils, the basic provision is also 20 cu's. The actual provision was calculated as 25 cu's. So the bonus for 4B is +5 cu's. This is bigger than the bonus for 4A, as we expected.

Looking now at 4C, 69 pupils would have a basic provision of $\frac{69}{3} = 23$ cu's. In fact the curriculum provided 31 cu's, giving a bonus for 4C of +8 cu's. This larger bonus means that 4C was given a greater provision of teaching power. Even though there are more pupils in this band, the school has more than provided sufficient extra groups to allow for this. The larger bonus means a smaller average class size, as we might expect for a band of less able pupils.

For the 4th Year as a whole, the bonus is $3 + 5 + 8 = +16$ cu's.

To summarize:

	4A (60)	4B (60)	4C (69)	4th Year (189)
cu's	23	25	31	79
basic	20	20	23	63
bonus	+3	+5	+8	+16

As you can see, the method combines the number of pupils and the number of teacher-periods and reduces them to one small number – moreover a number which can be compared from school to school regardless of the variations of the number of periods in the school week.

In looking at the results and deciding what corrective action, if any, you may wish to take, it often helps to draw bar-charts or histograms. In this case it is a 'transverse histogram' (Figure 12).

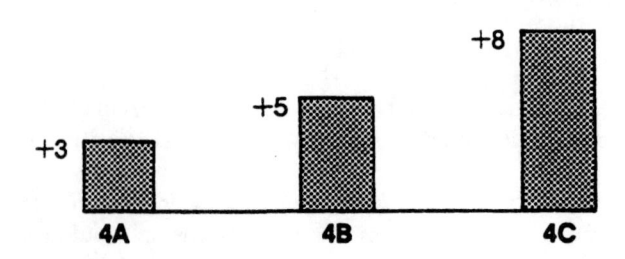

Figure 12

Staff deployment analysis 39

Before we look briefly at the analysis of lower school classes, here is a summary of the method:

1. For any class, band or year group (except the Sixth Form), count the number of teaching periods provided.
2. Convert to curriculum units by dividing by 4.44 (40-period week) or 3.88 (35-period week). This number is the *actual provision* of curriculum units.
3. Find the *basic provision* from 'number of pupils divided by three'.
4. The *bonus* is the actual provision minus the basic provision.

With your curriculum plan and an electronic calculator in front of you, this can be done in less than fifteen minutes.

3.3 Worked example — 1st Year

Treating the simpler curricula of lower school classes is usually easier. For example, consider a 1st Year curriculum:

1A	1B
(30)	(33)
RE_1	RE_1
Mu_2	Mu_2
F_5	F_5
Hum_5	Hum_5
Sc_6	Sc_6
A_2	A_2
E_6	E_6
M_6	M_6
Craft/Craft$_4$	Craft/Craft$_4$

$$PE/PE_3$$

Figure 13

The curriculum is based on a 40-period week and shows two classes, each divided into two groups for craft. The two classes are joined for PE (it is a mixed school).

As in the earlier example, in staff deployment analysis we are not interested in the names of the subjects (or the *quality* of the curriculum), only in the *quantity* of teaching power that is provided. The total for each of these classes is 44 periods.

The conversion factor for a 40-period week is 4.44, so the actual provision of curriculum units is $\frac{44}{4.44} = 10$ cu's for each class.

The basic provision for 1A (30 pupils) is $\frac{30}{3} = 10$ cu's, so this class has zero bonus. The basic provision for 1B (33 pupils) is $\frac{33}{3} = 11$ cu's, so this class has a

40 Timetabling

negative bonus (−1). To summarize:

	1A (30)	1B (33)
periods	44	44
cu's	10	10
basic	10	11
bonus	**0**	**−1**

It can be shown that a zero bonus (i.e. just the basic provision) means an *average* class size of 27 (see Appendix 2). A positive bonus means an average class size of less than 27; a negative bonus means an average class size of more than 27. Zero or negative bonuses are common in the junior years of British secondary schools — whether this should be the case is for each school to decide in the light of the analysis.

Continuing with the analysis for all parts of other year groups (excluding the Sixth Form) might give a picture like this:

Year:	1	2	3	4	5	
bonus:	−4	0	+3	+16	+16	(= 31 bonuses).

or, graphically, a 'longitudinal histogram':

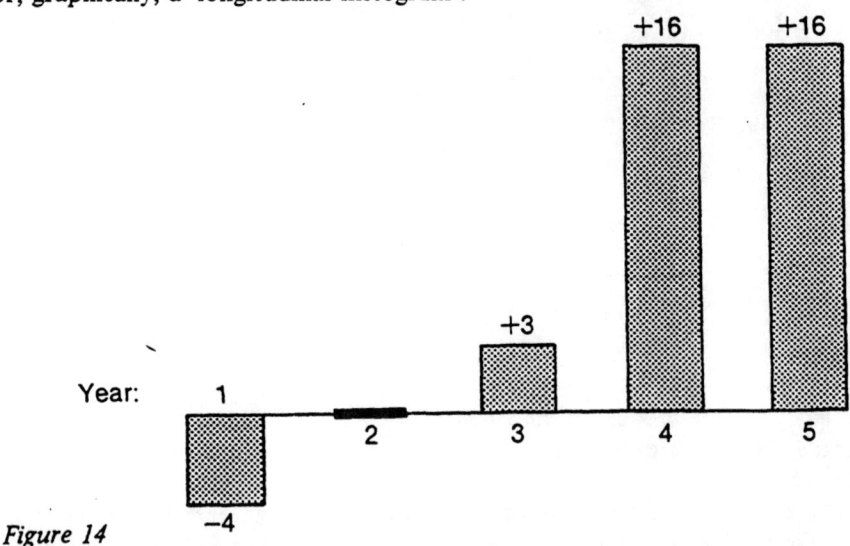

Figure 14

The school might then consider whether this is a fair distribution of the available staffing resources. It is clear that the 4th and 5th Years are being subsidized by the 1st Year (and perhaps the 2nd Year). The school can consider whether the total number of bonuses (31 in this case) might be distributed more equitably. We shall see in section 3.6 of this chapter how the total number of bonuses is connected to the total number of staff and the number of non-teaching periods.

3.4 Short cuts

In these examples I have used convenient numbers and always rounded off to the nearest whole number. Of course you could work in decimal places or fractions. LEA's and HMI's always seem happier working to at least one decimal place. I do not think this is necessary. We saw in the last example that although 1A and 1B had the same curriculum, the *three* extra pupils in 1B changed the bonus by *one* curriculum unit. This is a measure of the sensitivity of the method – if the population changes by 3, the bonus changes by 1.

Bearing this in mind, there is a method of counting curriculum units more quickly than by counting the number of periods and dividing by 4.44 or 3.88. In the 4th Year example (section 3.2), 4A was written down in 9 blocks of subjects which roughly correspond to the 9 curriculum units in a teaching week (even though the number of periods in a block varied from 3 to 7 instead of being a constant 4.44 periods). So we can simply count the total number of teaching groups in a band and this gives us the number of curriculum units that are provided. For example, counting the total number of teaching groups in 4A gives 23 (remembering to include 4A's share of Mathematics and English). This is the same as we found earlier. Sometimes there may be a small disparity in the numbers because in the earlier method we rounded up or down to the nearest whole number (for example, try this shorter method with 4B).

For the 1st Year example, this shorter method still works providing you ensure that the subjects are grouped (artificially and for this method only) into 9 bundles. In the example for 1A and 1B, this could be done by writing $(RE, Mu)_3$ as one 'subject'. Each pupil then takes 9 'subjects' although, due to craft, the actual provision of groups (or cu's) is 10 as we found earlier.

3.5 The Sixth Form

This method of staff deployment analysis cannot be applied usefully to the Sixth Form. This is because the students are normally allowed a variable amount of time for private study and this time is not staffed. Also, an average class size of 27 (our datum-line for zero bonus) is scarcely relevant to most Sixth Form groups.

For a traditional A-level Sixth Form, where the students are usually taught for four-fifths of the school week (3 A-levels + minority subjects, then private study), the method could be adapted to use $\frac{5}{4} \times 9 = 11$ cu's in the teaching week with a basic provision equal to the number of students (so that a zero bonus would mean an average class size of 9). However this method would seem to be of little value except in comparing traditional Sixth Forms with each other.

LEA's usually apply a staffing ratio of about 1:11 when considering Sixth Forms. Even at this level of staffing, it seems that in most schools the Sixth Form is subsidized by the main school (see also section 3.11).

If the students in your 'General Sixth' or 'non-A-level Sixth' are allowed little or no free time, then you can use the same method as for the 4th Year. The size of the bonuses may surprise you.

3.6 The contact ratio

We move now to a consideration of some of the formulae that can be used in analysing or synthesizing the curriculum.

First the definitions of some symbols:

N = number of pupils

T = number of teachers. This includes the full-time equivalent of any part-time teachers. Usually T does not include the Head.

Both N and T are fixed in the sense that the school usually does not have any direct control over them.

The ratio $T{:}N$ is the staffing ratio, determined by the LEA. Typically it is about 1:18.

x = number of curriculum units actually provided to the pupils
(where 1 cu = 4.44 periods in a 40-period week).

The essential information about a class can be summarised as N^x.

For example in section 3.2 we could have written:
$$4A = 60^{23}$$
We saw earlier that the basic provision $= \frac{N}{3}$ (and so the bonus $= x - \frac{N}{3}$)

c = the *contact ratio*. This is defined by:

$$c = \frac{\text{average teaching load of staff}}{\text{number of periods in the week}}$$

For example if the *average* teaching load of the staff in your school is 32 periods in a 40-period week (i.e. an average of 8 'free' periods), then $c = \frac{32}{40} = 0.80$

The national average for c has been quoted by HM Inspectorate as 0.77 (corresponding to $0.77 \times 40 = 31$ teaching periods in a 40-period week or $0.77 \times 35 = 27$ teaching periods in a 35-period week). The national average value of c has been decreasing over the years. Naturally, it varies from school to school: one might expect it to be lower in split-site schools. A rough survey of some schools in Manchester in 1977 gave values in the range $0.70 - 0.81$.

Remember that c refers to the *average* teaching load – for every Year-Tutor, Head of Department or Deputy Head who teaches below this ratio, other staff will have to teach above it.

To calculate the value of c for your school, calculate the total number of periods provided in the curriculum and divide this by the total number of periods that could be provided by the staff if they had no free periods. That is:

$$c = \frac{\text{number of periods provided in the curriculum}}{\text{number of full-time-equivalent staff} \times \text{number of periods in a week}}$$

The Headteacher is usually omitted when calculating c.
The full-time equivalent of part-time teachers is included.

The value of c also gives the *average* fraction of your staff that are teaching classes at any instant. Clearly the value of c affects the number of staff available to cover for absent colleagues. It also has implications for the degree of difficulty experienced in scheduling the timetable.

A quantity k, called the staff loading factor, is sometimes used. This is the reciprocal of c. i.e. $k = \frac{1}{c}$. If $c = 0.75$ then $k = 1.33$. The only advantage in considering this factor is if you decide to provide 40 extra periods on the curriculum (in a 40-period week) – perhaps an extra 1st Year form for your intake. You might think that you would need the equivalent of only one extra teacher. In fact you would need the equivalent of k extra staff because each of them would be teaching only a fraction c of the week.

3.7 The Curriculum Equation

Although the total number of staff is T, the *effective* number is only c multiplied by T. That is, cT. In effect you have cT staff teaching the whole week with no free periods. Since each of these effective teachers will provide 9 curriculum units (by definition), the total number of curriculum units $= 9cT$.
That is,
$$x = 9cT$$
This is the *Staffing Equation,* sometimes called the 'First Law' of the curriculum. This equation can be used in three different ways:

1. $x = 9cT =$ the number of curriculum units that can be provided by a staff of T teachers working at a contact ratio c. It can be applied to the whole school or just to a department.
    To calculate the number of bonuses, subtract $\frac{N}{3}$
    i.e. bonuses $= 9cT - \frac{N}{3}$

2. $T = \frac{x}{9c} =$ the number of teachers needed to provide x curriculum units when they are working at a contact ratio c. It can be used to to find the number of staff needed for a new school or for each part of a split-site school, or used to find the 'correct' size of a department.

3. $c = \frac{x}{9T} =$ the contact ratio that must be accepted if x curriculum units are to be provided by T staff.

3.8 Relative bonus $b\%$

In order to compare your school with others, the idea of a relative curriculum bonus is defined, as follows:

$$\text{Relative curriculum bonus } (b\%) = \frac{\text{total bonus curriculum units}}{\text{total basic curriculum units}} \times 100\%$$

For example, an 11–16 school of 900 pupils would have a basic provision of $\frac{900}{3} = 300$ cu's. If the curriculum actually provided 324 cu's then the bonus would be 24 cu's. The relative bonus ($b\%$) would then be $\frac{24}{300} \times 100\% = 8\%$.

This value may not be high enough to provide sufficient curricular flexibility. The experiences of HM Inspectorate suggest that relative bonuses below 10% will restrict the school's curriculum considerably, while values above 20% are generous and rare.

The lower limit of $b\% = 10\%$ implies a lower limit to the contact ratio c. This lower limit is $c = 0.0407$ multiplied by staffing ratio (see Appendix 2 for the proof). For example, if your LEA applies a staffing ratio of 1:18 (for the main school) then the lower limit for $c = 0.0407 \times 18 = 0.73$. If your value of c falls below this figure, then $b\%$ will fall below 10%, and you will lose the curricular flexibility that you need in order to provide a reasonable range of options.

3.9 Worked example

You are newly appointed to the Headship of Laura Norder High School (previous Head: Ivor Caine; Deputies: Ben Dover, A. Pauline Werke!). This is a 6-form-entry 11–16 school with 900 pupils (N). The LEA's staffing ratio is 1:18, so the teaching establishment is 50 staff (T). You devise your ideal curriculum and find it requires 400 curriculum units. What can you deduce?

Using the curriculum equation:
$$x = 9cT$$
$$400 = 9 \times c \times 50$$
$$c = \frac{400}{9 \times 50} = \frac{400}{450} = 0.88$$

This is equivalent to an *average* load of $0.88 \times 40 = 35$ periods in a 40-period week and must be considered to be too high. What would be possible?

If you decided on $c = 0.75$ ($= 30$ periods average in a 40-period week, giving a reasonable allowance of time to some staff for pastoral care etc.), then:

$$x = 9cT = 9 \times 0.75 \times 50 = 338 \text{ cu's.}$$

Since the school has 900 pupils (N), the basic provision $= \frac{N}{3} = 300$ cu's. Thus the bonus for the whole school is +38. You can then decide how to distribute these 38 bonuses between the five year-groups. Would you give +15 bonuses to the 4th Year and +15 to the 5th Year, leaving only +8 for the 1st, 2nd and 3rd Years? Or would you decide on a strong injection of resources into the 1st Year in an attempt to develop good work habits in your intake, hopefully to pay dividends later?

To compare this school with others we can calculate $b\%$, by:

$$b\% = \frac{\text{total bonus cu's}}{\text{total basic cu's}} \times 100\% = \frac{38}{300} \times 100\% = 12\tfrac{1}{2}\%$$

This is a reasonable value. It could be increased by increasing c (for example, if c is increased to 0.77, $b\%$ increases to $15\tfrac{1}{2}\%$). The variation of $b\%$ as c varies can be checked most quickly by using a nomogram.

3.10 The nomogram

It can be shown (see Appendix 2) that there is a relation between the staffing ratio ($\frac{N}{T}$), the contact ratio (c) and the relative bonus ($b\%$). This relationship can be plotted on a form of graph known as a nomogram (see page 47). For the present refer only to the three labels at the tops of the axes and ignore the labels at the bottom (these will be used in chapter 7).

The quantity plotted on the left-hand axis, $\frac{N}{T}$, is the staffing ratio. Typically it is in the region of 17 or 18. It is determined by the LEA and the school has no direct control over it. Mark the value of your staffing ratio on the $\frac{N}{T}$ axis.

The quantity plotted on the central axis is c, the contact ratio. This can vary over the range 0.70 – 0.80. As c varies, so does the relative bonus $b\%$ which is marked on the right-hand axis. *The three quantities are always connected by a straight line* (use a ruler or stretch a length of black cotton).

For example, suppose your staffing ratio is 1 : 18 and you wish to see the effect of having a contact ratio of 0.75. Draw a straight line from 18 on the left axis through 0.75 on the central axis. This line cuts the $b\%$ axis at $12\frac{1}{2}\%$, a reasonable value. (These are the same values that we used in the second part of the example in section 3.9).

Reducing the contact ratio to 0.73 gives a value for $b\%$ of less than 10% (unsatisfactory). If you wanted a $b\%$ value of 20% then you would have to accept a contact ratio of 0.80.

By pivoting your ruler or length of cotton about the LEA's value of $\frac{N}{T}$, acceptable values of c and $b\%$ may be found.

Once $b\%$ is determined, the number of bonuses that are available can be calculated from:

$$\text{bonus cu's} = \frac{b\% \times \text{number of pupils}}{300}$$

The school must then decide how to distribute these bonuses equitably.

3.11 Sixth Forms

As explained earlier, the Sixth Form presents special problems in using Staff Deployment Analysis. The usual method is to separate the Sixth Form provision from the main school as follows:

(a) Calculate the contact ratio as explained in section 3.6.
(b) Find the total number of teacher-periods in the Sixth Form curriculum.
(c) Multiply the contact ratio by 40 periods (or $c \times 35$ periods) to find the number of periods taught by an average teacher.
(d) Divide the number in (b) by the number in (c) to find the number of full-time-equivalent teachers for the Sixth Form.
(e) Subtract this number from the total full-time-equivalent staffing for your school and use the result as T for the main school (in the curriculum equation etc.)

Using the nomogram

Staffing (chapter 3)

1. Calculate (or ask LEA for) the staffing ratio $\dfrac{N}{T} = \dfrac{\text{number of pupils }(N)}{\text{number of staff }(T)}$

   (This is for the main school only – if you have a Sixth Form, see section 3.11).
2. Reading the label at the *top* of each axis and using a ruler, the nomogram will show what contact ratio (c) must be accepted to achieve a relative bonus ($b\%$) or vice versa. (See also section 3.10)
3. The national average for c has been quoted as 0.77 but it varies from school to school over the range 0.7 - 0.8
   The value of $b\%$ should be greater than 10% if the school is to have a reasonable curricular flexibility.
4. Once c is agreed, the number of curriculum units (x) to be provided can be calculated from the staffing equation: $x = 9cT$
   More conveniently, the number of bonuses to be distributed throughout the school can be calculated from:

   $$\text{bonuses} = \frac{b\% \times N}{300}$$

Rooming (chapter 7)

5. Calculate $\dfrac{N}{n} = \dfrac{\text{number of pupils }(N)}{\text{number of teaching spaces }(n)}$ (for main school only)
6. Referring to the label at the *bottom* of each axis, the nomogram will then show what rooming fraction (r) must be accepted for a given curriculum bonus ($b\%$) or vice versa.
7. If $r = 0.85$ then, on average, each room will be used for 85% of the week, and, on average, 85% of the teaching spaces will be in use at any time.
8. As r rises above 0.85 there are likely to be increasingly severe restrictions on the timetable.
   If $b\%$ falls below 10%, the school is unlikely to have sufficient curricular flexibility.
   Taken together, these values imply a critical value of $\dfrac{N}{n} = 21$ (see chapter 7)
9. If required, r could be used to calculate the number of curriculum units (x) to be provided, using the rooming equation: $x = 9rn$
   This equation can be applied to the whole main school or to specialist rooms within a department.
   The larger the value of r for the whole school, the more uniform must be the values of r for the individual departments.
10. Steps 2 and 6 should be iterated as necessary to obtain reasonable values of c, b, r.

Staff deployment analysis 47

The nomogram

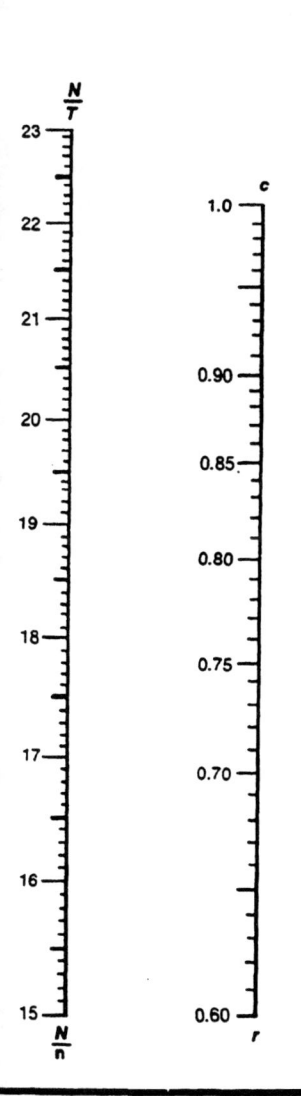

$\frac{N}{T}$

23
22
21
20
19
18
17
16
15

$\frac{N}{n}$

c

1.0
0.90
0.85
0.80
0.75
0.70
0.60

r

b%

23
22
21
20
19
18
17
16
15
14
13
12
11
10
9
8

b%

48 *Timetabling*

If you take the number found in (d) and divide it into the number of Sixth-Formers, the result is your staffing ratio for your Sixth Form. Comparing this with the LEA's value (usually about 11:1) allows you to decide whether your Sixth Form is being subsidized by the main school. A value of 9:1 means that the Sixth Form is taking more than its 'fair' share of teachers. This is commonly the case with Sixth Forms of less than 100 students.

3.12 Summary

The procedures described in this chapter need not be performed frequently – perhaps every second or third year if your situation is static. If the curricular structure changes or if your intake numbers change, then these methods will highlight the effects. It is a particularly interesting exercise when newly joining a school.

The calculations themselves require and make no judgements. Once the principles are understood, a computer program can be used to make the calculations automatically. Such a program is given in Appendix 10. The program will calculate the values of the various quantities for your school so that you may then use your professional judgement to decide on the best course of action.

$$1 \text{ curriculum unit} = \frac{\text{number of periods in teaching week}}{9}$$

$$\text{basic provision} = \frac{\text{number of pupils } (N)}{3}$$

$$\text{bonus cu's} = \text{actual provision of cu's } (x) - \text{basic provision.}$$

$$\text{contact ratio } (c) = \frac{\text{average teaching load of staff}}{\text{number of periods in the week}}$$

$$= \frac{\text{number of periods provided in the curriculum}}{\text{number of full-time-equivalent staff} \times \text{number of periods in the week}}$$

$$x = 9cT \quad \text{or} \quad T = \frac{x}{9c} \quad \text{or} \quad c = \frac{x}{9T}$$

$$\textit{relative bonus } b\% = \frac{\text{total bonus cu's}}{\text{total basic cu's}} \times 100\%$$

($b\%$ should be greater than 10%)

Further formulae can be found in chapter 7 and in Appendix 2.

4 Collecting the data

4.1 Introduction
4.2 Matching the departments to the curriculum
4.3 The Curriculum Plan
4.4 The Staffing Forms
4.5 Checking the Staffing Forms
4.6 The Staff Loading Chart

We have now reached a half-way stage in the overall timetabling process. We have decided the curricular pattern that we intend to provide, but have yet to begin the process of scheduling it. In order to proceed to the scheduling stage we must first assemble all the necessary data and then check this data for impossibilities.

The five main steps in the assembling and preliminary checking of the data are:

1 Checking that each department can cover the number of periods required by the curriculum.
2 Drawing up the Curriculum Plan which will show Heads of Departments what has to be covered by each department.
3 Providing Heads of Departments with Staffing Forms on which they can put their requests.
4 The initial checking of the Staffing Forms.
5 Drawing up a Staff Loading Chart to give an overall picture.

These steps are covered in the next five sections of this chapter.

4.2 Matching the departments to the curriculum

One of the first things we must check is that each department can cover the required number of periods in that subject. This is not merely a matter of ensuring that there are enough History teachers to cover the total number of periods of History : several things must be investigated. The questions to be considered include:

Are members of the department also Year-Tutors or House-Tutors requiring extra 'free' time?

Are there any part-timers who wish to change the number of teaching periods?

Have resignations or appointments of staff during the year changed the structure of the department?

Are there enough suitably qualified staff to take all the classes at all levels from university entrance examinations to remedial?

What is the position of staff who are shared between this department and another department? If the balance of periods between the departments is to change, how will this affect each department and the member of staff involved?

How many periods, if any, are surplus to the department? Can they be used to cover Games, RE, Form-periods, General Studies etc.?

How many periods, if any, are a deficit in the department? Can they be borrowed from any other department?

You will probably have done much of this checking while drawing up the option pools but it should always be done again at this stage. You may prefer to do it *after* drawing up the curriculum plan (section 4.3).

Methods of checking the departments vary from school to school. One method, in three steps, is shown below:

(a) *Find the number of periods needed to cover the subject this year.*

For example :
History Department

Year :	1	2	3	4	5	6
periods needed :	24	21	21	24	20	20 = 130

(+ 4 compared with last year)

(b) *Make suggestions about the teaching load of each member of the department, in order to find the total number of periods that are likely to be available.* It is best to use the same unique two-letter code for each teacher that you will use in scheduling the timetable.

For example:

If AF = 30 (Head of Department)
      JC = 28 (Year-Tutor)
      BP = 32
      EB = <u>32</u>
              122 ∴ Deficit of 8 periods.

The proposed teaching load should be based on the load usually given to

Heads of Department, Year-Tutors or House-Tutors, Deputy Heads etc. The numbers should be mathematically feasible. For example in the list shown above, if EB teaches History only in the Lower School where all the History is taught in bundles of 3 periods, then EB = 32 implies that he will teach 30 periods of History with 10 groups and then
either: 2 periods of History sharing a class with someone else
or: 2 periods of another subject, perhaps Games or RE

It is sometimes worth noting (and later providing to Heads of Departments as a guide) how the teaching load for a member of the department could break down into classes. For example (from the list above), assuming that History is provided for 3 periods per group in Lower School and 4 periods per group in Upper School, then:

BP = 32 (= 8 classes × 3 periods + 2 × 4 periods
   or 4 classes × 3 periods + 5 × 4 periods)

(c) *If the totals from part (a) and part (b) do not agree exactly, then make suggestions about possible solutions.*
For example:
History deficit = 8 periods

1. If AH in the English Department teaches 8 periods of History (she has some experience, is willing, English Department has some 'slack') then the totals balance but it leads to at least one split class (for EB).
2. If AH in the English Department teaches 10 periods of History (= 2 × 3 periods + 1 × 4 periods) then EB could do 2 periods of Games (he would like this).
3. JC, although Year-Tutor, could be asked to teach 30 periods this year, with AH = 8 periods of History and EB = 2 periods of Games.
Etc. etc.

When this has been done for all departments, a look at the alternatives should lead to a way of balancing all the departments and covering the necessary periods of Games, RE, General Studies etc. This process may well involve a certain amount of negotiation (sometimes delicate negotiation) between the Director of Studies, Heads of Departments and individual members of departments, as these 'musical chairs' moves are used to balance the staff against the curriculum.

4.3 Producing the Curriculum Plan

The Curriculum Plan is the document which shows, for all the classes in the school, the number of periods of each subject to be studied.
There is more than one way of doing this. I prefer to build up a booklet with one A4 sheet of paper to each year group. On each sheet I prefer to keep the time-axis vertical with the classes shown horizontally.

52 *Timetabling*

For example, the curriculum (for the bands 4A, 4B, 4C) that was shown in section 3.2 would appear as:

4A 60 = 31B + 29G	**4B** 60 = 29B + 31G	**4C** 69 = 41B + 28G
E_6 $\quad\quad$ E_6	E_6 $\quad\quad$ E_6	E_7 $\quad$ E_7 $\quad$ E_7
M_6 $\quad\quad$ M_6	M_6 $\quad\quad$ M_6	M_6 $\quad$ M_6 $\quad$ M_6
P or C or B_4	P or C or B or Sc_4	B or B or Sc or Sc_4
H or H or G_4	H or H or G_4	H or H or G_4
F or F or F_5	F or B or G_4	Art or Wwk or DSc or DSc Q
Art or TD or G_4	Art or Typ or P or Mwk_4	Nwk or TD or Typ or Typ_4
Mu or Ger or P_4	Wwk or TD or Nwk or Dsc Q	Mu or Nwk or Mwk or Mwk_4
PE $\quad$ PE_3	PE $\quad$ PE_3	PE $\quad$ PE $\quad$ PE_3
RE $\quad$ RE_1	RE $\quad$ RE_1	RE $\quad$ RE $\quad$ RE_1
Mu $\quad$ Mu_1	Mu $\quad$ Mu_1	Mu $\quad$ Mu $\quad$ Mu_1
Car $\quad$ Car_1	Car $\quad$ Car_1	Car $\quad$ Car $\quad$ Car_1
GSt $\quad$ GSt_1	GSt $\quad$ GSt_1	GSt $\quad$ GSt $\quad$ GSt_1

Figure 16

A Curriculum Plan should show:
the name of each form or band in the year group, with the number of pupils expected
the sets which are common to more than one form or band
the subjects for each form or band
the number of periods for each subject

You may also like to add the period breakdown to each rectangle in the Plan. For example: 2D = two double periods; D + 2S = one double and two singles. Similarly with T for triple periods, Q for quadruple periods.

The Curriculum Plan does not necessarily show the arrangement as it will finally appear on the printed timetable. For example, in the Plan shown above, the single periods of RE, Music, Careers and General Studies for 4A might well be timetabled as:

RE – Mu
Mu – Car
Car – GSt
GSt – RE
or some other workable arrangement.

The sheets of the Curriculum Plan, one sheet for each year-group, may be stapled together into a booklet. The timetabler's personal copy of this Curriculum Booklet will become his or her 'master' document once the names of staff are added to it (see section 4.5). In the booklet, the blank page opposite the

Collecting the data

plan of each year-group can be used for notes about part-timers, special assignments of classes (TV or swimming baths), special timetabling manoeuvres etc.

4.4 The Staffing Form

The next stage is to provide each Head of Department with three things:

(i) *A Curriculum Booklet*. In this, each Head of Department can see all the classes for which he or she will be responsible. The Curriculum Booklet may also draw attention (perhaps on the cover) to any changes in the structure of the curriculum. It may also include requests such as 'Heads of Departments are asked to produce a balanced distribution of experienced staff between Upper School and Lower School' or 'Heads of Departments are urged to teach at least one 1st Year class personally'. You may prefer to give copies of the Curriculum Booklet only to Heads of Departments at this stage or you may think it better to give one to all members of staff so that everyone is aware of what is proposed.

(ii) *Some information* on the expected teaching load of each member of the department. i.e. a list of the proposed number of periods for each member of the department as suggested in part (b) of section 4.2.

(iii) *A Staffing Form* on which the Head of Department can provide you with the data that you need. Ideally, before providing you with this information, the Head of Department will have applied the first timetable check (see chapter 5) to his department, so that he is aware of any problems arising and has done his best to solve them before filling in the Staffing Form.

The layout of the Staffing Form varies from school to school. One such layout is shown in Figures 17 and 18.

The top half of the Staffing Form (A4 or foolscap size) shows each class or band in the school, with two columns against each (Figure 17).

In the first column after the class name, the Head of Department writes the initials of the teacher he wishes to teach that class. If it is essential that the class is taught by that teacher then an asterisk is marked in the second column. (This will

\multicolumn{4}{c	}{Staffing Form for History. Department 19..}			
1A$_1$	AF	\} any order	4A	AF	*
1A$_2$	JC			JC	*
1a$_1$	EB		4B	BP	\}
1a$_2$	BP			AH	
1B$_1$	AF				
1B$_2$	JC	\} "	4C	BP	\}
1β$_1$	EB			AF	
1β$_2$	BP				
2A	AF	←	5A	AF	*
2a	BP			BP	*

Figure 17

54 Timetabling

usually apply to all the 5th Year groups and some of the 4th Year groups.)

If it is not essential that the class is taken by the teacher shown in column 1, then the initials of another teacher can be shown in column 2. Alternatively, two or more teachers who could interchange classes can be linked in column 2 by arrows or brackets. This can save time later if the timetabler wishes to make a change in the staffing and knows some of the changes that will be acceptable to the department.

The lower part of the Staffing Form shows the number of periods for each member of the department:

Preferred rooms		Staff (initials)	Numbers of teaching periods (in pencil please)								
Lower School	Upper School		1	2	3	4	5	6G	6L	6U	Totals
25	7	AF	6			8	8			8	30
24	8	JC	6	3	3	4	4		8		28
24	8	BP	6	3	3	8	8	4			32
25		EB	6	12	12						30(+26a)
24	7	AH			3	3	4				10(+22E)
Totals:			24	21	21	24	20	4	8	8	=130

Figure 18

For each member of the department, a horizontal line shows the distribution of his teaching periods throughout the school. The 'rooms' section at the left (shown here for a split-site school) may not be necessary.

The reverse side of the Staffing Form may contain some or all of the following requests to Heads of Departments:

to use non-overlapping teacher teams for Maths and English etc., as much as possible (see chapter 5)
to apply the first timetable check (chapter 5) if you have previously explained this test as part of an in-service training programme
to keep part-time teachers out of option blocks or teams of teachers
to check that the department has staffed all the groups for which it is responsible
to note briefly any specific complaints about the current timetable
to note in detail any timetabling limitations that will affect the department for the coming year:
    e.g. days and times for part-time teachers
        essential days and times for particular lessons (TV, swimming etc.)
        requests for particular classes to be timetabled in parallel or grouped in a particular way for team-teaching
to return the Staffing Form as soon as possible

4.5 Checking the Staffing Forms

When the forms are returned, it is wise to check everything. For example:

Are the initials and asterisks on the upper part of the form clearly attached to classes?

Does the distribution of each teacher on the upper part of the form correspond to the distribution of the same teacher on the lower part?

Is the arithmetic of the bottom part correct? The totals underneath each year-group should correspond to the totals calculated in part (a) of section 4.2 (page 50).

The totals in the right-hand column should correspond to the final decisions made in part (b) of section 4.2. These two sets of totals should give the same grand total for the department in the bottom right-hand corner of the Staffing Form.

Are you quite sure which teachers are part-time? It is best to put a ring round their initials. Are you quite sure which days and times they are available?

Are you quite sure about the times requested for swimming, TV programmes, links with the local Further Education college etc.?

Is there anything in the complaints about the current timetable that may affect your approach to the new timetable?

Once the checking is completed, the initials of the members of staff can be added to the timetabler's copy of the Curriculum Booklet. This is the Master Booklet which will contain all the information that has to be timetabled. The Master Booklet will be at the timetabler's side throughout the next few weeks of work.

The staff initials should be added in pencil (nothing is finally decided yet) into the rectangles on each sheet of the Master Curriculum Booklet, next to the appropriate subject. It helps to ring the initials of part-timers in red. The days and times of availability of part-timers can be collected on to one blank page of the booklet for easy reference. Requests for particular times for swimming, TV etc., should be marked against the relevant classes.

4.6 The Staff Loading Chart

This is the second 'master' document. It shows for all members of staff their teaching load, the classes they are due to teach, the Form-Tutors of each class and in the case of a split-site school, the weighting of staff by periods between the buildings.

There are different ways of doing this but I think the best is that shown in Figure 19.

As before, *classes* are shown horizontally with *staff* (grouped by departments) shown vertically. The size of the chart obviously depends on the size of the school, but even large schools will fit comfortably on to two sheets (Sellotaped together) of double-leaf squared paper such as that found in teachers' mark books.

56 Timetabling

	Name	Total	LS-US	base	1A 1a 1B 1ß	2A 2a 2B 2ß	3A .
M	Alcock	30	6-24	u	M_6		
A	Bull	32	26-6	L	M_6	M_6 (M_6)	
T	Carr	32	20-12	L	E_6		M_6
H	(Driver)	12	12-0	(L)	M_4		
S	XM	26	20-6	u	M_6 M_2	M_6	

Figure 19

The first columns, at the left, show the name of the department and the member of staff, followed by his or her total teaching load.

The next two columns are relevant only to a split-site school. The first of these two columns shows the split (in periods) between the Lower School site and the Upper School site. This will be important information at the scheduling stage when we are determining priorities. The second of these two columns simply shows in which building the teacher will be based for registration and administrative purposes.

The remaining columns of the chart show, for each class and for each teacher, the subject and the number of periods.

For example, in the Maths Department of the split-site school shown in the diagram above, Alcock is teaching for a total of 30 periods; 6 periods in the Lower School, 24 in Upper School, so he is based in Upper School. The 6 periods he is to teach in Lower School will be spent teaching Maths (M) to class 1B. Bull is teaching 32 periods; based in Lower School; some of his Lower School classes are shown; in each case he is teaching Maths. The circle, added at a later date, shows that Bull is to be the Form-Tutor of 2B. Carr is to teach 32 periods, split 20–12 between the buildings (this is a more difficult split and so he will have a higher priority at the scheduling stage than Alcock and Bull). Carr is based in Lower School and is evidently a member of the Maths Department but also teaches English for 6 periods to 1A. Driver is a part-timer (the name is ringed) teaching only 12 periods. XM (X-Maths) is an unknown person, yet to be appointed, probably a probationer with only 26 teaching periods. Unfortunately Driver and XM have to split the teaching of a class (1ß) between them.

The chart should balance arithmetically both horizontally and vertically. Horizontally, for each teacher, the totals of the classes should agree with the 'total' column; vertically, for each class, the totals of the subjects should agree with the total number of periods in a teaching week.

The Staff Loading Chart is useful in many ways during the timetabling process. For the Head it shows at a glance the teaching load of each member of staff and the intended distribution throughout the classes of the school. The Head may wish to make changes here. The Chart is useful when deciding Form-Tutors, if you wish to ensure that each Form-Tutor also teaches his form. (The final result of choosing Form-Tutors must be one ring in each class column). The Chart is useful in checking the total full-time-equivalent number of staff in order to agree with the LEA's staffing allocation. In a split-site school the Chart is useful when deciding on an order of priorities for the scheduling of staff that commute between buildings.

Having obtained the data and checked the arithmetic, the timetabler naturally feels an urge to move immediately to the scheduling stage. This is a mistake. Almost certainly there are mathematical impossibilities in the data. During the last few years some simple tests have been devised to identify some of these impossibilities so that they can be removed by modifying the data *before* the difficult task of scheduling begins. These tests are explained in the next four chapters.

5 Timetable test 1

The Combing Chart

5.1 Introduction
5.2 Teacher teams
5.3 The Principle of Compatibility
5.4 Choosing teacher teams — worked example
5.5 The Combing Chart — worked example
5.6 The Combing Chart for more than one department — worked example
5.7 Schematic Diagrams
5.8 The principle of compatibility and time
5.9 The principle of compatibility and class-combinations
5.10 The principle of compatibility and room-combinations
5.11 Summary

The sets of data received on the Staffing Forms are almost certainly incompatible. Because of the wide range of options that we offer in our schools and because we usually allow departments some freedom in choosing the staff to teach the groups, the sets of data we receive almost certainly contain some mathematical impossibilities. These impossibilities will force us to compromise, either at this stage or later during the scheduling stage.

All scheduling is likely to involve some compromise, although obviously we wish the compromising to be as inconsequential as possible. Compromises made in a logical way at this present stage are likely to have less consequence and be more acceptable to the staff than compromises forced on the timetabler during the scheduling stage.

The compromises that have come to be accepted by the teaching staff vary somewhat from school to school. Timetablers naturally vary in the amount of patience and ingenuity they can maintain in order to obtain a better solution. Some of the compromises that may be forced during scheduling are listed here:

1 *Alteration to the requested period spread.* This happens most frequently to Modern Languages.
   E.g. French scheduled for 5 periods on 4 days instead of 1 period per day.
2 *Alteration to the requested period breakdown.*
   e.g. Art or Science scheduled as single periods in the 1st Year although doubles were requested.
3 *Specialist subjects taught in ordinary classrooms.*
   e.g. all four periods of Physics taught in a classroom.
4 *The requested teacher replaced by an alternative in the same department.*
   e.g. a probationary teacher replaces the Head of Department for a tough 3rd Year class.

5   *The requested teacher replaced by an alternative in the same department for some periods during the week.*
    e.g. class 3A has two teachers for Maths.
6   *The requested teacher replaced by a member of another department.*
    e.g. some time ago, a Deputy was heard to say (at the scheduling stage): 'Those two Craft teachers will have to teach Maths.'
7   *Setting scheduled for only some of the periods.*
    e.g. 4th Year Maths setted for only 4 out of the 6 periods.
8   *Multiple periods spanning a break or a lunchtime.*
    e.g. a double period of Science across a break.
9   *Alteration to the expected number of periods.*
    e.g. Lower Sixth Chemistry allocated only 6 periods instead of the usual 8 periods.
10 *Inability to allocate any teacher.*
    e.g. a Deputy was heard to say (at the scheduling stage):
    'Office Practice for the 4th Year will have to be cancelled.'

There is no known method of determining whether a given set of data can be timetabled without compromise (other than by completing a full timetable). However, there are tests which will detect some of the impossibilities *and pinpoint the reasons for them.*

In considering these feasibility tests it is important to remember that it is *teachers* that clash, not subjects. That is, clashes are not introduced directly by the curriculum on which we have decided, but only indirectly by way of the teachers who are chosen to staff the groups. For some groups the Department's choice of a teacher will be made for sound educational reasons; for other groups the choice may be arbitrary. Once the feasibility tests have pinpointed an area of difficulty, one can look for simple and acceptable modifications to the data on the Staffing Forms.

These modifications may be crucial but simple. Perhaps, by happenstance, a certain teacher is due to teach 1C, according to the Staffing Form. For timetabling, the feasibility tests show that it would be far better if he taught 1B instead. The Head of Department does not mind, the teacher does not mind, but for the timetabler the difference could be crucial.

5.2   Teacher teams

Teams of teachers are obviously more difficult to schedule than single teachers. The number and size of the teacher teams in our schools tend to increase as Heads of Departments request them for a variety of reasons:

(a)   to allow setting or team teaching, e.g. in Mathematics, English, Languages
(b)   to allow a choice of subjects, e.g. in the option pools
(c)   to allow separation by sex, e.g. for PE
(d)   to reduce class size, e.g. if two classes are scheduled together and allocated three teachers
(e)   to allow a cycle of rotation during the year, e.g. in Art and Crafts

60 Timetabling

In choosing the teams for these activities, we want the teams to be compatible so that they can be timetabled within the 35 or 40 periods in a week. For example, consider a remedial department consisting of three teachers, numbered 1, 2, 3. Each is due to teach for 30 periods (in a 40-period week). On the Staffing Form, the Head of Department requests that:

teachers 1 and 2 teach together for 15 periods
and teachers 2 and 3 teach together for 15 periods
and teachers 1 and 3 teach together for 15 periods
Question: is this possible?

To see the situation clearly, consider a diagram of teachers against time as shown in Figure 20. The vertical axis shows the three teachers. The horizontal axis shows a length of time in periods. By drawing a horizontal bar for each teacher in a teacher team, we can see the total number of periods needed for this remedial department.

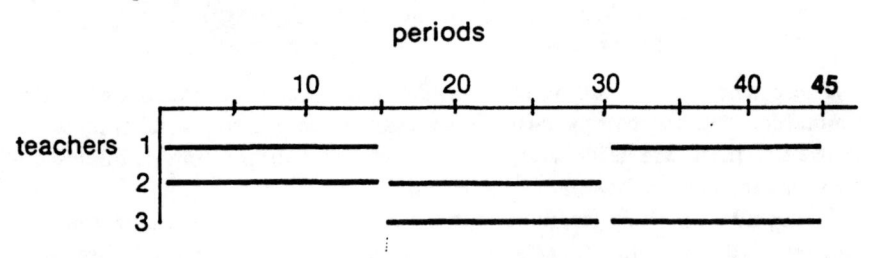

Figure 20

We can see that this arrangement requires 45 periods (even though each teacher teaches only 30 periods). It could not possibly fit into a 40-period week. The chosen teams were not compatible with the available timeframe.

Now consider another example. A small Mathematics department consists of 6 teachers, numbered 1 to 6. Each teacher is to teach for 30 periods. They are in an 11-16 school where each of the five year-groups is divided into 2 half-year bands (called A and B). Each band requires a team of 3 teachers. The Head of Department might request the teams shown in Figure 21.

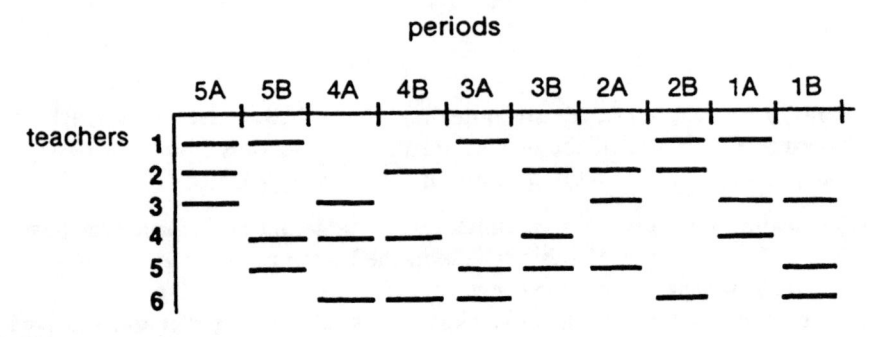

Figure 21

The chart shows that the team for 5th Year band A is made of teachers 1, 2, 3. For band 5B, the teachers are 1, 4, 5. These two teams cannot teach at the same time because they have teacher 1 in common (and teacher 1 cannot teach two classes at the same time).

For 4A the teachers are 3, 4, 6. This team cannot teach at the same time as the 5A team (because of teacher 3), nor can this team teach at the same time as the 5B team (because of teacher 4). The three teams considered so far would need $3 \times 6 = 18$ periods of the week.

Inspecting the other teams one by one shows that *none* of them can teach at the same time as any other team. Each team overlaps every other team.

Each teacher teaches five classes, each of 6 periods, and so teaches 30 periods per week. However, since no team can exist at the same time as any other team, the total length of time needed for the teams to teach all 10 bands is $10 \times 6 = 60$ periods. In a 40-period week this is clearly impossible.

This example is an extreme case where all the teams clash. Now consider an ideal situation, unlikely to be obtained in practice but something to aim for. Figure 22 shows the same Maths department with the same 6 teachers teaching the same number of groups.

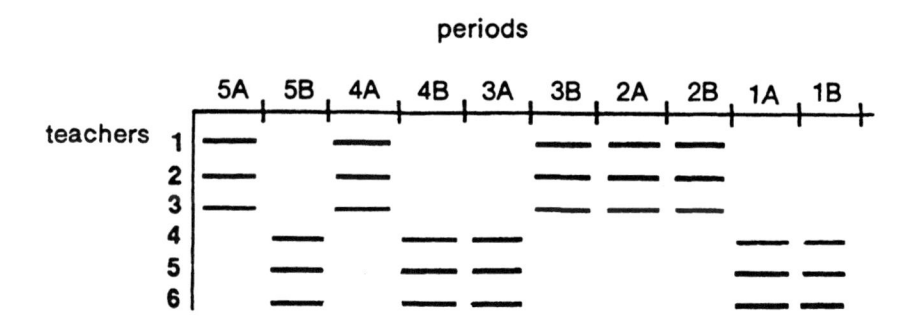

Figure 22

In this diagram the team for 5A does not overlap the team for 5B. The teams are said to be non-overlapping or *disjoint* or compatible. This means that 5A and 5B can be timetabled at the same time. Similarly with 4A, 4B etc.

Comparing the two diagrams above for this Maths department, we can see the difference between them: the second diagram can be squeezed up by sliding the 4, 5, 6 teams to the left, under the 1, 2, 3 teams. The whole diagram will then fit into a time of only 30 periods, as shown in Figure 23.

These diagrams are called 'Combing Charts'. The horizontal bars for the teams can be thought of as the teeth of combs which allow or prevent other teams moving or 'combing' to the left.

62 Timetabling

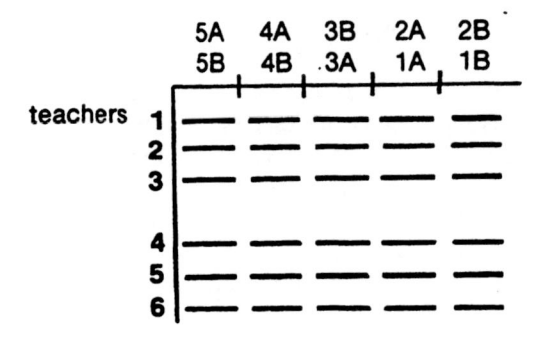

```
                    periods

            5A   4A   3B   2A   2B
            5B   4B   3A   1A   1B
teachers  1 ─── ─── ─── ─── ───
          2 ─── ─── ─── ─── ───
          3 ─── ─── ─── ─── ───

          4 ─── ─── ─── ─── ───
          5 ─── ─── ─── ─── ───
          6 ─── ─── ─── ─── ───
```

Figure 23

It is clear that these non-overlapping, compatible teams give much greater flexibility at the scheduling stage. In fact there are two advantages with non-overlapping teams:

(a) Non-overlapping teams will fit into a smaller number of periods (overlapping teams may not fit into the school week).
(b) There is a greater number of different ways of fitting non-overlapping teams. In the last diagram, the labels show 5A paired with 5B, but 5A could well be paired with 4B while 5B could be paired with 2A etc. This interchangeability gives much greater flexibility at the scheduling stage.

5.3 The principle of compatibility

In the light of the previous section let us see how a department might choose *ideal* teacher teams. Consider a large department — English, Maths or perhaps Science — consisting of 12 teachers, numbered 1-12. Suppose that for one of the year-groups we need a team of 6 teachers. Clearly there are many ways of choosing 6 teachers, but suppose we choose the teachers numbered from 1 to 6. This team is marked as team A in Figure 24. Suppose now that we need a team of 6 teachers for another year-group. There are only two possibilities if we want non-overlapping teams — either we choose the team of the same 6 teachers (team A) or we choose the team of the *other* 6 teachers (team B).

The teams are subsets of the department. Because team A and team B are non-overlapping teams they are called *disjoint subsets*. In choosing other teams in this department, we should follow the same principle.

Suppose, for other parts of the school, we need teams of 3 teachers. Ideally each 3-team should be chosen from *within* one of the 6-teams. For example, in Figure 24, 3-team P (teachers 1, 2, 3) is entirely within 6-team A. This means that

Timetable test 1 – the Combing Chart 63

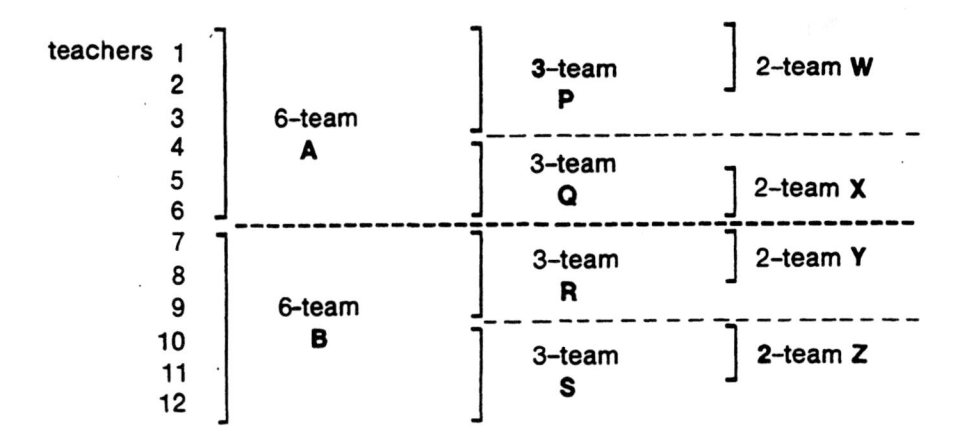

```
teachers  1  ⎤          ⎤  3-team  ⎤  2-team W
          2  ⎥          ⎥     P    ⎦
          3  ⎥  6-team  ⎦ _ _ _ _ _ _ _ _ _ _ _ _ _
          4  ⎥    A     ⎤  3-team
          5  ⎥          ⎥     Q    ⎤  2-team X
          6  ⎦          ⎦          ⎦ _ _ _ _ _ _ _
          7  ⎤          ⎤  3-team  ⎤  2-team Y
          8  ⎥          ⎥     R    ⎦
          9  ⎥  6-team  ⎦ _ _ _ _ _ _ _ _ _ _ _ _ _
         10  ⎥    B     ⎤  3-team
         11  ⎥          ⎥     S    ⎤  2-team Z
         12  ⎦          ⎦          ⎦
```

Figure 24

3-team P can teach at the same time as 6-team B, if we wish to schedule them that way. Choosing a 3-team such as teachers 1, 2, 7 would be less satisfactory because it would clash with both team A and team B.

Once 3-team P is chosen to be teachers 1, 2, 3 (as in the diagram), the only other disjoint subset of team A is 3-team Q (teachers 4, 5, 6). Similarly teams R and S are disjoint subsets of team B.

When it comes to choosing 2-teams, these should be chosen from *within* the 3-teams, as shown. At each level, each team should be chosen from *within* a larger team. In the diagram the horizontal dashed lines show the boundaries which should not be crossed.

This principle is called the *Principle of Compatibility*. It can be applied to sets of resources other than teachers, as we shall see in later sections of this chapter. The principle states that, *to fit sets of resources into the minimum number of periods, with the maximum flexibility, disjoint subsets should be chosen.*

In applying the principle to the staffing of your school, two points should be noted:

1 The rigid application of the principle is an ideal: there are likely to be sound educational reasons preventing your teacher teams from being entirely non-overlapping. However, it is important for Heads of Departments to realise that each departure from the principle implies a loss of flexibility, with a consequent possibility of compromises in the final timetable. If such compromising forces a change of teacher, then the change will always be towards a greater obedience to the principle.
2 In applying the principle, it is the choice of the largest team that is the most critical. In the example, the initial choice of 6-team A limited the possibilities for all the other teams.

5.4 Choosing teacher teams — worked example

You are the Head of the English Department at the Laura Norder High School. The department is composed of 10 teachers, numbered 1–10. The timetabling of your department has been difficult and unsatisfactory in recent years and you resolve to improve the situation.

Teachers 1, 3, 5, 7, 9 are due to continue with their classes into the new 5th Year (as a team of 5).

(a) You need to choose a team of 5 for the new 4th Year.
    What are the alternatives? Which is the better alternative?
(b) You remember that you have promised teachers 9 and 10 that they can teach the new 4th Year. What do you do?
(c) For the 3rd Year, you need to choose a team of 4.
    Teachers 1 and 2 take several withdrawal groups.
    Teacher 3 is the 3rd Year Tutor.
    Which team would you choose?
(d) For the 1st Year a team of 6 is needed.
    Suggest an item for the agenda of the next meeting of the School's Curriculum Study Group.

If we assume that we need consider only the educational factors that have been mentioned in the questions, then I suggest the solutions should be:

(a) Since the 5th Year has a 5-team of all the odd-numbered teachers, then the choice is either all the *odd* teachers or all the *even* teachers.
    If the odd team is chosen again, then the even team will not teach any of the Upper School classes. In some schools this may be preferred. However, if all members of the department are to be given the chance of teaching 4th- and 5th-Year pupils, then the even team must be chosen.
(b) If you decide on the even team then teacher 9 (odd) must be told of your decision, with reasons. Ideally all members of the department should be made aware of the principle of compatibility and the ways in which it affects the timetable. As Head of Department you might also resolve not to make any promises in future until your position is clear.
(c) Since teacher 3 (odd) is the 3rd Year Tutor, the 4-team should be chosen from *within* the odd 5-team (so that it will be disjoint with the even 5-team). As teacher 1 is involved in withdrawal work, the 4-team should be teachers 3, 5, 7, 9.
(d) A team of 6 could be chosen for the 1st Year but it could not be disjoint with the 5-teams for the 4th Year and 5th Year. If despite this a 6-team was chosen, then the best choice would be the 6 members of the department who were not in the 4-team for the 3rd Year. Then at least the 3rd Year and the 1st Year could be scheduled at the same time.
However, for greater flexibility the 1st Year team should be a disjoint subset of the other teams. It might be worthwhile suggesting to the School's Curriculum Study Group that there would be benefits to your department

and to the whole school if the 1st Year was scheduled as two half-year groups, each requiring disjoint 3-teams.

If, in practice, not all the teams are disjoint subsets then we need a feasibility test to apply to the department. For this we use a Combing Chart.

5.5 The Combing Chart — worked example

In practice we do not get ideal teacher teams. Even where Heads of Departments understand the principle of compatibility, there will usually be some reason why the teams are not perfectly disjoint. We need a feasibility test to apply to a department to see if the teacher teams will fit into the school week. This test ('timetable check number 1') consists of drawing a Combing Chart like Figures 20-23 in section 5.2.

For example, consider a Mathematics department of 6 teachers staffed as in Figure 25.

Year and band (6 periods each)	Teachers
5A	1, 3, 4
5B	3, 5, 6
4A	1, 2, 3
4B	4, 5, 6
3A	1, 2, 3
3B	2, 4, 5
2A	1, 5, 6
2B	1, 2, 6
1A	4, 5, 6
1B	2, 3, 4

Figure 25

To draw the Combing Chart, we draw two axes (as in Section 5.2, Figures 20-23): teachers vertically and time horizontally. We usually begin with the most complicated teacher team. In this example all the teams are equal in size so we begin with the 'least-alterable' — the 5th Year. For 5A we draw horizontal lines, each 6 periods long, opposite each of the teachers involved (Figure 26).

At this point we are not considering the period breakdown; that is, we are not considering whether the 6 periods will be taught as 3 doubles or 6 singles etc. There is little point in looking at the finer detail until the main structure appears feasible.

66 Timetabling

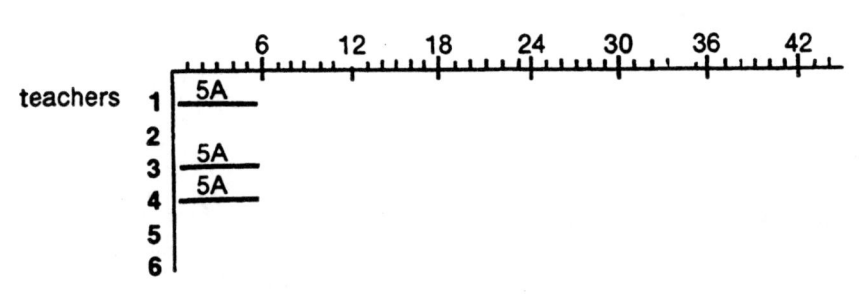

```
                          periods
                  6    12    18    24    30    36    42
teachers  1 | 5A
          2 |
          3 | 5A
          4 | 5A
          5 |
          6 |
```

Figure 26

The next team to be added, 5B, has teacher 3 in common with the team for 5A and so it must go into a new block of time. Similarly, 4A has teachers 1, 3 in common with 5A and teacher 3 in common with 5B, so that 4A team must use a further block of time. Similarly the 4B team clashes with the teams for 5A and 5B; however it does not clash with the 4A team and so it can fit into the *same* block of time as 4A. If you care to continue this process with the other teams, you should get a final picture as in Figure 27.

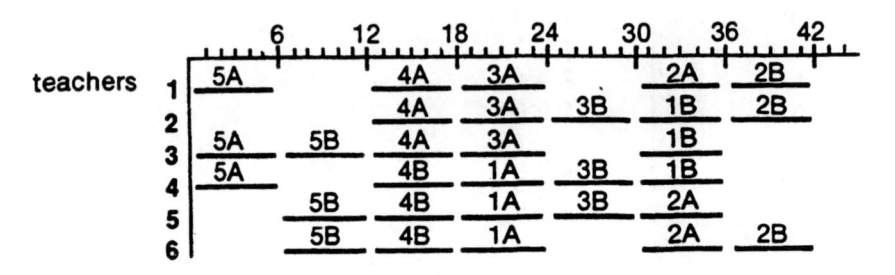

```
                          periods
                  6    12    18    24    30    36    42
teachers  1 | 5A         4A   3A         2A   2B
          2 |            4A   3A   3B    1B   2B
          3 | 5A   5B    4A   3A         1B
          4 | 5A         4B   1A   3B    1B
          5 |      5B    4B   1A   3B    2A
          6 |      5B    4B   1A         2A   2B
```

Figure 27

The columns, each 6 periods wide, could have occurred in a different order if you had considered the classes in a different order but the chart would be essentially the same. Clearly the object is to 'comb' the teams to the left as much as possible, into a shorter period of time.

In this example 42 periods are needed — a mathematical impossibility in a 40 period week. The Head of Department can see why his teams must be changed (without feeling suspicious about a timetabler saying 'It can't be done'). Further, the Head of Department can see which teachers to interchange to improve the situation.

The Head of Department may wish to adjust one team in order to bring the total time-span down to 36 periods. For the timetabler this will not be enough. True, it allows a solution for this department, but this department has to dovetail into other departments. Leaving this department with a period-spread of 36 periods will not allow a total solution unless this department is given the highest priority in scheduling (and then other departments will suffer compromises as a result). The rule seems to be: *if the maximum teaching load of a member of the department is n periods, then the Combing Chart for that department should fit into n periods.*

In our example, the maximum teaching load for anyone is 30 periods, so the chart should comb down to 30 periods. This could be achieved by interchanging teacher 4 in the 3B team with teacher 6 in the 2B team. Then the 3B team will fit against the 5A team and the 2B team will fit against the 5B team, the whole fitting into 30 periods.

Even this is not ideal as it gives an almost unique pairing of classes — the only alternatives to the pairings shown would be 4A-with-1A and 3A-with-4B. We want the chart not only to comb as much as possible to the left, but also to comb to the left with as many permutations as possible. Unless there are strong educational reasons against it, interchanging teachers 1 and 4 between the teams for 2A and 1B would improve the situation by making these teams compatible with the teams for 4A, 4B, 3A, 1A.

When making changes on the Combing Chart, it is useful to remember that if there is an unavoidable conflict between two teams, it is worthwhile positively compounding the conflict: two clashes are no worse than one. When taken to the limit this approach leads to non-overlapping teams.

The Combing Chart is the first main timetabling check. It is valuable for all members of staff to have some knowledge of the principle: it can form the basis of a useful in-service training meeting. Certainly the Head of each large department should be expected to draw up his own Combing Chart before completing the Staffing Form.

A computer can be used to draw a Combing Chart (see Appendix 11). Such a program is not outstandingly useful because often there is more to be learned in the drawing of the chart than merely in the completing of it.

5.6 The Combing Chart for more than one department — worked example

'General Subjects' teachers can cause difficulties because they link two or more departments together. Since such teachers are likely to become more common as falling rolls reduce the sizes of our schools, it is worthwhile noting some ways of reducing the conflicts that they cause. Consider a case where a teacher 'HG' offers both History and Geography. Clashes are less likely to occur in scheduling if the following rules are observed:

(a) Teacher HG should not be a member of a team in either the History

department or the Geography department — that is, he should teach pure class activities only.
(b) If teacher HG must be a member of a team, try to limit this to only one team in each department.
(c) Whether teacher HG teaches in a team or not, try to arrange for him to teach the *same* class for *both* subjects. This does not eliminate the teacher conflict, but it does link it to a conflict which already exists (the conflict between a class and itself) and so it reduces the total number of conflicts. For example if HG teaches 3A for History and 3B for Geography, then 3A History cannot occur simultaneously with 3B Geography. However, if HG teaches 3A for both History and Geography then, because of HG, 3A History cannot occur simultaneously with 3A Geography — but it never could do that because 3A cannot have two subjects simultaneously.

In cases where a teacher is shared by two departments, a Combing Chart drawn by each Head of Department will not show the full picture. To see that, the timetabler should draw a Combing Chart for both departments combined.

The timetabler may also wish to draw a large Combing Chart to investigate the teams in the option pools. This is particularly useful when there are interchangeable teachers. For example, in 4th Year band A there may be two Biology groups, one in pool 3 and one in pool 5. The Head of Department has requested teachers AB and CD for these groups but does not care which teacher takes which group. For you, the timetabler, one arrangement might be very much better than the other. A Combing Chart of the teacher teams in the option pools will help you to decide which is the better arrangement for scheduling.

Consider an example. The 5th Year and 4th Year teacher teams in Figure 28 are to be timetabled across a full year-group in each case.

	teachers	
5th Year team 1 (4 periods)	1, 4, 8, 10	
5th Year team 2 (4 periods)	2, 5, 9, 11	12 periods
5th Year team 3 (4 periods)	3, 6, 7, 12	
4th Year team 1 (4 periods)	2, 5, 7, 10	
4th Year team 2 (4 periods)	2, 3, 7 with 8 *or* 9	12 periods
4th Year team 3 (4 periods)	1, 4, 6 with 9 *or* 8	

Figure 28

These teams could be the teams for Maths or English sets or the teams for option pools. In 4th Year team 2 and team 3 there are alternatives: the Head of Department has specified that teacher 8 should teach one group and teacher 9 the other group, but it does not matter which. We can draw a Combing Chart to find the better arrangement.

Usually it is best to begin with the largest teacher team. Here they are equal in size so we begin with the 5th Year teams. A word of warning here: the 5th Year

Timetable test 1 – the Combing Chart

teams do not have any teachers in common and so it might be thought that they could be combed to the left of the chart and all fitted into the same 4-period block. This is not possible. The 5th Year teams are all due to teach the same pupils and cannot do so simultaneously.

The 5th Year teams will fit into 12 periods. The 4th Year teams would also fit into 12 periods. Ideally all the teams should fit into the same 12 periods. This would be the best case. The worst case would be if the teams were entirely incompatible, in which case 24 periods would be needed for these teams.

To find the number of periods actually needed, we can continue by trying to fit in 4th Year team 1. This clashes with each of the 5th Year teams and so cannot be combed to the left but needs an extra 4-period space (Figure 29).

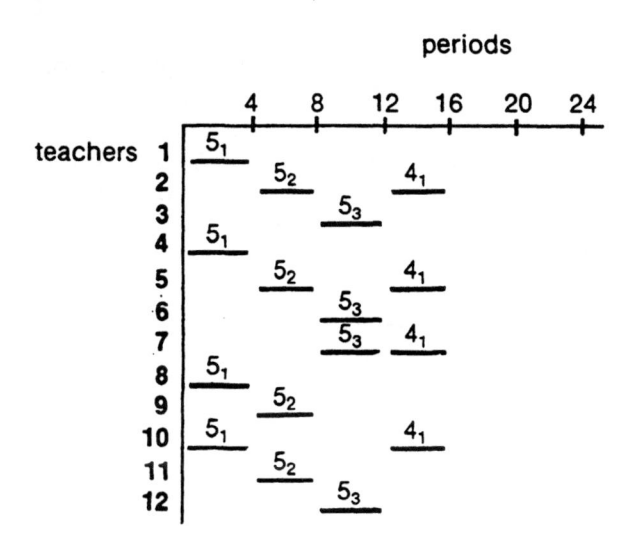

Figure 29

Now consider 4th Year team 2 and team 3. Let us begin by looking at the first alternatives for the teachers (i.e. teacher 8 in team 2 and teachers 9 in team 3). In this case both teams clash with everything fitted so far. 24 periods would be needed to fit the teams and the solution space is considerably reduced.

Now consider the other alternative (teacher 9 in team 2 and teacher 8 in team 3). Now 4th Year team 2 will fit against 5th Year team 1 and 4th Year team 3 will fit against 5th Year team 2 (it is left to the reader to draw in the bars on the diagram).

A total of 16 periods is needed. Although this is less than the first alternative, it is still not a very good solution. The diagram shows a unique fit; there is no flexibility; none of the teams can pair up in any way other than those shown. Ideally the teams ought to be able to pair up in many different ways (as discussed

70 Timetabling

in section 5.2). Of course in this example we have looked only at some of the teacher teams. When all the other teams for the 5th Year and 4th Year are fitted, it may be that the same combinations of teachers may appear, so allowing alternative pairings of teams. The more the principle of compatibility is followed, the more these alternative pairings will occur, giving more flexibility in scheduling.

In looking at these Combing Charts we have so far ignored the effect of different *period-breakdown* — that is, we have assumed that each group is taught in one large block of time (4 periods for each group in the current example). In practice this is not the case. If all the groups are taught in double periods or all the groups are taught in single periods then there is no problem. In fact some of the groups will be taught in single periods, some in double periods and some in triple or quadruple periods. This means that even if your Combing Chart fits into the length of the school week, it still may not be possible to schedule it into the school week. Consider the effect of varying period-breakdown in the current example. Suppose 5th Year team 1 is Craft, to be taught in one quadruple period while 4th Year team 2 is Science, to be taught in two double periods. Now all the periods for 4th Year team 2 will not fit against 5th Year team 1. Only one double will fit against 5th Year team 1 and the other double must go at the end, making a total of 18 periods now (Figure 30).

In general there is little point in looking at the finer detail of period-breakdown until the main structure appears feasible.

Some timetablers like to draw a Combing Chart showing *all* the teacher teams in the school (ignoring period-breakdown, at least initially). How rewarding this might be depends on the size of your school. Although a large school will fit on to

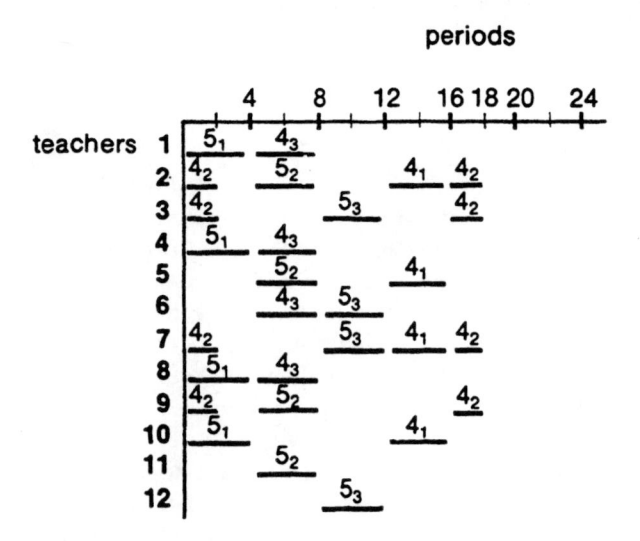

Figure 30

Timetable test 1 - the Combing Chart 71

two pieces of A4 paper, the number of possible combinations of teacher teams can make it very confusing. Using coloured felt-tip pens to identify subjects helps considerably.

(A much simpler way of investigating the teachers teams for the option pools is given in chapter 6, the Conflict Matrix).

When looking at the whole school, instead of using a Combing Chart (plotting *teachers* against time), some timetablers prefer to use a similar diagram but plotting *classes* against time. This is called a Schematic Diagram.

5.7 Schematic Diagrams

A Schematic Diagram is like a simplified school timetable. It plots classes against time but it ignores (at least initially) some of the essential features of the final timetable. A Schematic Diagram completely ignores the effects of period-breakdown, the effects of part-time teachers, the effects of fixed times for swimming and the requirement for the distribution of classes over the school week.

Schematic Diagrams can be useful in answering "What if........?" questions, particularly when a major change in the curriculum is being considered. In drawing a Schematic Diagram the classes are shown simply as blocks of time, for example as in Figure 31.

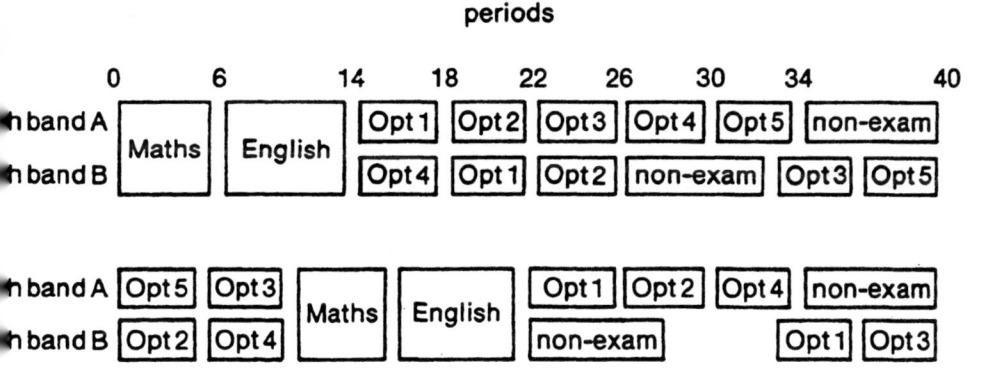

```
                              periods
       0        6        14    18   22   26   30   34     40
band A  ┌──────┬────────┬────┬────┬────┬────┬────┬─────────┐
        │Maths │English │Opt1│Opt2│Opt3│Opt4│Opt5│non-exam │
band B  │      │        │Opt4│Opt1│Opt2│non-exam│Opt3│Opt5│
        └──────┴────────┴────┴────┴────┴────────┴────┴────┘

band A  │Opt5│Opt3│         │       │Opt1│Opt2│Opt4│non-exam│
              Maths  English
band B  │Opt2│Opt4│         │       │non-exam │    │Opt1│Opt3│
```

Figure 31

This rather simple Schematic Diagram shows that 5A and 5B are combined for Maths and English. It shows that 5A option 1 can occur simultaneously with 5B option 4 — that is, there are no teacher-clashes between these two activities (the Conflict Matrix, chapter 6, helps here). When filling in a Schematic Diagram, great care must be taken to ensure that there are no clashes with other groups above or below. It helps to have movable pieces of coloured card or magnetic plastic with the names of the teachers marked (see also chapter 9).

If the example shown in Figure 31 is supposed to be completed and to have no

72 Timetabling

other alternative arrangement, then it shows that 4B option pool 5 cannot be fitted (perhaps because it is a heterogeneous pool). Even if a Schematic Diagram can be completed then a unique fit is not good news — the constraints of period-breakdown and part-time staff have yet to be imposed. It should be possible to complete the diagram in more than one way. The number of different ways it can be completed gives a measure of the flexibility you will have at the scheduling stage.

Another deduction that might be made from the Schematic Diagram shown in Figure 31 is that there may be a difficulty because of the simultaneous occurrence in 5A and 4A of 'non-exam' (RE, PE, Careers, General Studies, Music etc.). This may mean that the timetable needs four gymnasia or five RE teachers at the same time. A smaller Schematic Diagram, to look at 'non-exam', will show the possibilities. For those who wish to look at Schematic Diagrams in more detail, there are references in the bibliography.

5.8 The principle of compatibility and time

The school week is divided into subsets of periods by days, breaks and lunch-hours. These subsets are clearly disjoint and non-overlapping. The ways in which departments specify the period-breakdowns for their subjects must be compatible with the way in which the school week is divided.

For example, in a school operating a 35-period week with a 2-2-3 day, a Craft department might request 3 triple periods and 13 double periods for a particular room. This might appear to be possible (if difficult) because $(3 \times 3) + (13 \times 2) = 35$ periods. However a diagram shows it to be impossible (Figure 32).

In a similar way, a Head of Department might request 5 double periods for a part-timer who is available only for four afternoons per week.

If we consider now a 40-period week, similar considerations show that a 3-2-3 day is not a good one for scheduling unless there is a large number of triple periods. For a timetable requiring many double periods, it is poor. A Head of Department may specify a particular science laboratory or craft room for 16

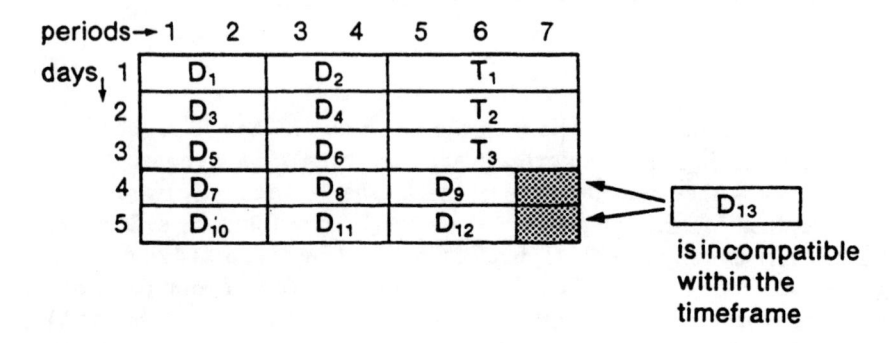

periods →	1	2	3	4	5	6	7
days 1	D_1		D_2		T_1		
2	D_3		D_4		T_2		
3	D_5		D_6		T_3		
4	D_7		D_8		D_9		▓
5	D_{10}		D_{11}		D_{12}		▓

D_{13} is incompatible within the timeframe

Figure 32

double periods in a 5-day week: with either a 2-2-3 day or a 3-2-3 day that is impossible. If a teacher or a room is to be used only for double periods, each can be used for a maximum of 30 periods per week in a 2-2-3 or a 3-2-3 arrangement.

For most schools, a 2-2-4 day or a 2-2-2-2 day is easiest to schedule, but this consideration may be over-ridden by other factors (e.g. the public transport services or other factors demanding a short afternoon).

The fitting of a department's requests into the time periods of a school week can be checked when the Combing Chart is drawn (section 5.5). Instead of leaving the horizontal axis as simply 0–40 periods, it can be divided by vertical lines into 3-2-3 or 2-2-2-2 days etc. Then the horizontal bars should be drawn in such a way that they do not cross any of these vertical lines. As mentioned earlier, it is best if Heads of Departments do this — then they will appreciate the necessity for change if their specification will not fit. A pro forma ruled sheet (sometimes called a Visual Planner) can be provided to the Heads of Departments with the Staffing Form.

Some schools have begun using staggered lunch breaks, or early starts and late finishes on some days for some year-groups. These tactics can give greater flexibility to the timetable and allow more efficient use of the limited resources of a school. (See also section 9.13.)

There is a further consideration regarding time: this is concerned with the time span of each option pool and the compulsory core subjects. There will be a more compatible arrangement, easier to timetable, if all the option pools and the compulsory core subjects are equal in time or are simple multiples or sub-multiples of each other. For example, the schematic diagram in section 5.7 would have been easier to fit if each of the option pools and the 'non-exam' had been 4 periods, with each of the Maths and English equal to 8 periods.

5.9 The principle of compatibility and class-combinations

Whenever classes are combined together for setting, team-teaching, options etc., the principle of compatibility can be applied to the ways in which they are combined. The class-combinations should be disjoint, non-overlapping.

For example, consider the proposal in Figure 33 for the grouping of English and Mathematics in the 4th Year.

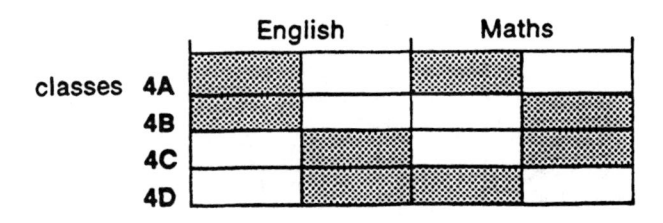

Figure 33

74 Timetabling

This will be difficult to schedule because the class-combinations for English and Maths are overlapping: each of the Maths combinations clashes with *both* of the English combinations. Clearly a consistent combination of classes would be easier to timetable.

As a more common example, consider Figure 34.

classes	ENGLISH	MATHS	FRENCH		PE
3A			etc.		
3B					
3C					PE
3D	ENGLISH	MATHS	FRENCH etc.		
3E					PE
3F					

Figure 34

If the classes are grouped as triplets for most of the week, changing to pairs for PE can lead to difficulties (PE for 3CD clashes with *both* half-year-groups). For compatibility the class-combinations for P.E. should be a subset *within* the other class-combinations.

In some cases, class-combinations within year-groups may be non-overlapping but still cause clashes with other year-groups because of the way they are staffed. For example, for English the classes might be staffed as in Figure 35.

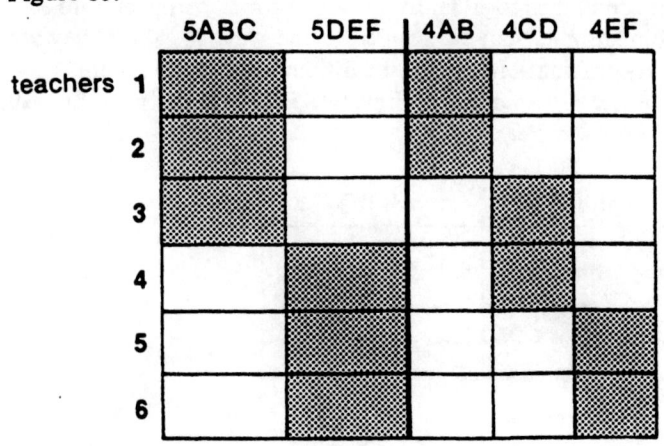

	5ABC	5DEF	4AB	4CD	4EF
teachers 1	■		■		
2	■		■		
3	■			■	
4		■		■	
5		■			■
6		■			■

Figure 35

In this case the class-combinations within the 5th Year are non-overlapping, as required by the principle of compatibility. The 4th Year class-combination are also disjoint within the 4th Year. However, because of the way they are staffed, 4CD clashes with both 5th Year teams.

5.10 The principle of compatibility and room-combinations

We have seen that the principle of compatibility has implications for the grouping of teachers, units of time and classes. It also has implications for the grouping of rooms. If a school were to teach classes entirely in specialist rooms then the principle would apply as severely to room-combinations as it does to teacher-combinations and class-combinations. It helps the timetabler if there is a suite of Maths rooms and the number of rooms corresponds to the number of staff in the teacher teams, but this is by no means essential. In practice, schools use alternative classrooms for many subjects.

Subjects such as Science, Craft, PE and Music will always be subject to rooming constraints, but the major constraint is usually one of total usage in the school week. This is discussed in chapter 7.

5.11 Summary

The principle of compatibility applies to teacher-teams, period-combinations in the school day, class-combinations and room-combinations. Strict adherence to the principle is usually impossible in practice but the greater the departure from the principle, the greater the loss in flexibility with a consequent loss in quality in the timetable.

The *first* of the timetable feasibility tests is the Combing Chart (section 5.5). Normally this test should be completed by each Head of Department so that each can see the implications of staffing decisions and can see why changes may be necessary.

It is possible for the timetabler to use the Combing Chart to check several interlocking departments and even the entire upper school option scheme. However such a chart will be very complicated and a better method is to use the *second* timetable feasibility test — the Conflict Matrix.

6 Timetable test 2
The Conflict Matrix

6.1 Introduction
6.2 The Conflict Matrix — worked example
6.3 Conflict Matrices for more than two year-groups
6.4 Including the effect of period-breakdown — worked example
6.5 Including the effect of other resources — rooms, equipment, part-time teachers
6.6 Using a microcomputer
6.7 Summary

Because the option pools require the simultaneous use of many resources, they tend to dominate the timetable and are given a high priority in scheduling. It is therefore particularly important to know whether the proposed staffing of the option pools is feasible.

The principle of compatibility and the Combing Chart are invaluable aids in choosing and testing the teacher teams within a department. However the Combing Chart can become complicated when used to check teams from the several departments in the option pools. A simpler method of investigating the mixed teams in option pools is to draw up a *Clash Table* or *Conflict Matrix*. The grander title is usually used, to distinguish it from the Clash Table used earlier to investigate the pupils' choices.

Initially the Conflict Matrix considers only the staffing of the teacher teams. If this proves feasible then other factors — period-breakdown, rooms, even teaching equipment — can be included. As well as identifying particular areas of conflict at an early stage, so saving time at the scheduling stage, the Conflict Matrix also helps the timetabler to decide which parts of the option scheme have the highest priority and should be scheduled first.

6.2 The Conflict Matrix — worked example

To simplify the example, consider a school in which the staffing for each of the 4th and 5th Years consists of only five teacher teams. Each of these teacher teams teaches across the full year group. The teams are as follows:

		teachers
4th Year:	Team 1	1, 3, 11, 15, 31
	Team 2	12, 24, 30, 32, 35
	Team 3	13, 14, 18, 20, 38
	Team 4	2, 14, 15, 20, 22
	Team 5	4, 11, 12, 13, 18
5th Year:	Team 1	1, 2, 3, 4, 5
	Team 2	6, 7, 8, 9, 10
	Team 3	11, 12, 13, 14, 15
	Team 4	16, 17, 18, 19, 20
	Team 5	21, 22, 23, 24, 25

Figure 36

The first question to be considered is: does this represent a feasible or an infeasible situation? To answer this we produce a Conflict Matrix by first drawing a grid of squares and then labelling each column with a 5th Year team and each row with a 4th Year team (Figure 37).

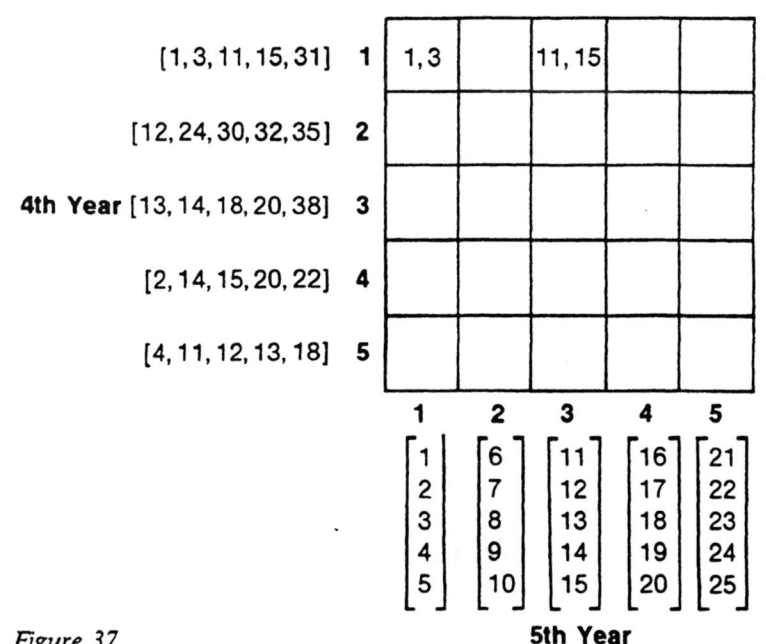

Figure 37

78 *Timetabling*

Then consider each cell of the matrix in turn. If that 4th Year team and that 5th Year team have a teacher in common, then that cell should be marked. It can be marked with a cross to show the clash; more usefully it can be marked with the names of the teachers who are causing the clash. This has been done for the first row of the matrix; you may like to complete the other cells yourself before looking at the result shown in Figure 38.

When all the clashes have been marked in, it is time to consider what the pattern means.

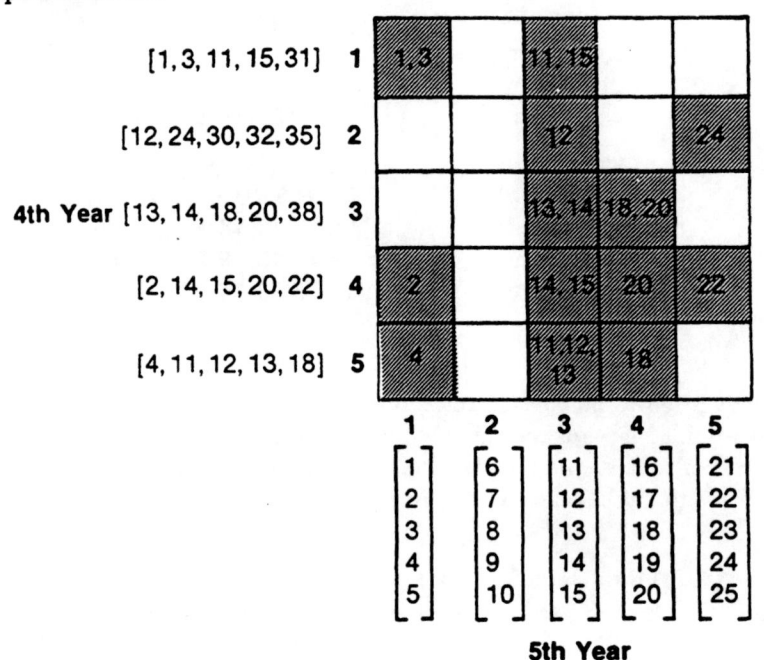

```
                                          1      2      3       4      5
              [1, 3, 11, 15, 31]   1  | 1,3  |      | 11,15 |      |      |
              [12, 24, 30, 32, 35] 2  |      |      |  12   |      |  24  |
   4th Year   [13, 14, 18, 20, 38] 3  |      |      | 13,14 | 18,20|      |
              [2, 14, 15, 20, 22]  4  |  2   |      | 14,15 |  20  |  22  |
              [4, 11, 12, 13, 18]  5  |  4   |      |11,12, |  18  |      |
                                                    |  13   |      |      |
                                          1      2      3       4      5
                                        ⎡1⎤    ⎡6⎤   ⎡11⎤   ⎡16⎤   ⎡21⎤
                                        ⎢2⎥    ⎢7⎥   ⎢12⎥   ⎢17⎥   ⎢22⎥
                                        ⎢3⎥    ⎢8⎥   ⎢13⎥   ⎢18⎥   ⎢23⎥
                                        ⎢4⎥    ⎢9⎥   ⎢14⎥   ⎢19⎥   ⎢24⎥
                                        ⎣5⎦    ⎣10⎦  ⎣15⎦   ⎣20⎦   ⎣25⎦
                                                     5th Year
```

Figure 38

For the school in the example, this pattern is bad news: if the 4th Year curriculum consists only of the teams shown, *none* of the 4th Year teams can fit against 5th-Year-team-3 (5_3). Something must be done about this impossibility. In practice this would involve inspection of the teacher teams and discussion with Heads of Department to see which members of team 5_3 need not be members of the 4th Year teams.

In the absence of other information, it would seem simplest to do something about teacher 12. (Of all the clashes between 5_3 and the 4th Year teams, the clash with 4_2 involves only one teacher: teacher 12.) There are two ways of removing the clash caused by teacher 12:

1 *Deletion.* Allow teacher 12 to remain in team 5_3 but remove him from team 4_2 (or vice versa).
2 *Interchange.* Perhaps teacher 12 and teacher 38 are both due to teach Biology in the 4th Year pools. If it does not matter who takes which group,

then interchanging them removes the clash between 5_3 and 4_2. It adds a clash between 5_3 and 4_3 but three clashes are no worse than two. As with the Combing Chart, it is always worthwhile positively compounding conflicts to give flexibility elsewhere.

If we suppose that in one of these ways the clash is removed between 5_3 and 4_2, then these two teams can be scheduled to occur simultaneously *providing they have the same period-breakdown.*

Looking further at the diagram, we can see that 5_2 seems to have a lot of flexibility because there are no clashes in that column. In fact, that flexibility is illusory: when we look at 4_4 we see that it has only one blank cell. So 4_4 must occur simultaneously with 5_2, providing that they have the same period-breakdown.

This illustrates the steps used in the initial analysis of the matrix:

1 Ensure that each team has at least one empty cell.
2 If a team has only one empty cell then it must occur simultaneously with another team, providing the teams have the same period-breakdown. The empty cell lies at the 'crossroads' where the teams meet.

Continuing with the analysis of this matrix, we find that other teams now have only one empty cell. Now that 5_2 has been paired off, 4_5 has only one empty cell: it must be paired with 5_5. Similarly 4_3 must be paired with 5_1. Finally 4_1 goes with 5_4. This is summarised in Figure 39, in which the circles show the empty cells which are common to the paired teams. The numbers in the circles show the order in which they were paired and discussed in the preceding paragraphs.

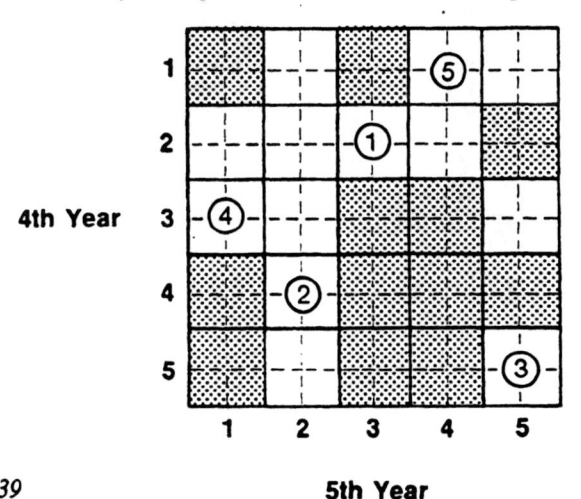

Figure 39

This analysis leads to a *unique* solution — not a good situation as the effects of period-breakdown, part-time teachers, rooms and other resources have yet to be considered. In reality, at this stage you should expect to find several ways in which the teams could be paired.

80 Timetabling

The Conflict Matrix can include any team of teachers. If any English or Mathematics Teachers also teach in the option pools then the teams for the English and Maths sets must be included.

6.3 Conflict Matrices for more than two year-groups

If your 4th Year or your 5th Year is divided into two or more bands then more than one Conflict Matrix will have to be drawn. If your school has a Sixth Form then you will wish to see how the Sixth Form teams fit against the 4th Year and against the 5th Year. Taking n groups two at a time, the number of Conflict Matrices required is $\frac{1}{2}n(n-1)$. One way of drawing these matrices manually is shown in Figure 40.

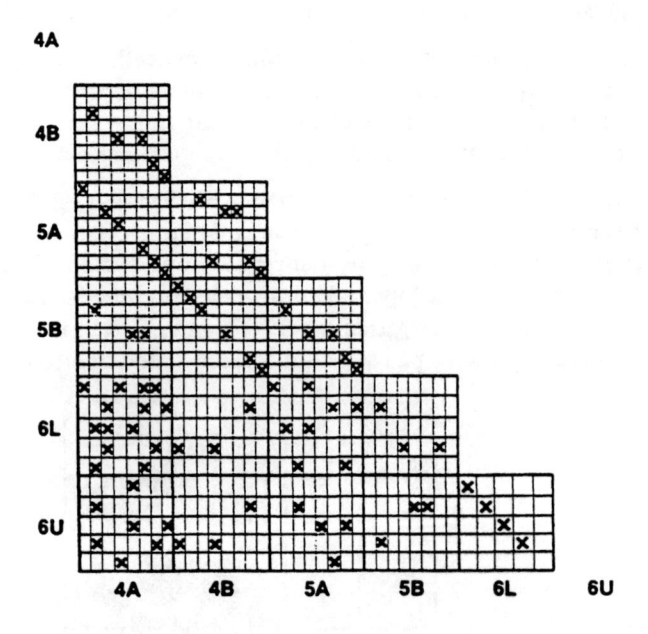

Figure 40

In this example the clashes are shown simply by crosses. This layout gives the conflicts for each pair of classes with the minimum amount of paperwork.
As well as the options teams, the English and Mathematics teams should be included. You might wish to include lower school teacher teams also.
It is clear that such a diagram is much more difficult to analyse clearly — cruder analysis will have to suffice. Two things can be seen clearly:

1 The total number of clashes, when compared with the same diagram for previous years, gives a crude measure of relative difficulty. It is useful to know from the beginning whether this year's timetable is likely to be 'slightly

easier' or 'much more difficult' than last year's. The total number of clashes will naturally be greater if you have heterogeneous option pools and if you change the pools from year to year.

2 The pattern of the clashes gives the timetabler some idea of the priority that should be given to different areas when it comes to the scheduling stage. For example, in the diagram, the number of clashes in the 6L–4A block is greater than in any other block. This means that, to schedule the teams, a higher priority must be given to fitting the 4A teams against the 6L teams. Yet this is a *scheduling* priority and you may feel that a higher *educational* priority should be given to the 5th Year and the 6U teams because their classes have already embarked on two-year courses. This may lead you to try to reduce the clashes in the 6L–4A block at this stage, rather than allow them to distort the timetable at the scheduling stage.

Whether staff changes are made at this stage or not, the timetabler will find it useful to have the Conflict Matrices to hand when he begins the scheduling stage. The matrices show directly which two teams cannot fit together on the timetable, but they can also be used to see the clashes between three or more teams. For example, suppose you have scheduled 6L-team-2 and 6U-team-3 to occur simultaneously and the matrices show that:

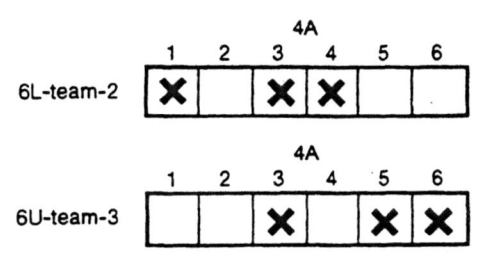

```
                    4A
              1  2  3  4  5  6
6L-team-2  [ X |  | X | X |  |  ]

                    4A
              1  2  3  4  5  6
6U-team-3  [   |  | X |  | X | X ]
```

Then adding the matrices together, we get:

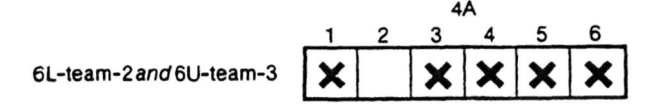

```
                            4A
                      1  2  3  4  5  6
6L-team-2 and 6U-team-3  [ X |  | X | X | X | X ]
```

This shows that if 6L-team-2 and 6U-team-3 are scheduled together, then of the 4A teams, only team 2 can occur at the same time (and only if the period-breakdown is the same).

6.4 Including the effect of period-breakdown — worked example

If a Conflict Matrix proves to be feasible when the teacher teams have been considered, you may wish to see the effect of including the period-breakdown for each team. This is done by writing the period-breakdowns on the other two sides of the matrix, using a simple code: **S** for single periods, **D** for double periods, **T** for triple and **Q** for quadruple periods.

82 *Timetabling*

For example, consider the simplified Conflict Matrix in Figure 41.

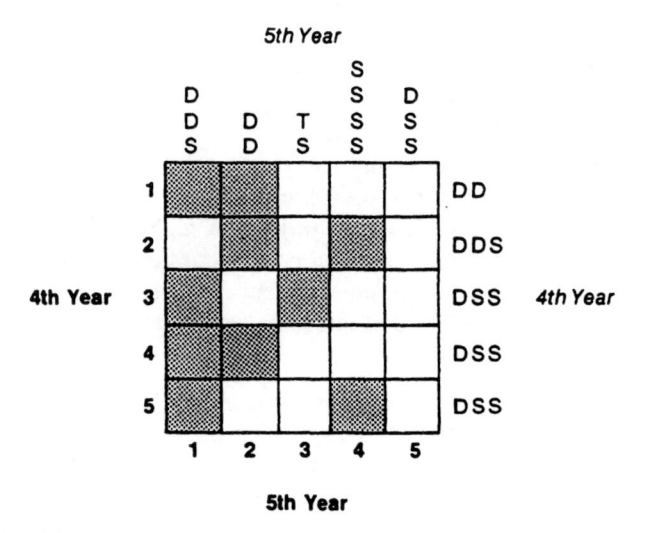

```
                    5th Year
                       S
          D            S    D
          D    D   T   S    S
          S    D   S   S    S
      1  ▓▓   ▓▓                  DD
      2        ▓▓      ▓▓         DDS
4th Year 3 ▓▓        ▓▓           DSS   4th Year
      4  ▓▓   ▓▓                  DSS
      5  ▓▓            ▓▓         DSS
          1    2   3   4    5
                    5th Year
```

Figure 41

This is a deliberately simplified diagram showing the effects of five teams in each year. The names of the teachers in the teams have been omitted: the clashes that they cause are shown by the shading.

The period-breakdown is as shown: the 5th Year periods are shown at the top, the 4th Year periods to the right. For example, 5th-Year-team-1 (which will be written as 5_1) teaches for 5 periods — 2 doubles and one single period.

To investigate the feasibility of this matrix, consider first the team with the least flexibility. This is the team 5_1 — it has only one empty cell. This means that 5_1 must be scheduled to occur simultaneously with 4_2. Fortunately they have the same period-breakdown and so this is possible. That is, each D of 5_1 will fit against a D of 4_2 and the S of 5_1 will fit against the S of 4_2. This can be shown in the matrix by marking 'DDS' in the empty cell and crossing out the DDS above 5_1 and the DDS to the right of 4_2. It is useful to sketch a Schematic Diagram at the same time (see section 5.7). The Schematic Diagram will begin by showing 4_2 under 5_1 (for 5 periods).

The next team to consider is 5_2. This team needs DD. It has two empty cells, against 4_3 and 4_5. There are 4 ways in which the DD of 5_2 can be paired with parts of 4_3 and 4_5. The 4 ways are:

(a) One D of 5_2 with the D of 4_3; then the other D of 5_2 with the D of 4_5.
(b) One D of 5_2 with the D of 4_3; then the other D of 5_2 with one S from 4_3 and one S from 4_5.
(c) One D of 5_2 with the D of 4_5; then the other D of 5_2 with one S from 4_3 and one S from 4_5.
(d) One D of 5_2 with one S of 4_3 and one S of 4_5; then the other D of 5_2 with the other S of 4_3 and the other S from 4_5.

Timetable test 2 – the Conflict Matrix

Since there is little to choose between them, let us choose (a) (it looks the simplest). Whenever you make an arbitrary decision like this, you should carefully record it and the alternatives so that if you reach an impossible situation (a cul-de-sac on the diagram) you can retrace your steps and take another alternative.

Choosing (a) we can mark a D in the empty cell shared by 5_2 and 4_3 and a second D in the empty cell shared by 5_2 and 4_5. We also cross out the DD above 5_2 and one D from the DSS of 4_3 and one D from the DSS of 4_5. The Schematic Diagram will show the same pairing of teams.

It is usually best to proceed by alternate vertical and horizontal movements. Having moved vertically down the 5_2 column, let us now move horizontally along the 4_5 row. 4_5 needs two more singles to complete it: one S with 5_3 and one S with 5_5.

The next step is to move up the 5_3 column. The triple of 5_3 can be matched with a double of 4_1 plus a single of 4_4. At this stage the matrix looks like Figure 42.

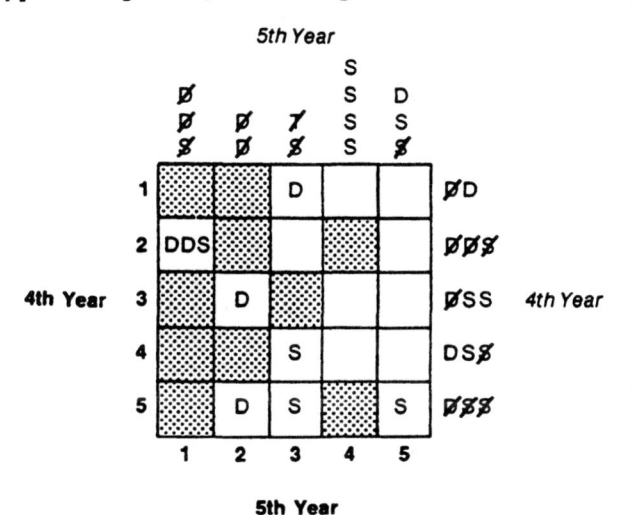

Figure 42

It is left to the reader to complete the diagram — the next step would seem to be to move along the 4_1 row or the 4_4 row. (There is more than one way of completing the last two columns of the matrix.)

The Schematic Diagram in Figure 43 shows one of the possible solutions:

Figure 43

The fact that more than one Schematic Diagram can be obtained indicates that there will be some flexibility at the scheduling stage. In effect, the final timetable will consist of vertical slices of one of these Schematic Diagrams, rearranged to take into account the period-spread throughout the week, the effect of part-time staff, etc.

If any part of the Conflict Matrix gives only one possible pairing — like 5_1 and 4_2 in the example — then those two teams should be treated at the scheduling stage as a single item (see chapter 9).

For those who wish to follow this method in more detail, into 'Schematic Matrices', there are references in the bibliography.

6.5 Including the effect of other resources — rooms, equipment, part-time teachers

If, after including the teacher teams and the period-breakdowns, the Conflict Matrix still proves to be feasible, then you may wish to see the effect of including other resources.

For example, you may have two teachers of Music but only one Music Room. You may have two people teaching Computer Studies but only one microcomputer. These clashes can be shown on the matrix in the same way that teacher clashes are shown. Normally, however, they should not be treated as absolute conflicts — for example, the Music teachers could take turns in using the Music Room, while 'theory' lessons take place in another room.

Normally the effects of part-time teachers cannot be shown on the Conflict Matrix. However, if you have two part-timers in the options scheme (most unfortunate) and if the times that they are available do not overlap, then this is an absolute conflict that can be marked in the matrix.

6.6 Using a microcomputer

As in the case of the earlier Clash Table, a microcomputer can simplify the business of drawing Conflict Matrices. A suitable program is given in Appendix 12. This program is particularly useful when several matrices have to be drawn. In use, the computer is given the initials of the teachers in each of the teams. It may also be given the period-breakdown for each team and details of special rooms or teaching resources. Then if the names of any two year-groups or bands are typed in, the machine automatically draws the correct Conflict Matrix on the television screen, and on a printer if one is fitted. The printed copies are useful both at this stage and during the scheduling stage.

6.7 Summary

Although a Combing Chart is useful for checking teams within a department, when many departments come together in the options scheme a Conflict Matrix is more useful.

A Conflict Matrix is particularly useful when the option pools apply across a full year-group. The matrix allows the timetabler to check the feasibility of the staffing of the pools. Period-breakdown, rooms and other resources can also be included.

A Conflict Matrix is a useful preliminary to drawing a Schematic Diagram (see also section 5.6).

7 Timetable test 3
Accommodation

7.1 Introduction
7.2 The rooming fraction
7.3 Priorities — worked example
7.4 The rooming equation
7.5 The nomogram
7.6 Johnson's Rule
7.7 Worked example
7.8 Summary

In chapter 3 we saw how the curricular provision of a school depends on the number of teachers. The curricular provision also depends upon other resources; in particular it depends upon the accommodation that is available.

By definition, each class that is taught needs a teacher. In the same way each class also needs a teaching space whether this is a classroom, laboratory, workshop, gymnasium, swimming pool, playing field or cross-country course. In this chapter the word 'room' will be used whatever the type of teaching space.

Staff do not teach for every period in the week; on average they teach for a fraction c of the school week (see section 3.6). In the same way, rooms are not occupied for every period in the week; on average they are used for a fraction r of the school week. This fraction r is called the *rooming fraction*. Its value is crucial in determining success or failure at the scheduling stage.

7.2 The rooming fraction

The rooming fraction r is defined by:

$$r = \frac{\text{average usage of rooms (in periods)}}{\text{number of periods in the school week}}$$

For example, if the *average* usage of the rooms in your school is 34 periods in a 40-period week, then $r = \frac{34}{40} = 0.85$. This is a typical value.

Remember that r refers to the *average* usage of accommodation — for every needlework room, library or drama studio that is used below this fraction of the week, other rooms will have to be used above it.

To calculate the value of r for your school, calculate the total number of periods provided in the curriculum and divide this by the total number of periods for which the rooms could be used if they were never empty. That is:

$$r = \frac{\text{number of periods provided in the curriculum}}{\text{number of teaching spaces} \times \text{number of periods in a week}}$$

Remember to include all the 'rooms' that are used for teaching. For example, if the playing fields, on average, are occupied by two classes, then count the playing fields as two rooms.

The value of r also gives the *average* fraction of rooms that are occupied at any time. For example, if $r = 0.85$, then (on average) 85% of the rooms are occupied at any time.

Clearly the value of r has implications for the timetable. If the value of r rises too high then the timetabler will have to make some compromises at the scheduling stage. As r increases, more and more specialist subjects have to be taught in non-specialist rooms (or vice-versa).

Observation and analysis by a group of HM Inspectors led them to suggest that r could rise to 0.85 without compromising educational objectives. However, *as r rises above 0.85 there are likely to be increasingly severe restrictions on the curriculum and the timetable.*

As r rises above 0.85 there will be restrictions on your curriculum (as distinct from restrictions on your scheduling). These restrictions arise from a mismatch between your ideas about the curriculum and the architect's ideas. This can be explained best by referring to Figure 44. This shows values of r for two different schools.

In school A, due to falling rolls, r is very low. The overall value of r for all types of accommodation is only 0.60. That is, on average, only 60% of the rooms are occupied. Because the overall value is low, values of r for individual types of room can vary widely. For example, if the school's curriculum requires it, the science laboratories can be timetabled at over 90% usage — the timetabler would give them a high priority at the scheduling stage, knowing that there would be ample flexibility later because the classrooms would have only 40% usage. Such a school can decide its own curriculum, to a large degree independently of the architect's designs.

88 *Timetabling*

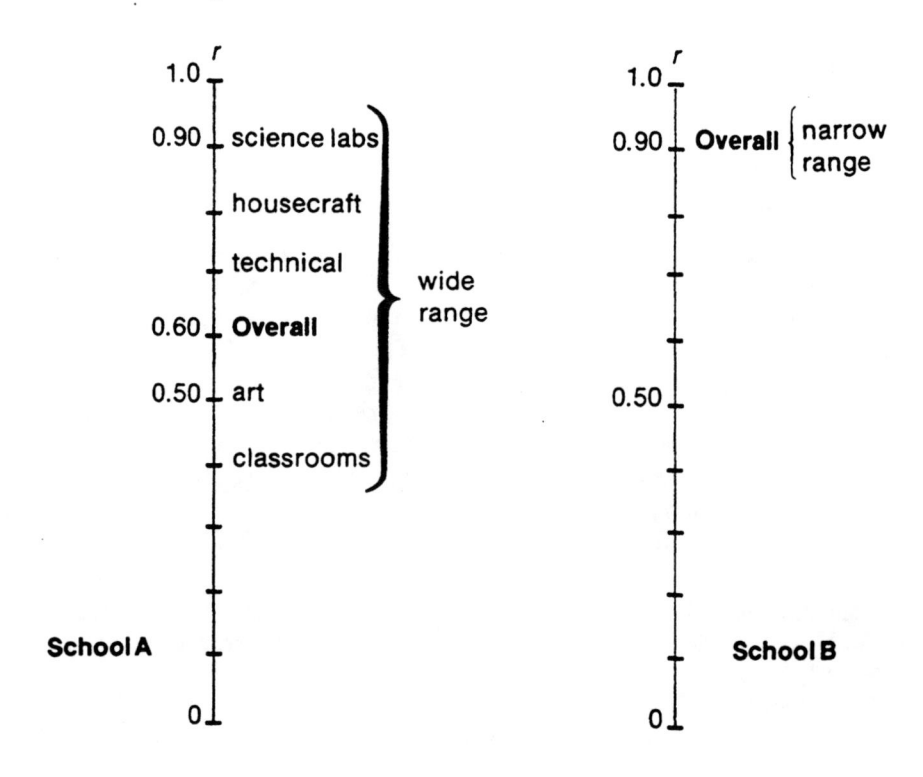

Figure 44

However in school B the overall value of r is 0.90. Because the overall value is so high, all types of room must be used at about 90% usage. Specialist rooms could not be timetabled at much over 90% because the timetabler would not have much flexibility with ordinary classrooms — they also have to be timetabled at about 90% usage. All types of room are forced into a narrow range of values of r. The needlework room will have to be used for 90% of the week, whether the school likes it or not; the woodwork rooms will have to be used for 90% of the week, whether the school likes it or not. The curriculum must conform more closely to the architect's design. This is one area where schools will gain as rolls fall.

In most schools the science laboratories are used at a high value of r. This is because laboratories cost about twice as much to build as general classrooms. HM Inspectorate suggest that science laboratories may be timetabled at 90% usage if support services are good; otherwise they suggest that 70% may be the upper limit.

It is worth remembering that the structure of the school day can limit the rooming fraction. As we saw in section 5.8, with a 2-3-3 or a 3-2-3 day, the maximum number of double periods is 15. That is, a maximum of 30 periods out of 40. This gives a maximum rooming fraction of 0.75 if the accommodation is used only for double periods.

7.3 Priorities — worked example

One of the difficulties at the scheduling stage is deciding an order of priority for fitting different parts of the data. The rooming fraction can help to clarify this. The timetabler should calculate the overall value of r and the individual values of r for different types of accommodation, using the same equation as before:

$$r = \frac{\text{number of periods to be timetabled}}{\text{number of teaching spaces} \times \text{number of periods in a week}}$$

Then the values of r for different types of accommodation can be arranged into a list showing the order of priority for scheduling (assuming for the moment that all other factors are equal).

Consider an example. You are the new Head of the English Department of the Laura Norder High School. All 12 members of the English Department are teaching 30 periods (in a 40 period week). The departmental suite consists of 10 rooms.

The Head of Science tells you that his department teaches 300 periods in 8 laboratories.

The Head of Art complains that, although he has 4 Art rooms, only 96 periods of Art are shown on the Curriculum Plan.

What do you deduce?

For the English department:

$$r = \frac{\text{number of periods timetabled}}{\text{number of rooms} \times 40}$$

$$= \frac{12 \times 30}{10 \times 40}$$

$$= \frac{360}{400}$$

$$= 0.90$$

This 90% room usage is high but the consequences for the department have to be judged in comparison with other departments.

For the Science department:

$$r = \frac{300}{8 \times 40} = 0.94$$

This is very high. Clearly, for priority in scheduling, science will take precedence over English (particularly as Science lessons require a laboratory more than English lessons require an English room).

For the Art department:

$$r = \frac{96}{4 \times 40} = 0.60$$

Clearly the order of priority for these three departments is:

1. Science
2. English
3. Art

Whether the English department will be given a high priority after science depends on the value of r for other departments. If the overall value of r is high, English classes may have a low priority on this basis (although other factors such as teacher-teams may increase the priority). If the overall value of r is reasonable (0.85 or less) then several departments will have a low r (to balance the Science and English). This might suggest that there is a mismatch between the curriculum and the allocation of rooms. Perhaps another department should donate a room to the English department. If all the rooms are treated as specialist rooms, as implied in this example, then the principle of compatibility applies to them (see section 5.10).

7.4 Rooming Equation

In section 3.7 we saw that the number of curriculum units (x) that can be provided depends on the number of teachers (T) and their contact ratio (c). This led us to the staffing equation: $x = 9cT$.

There is a corresponding equation for rooms. The number of curriculum units (x) that can be accommodated depends on the number of teaching spaces (n) and their rooming fraction (r).

Although the total number of rooms is n, the effective number is only n multiplied by r. That is, rn. In effect we have rn rooms being used all the time. Each of these effective rooms can accommodate 9 curriculum units in a school week, giving a total of $9rn$ curriculum units.

That is:

$$x = 9rn$$

This is the Rooming Equation, sometimes called the 'Second Law' of the curriculum.

As it stands, the equation will tell you the number of curriculum units that can be accommodated in n rooms at a rooming fraction r. This can be applied to the whole main school or to specialist rooms within a department. As in section 7.2, n must include all the teaching spaces that you use.

Alternatively the subject of the equation can be changed to r:

$$r = \frac{x}{9n}$$

If x was determined from the curriculum (section 3.2) or from the staffing equation (section 3.7) then r can be calculated from this equation.

Remember that since x applies only to the main school, so also does n. If you have a Sixth Form, then a corresponding number of rooms will have to be subtracted from the total accommodation. This can be done by looking at the current timetable and finding the average number of rooms occupied by the Sixth Form classes.

By comparing the Staffing Equation ($x = 9cT$) with the Rooming Equation ($x = 9rn$), we can see that:

$$cT = rn$$

or $T = \dfrac{rn}{c} = $ the number of staff, working at a contact ratio c, that can be accommodated in n rooms at a rooming fraction r

This can be used to find the 'correct' size of a specialist department. For example, if 7 laboratories are to be used at 90% usage when the contact ratio is 0.75, then

$$T = \frac{0.90 \times 7}{0.75} = 8.4 \text{ staff}$$

If there are 9 full-time Science teachers then 0.6 of a teacher ($= 18$ periods) will be timetabled out of a laboratory.

Some other curriculum equations are shown in Appendix 2. For example: $x < 7.7n$. That is, to keep r less than 0.85, the number of curriculum units provided by the school or by a department must be less than the number of rooms multiplied by 7.7.

7.5 The nomogram

In section 3.10 we saw how a nomogram connects the staffing ratio ($\frac{N}{T}$), the contact ratio (c) and the relative bonus ($b\%$). The same nomogram, on page 47 can also be applied to rooms.

This time the labels at the *bottom* of the axes are used. The quantity plotted on the left hand axis is $\frac{N}{n}$, the number of pupils divided by the number of teaching spaces (in each case for the main school only). This value is usually in the range 16–22. It is determined by the LEA: the school has little direct control over it.

The quantity on the right hand axis is still $b\%$. This quantity was found when the nomogram was used in section 3.10. Joining the quantities on the left and right axes by a straight line gives the intercept on the central axis, which is r, the rooming fraction.

For example, suppose that your school has $\frac{N}{n} = 20.5$ and it is proposed to have $b\% = 18\frac{1}{2}\%$. Draw a straight line from 20.5 on the left axis to $18\frac{1}{2}$ on the right axis. This cuts the central axis at $r = 0.90$. This is rather high but the only ways of reducing it are to obtain more accommodation or to reduce $b\%$ by reducing the contact ratio.

To summarize the use of the nomogram:

1. Calculate $\frac{N}{T}$ and $\frac{N}{n}$
2. Using the top labels and knowing $\frac{N}{T}$, decide c and $b\%$.
3. Using the bottom labels and knowing $\frac{N}{n}$ and $b\%$, decide r.
4. Iterate as necessary to achieve reasonable values of c, $b\%$, r.

7.6 Johnson's Rule

Still looking at the nomogram (page 47) and considering the labels at the bottom of the axes, we can see that two of them (r and $b\%$) have critical values.

The $b\%$ axis should have a *minimum* value of 10% if the school is to retain sufficient curricular flexibility for its option scheme (see section 3.8). The r axis should have a *maximum* value of 0.85 if the school is to retain sufficient scheduling flexibility to keep rooming compromises within acceptable limits.

When taken together these two limits give a *maximum* value to the quantity $\frac{N}{n}$. Joining $b\% = 10\%$ and $r = 0.85$ on the nomogram, the line cuts the $\frac{N}{n}$ axis at just under 21. That is,

$$\frac{N}{n} < 21 \quad \text{or} \quad N < 21n$$

This is Johnson's Rule: *If the number of pupils divided by the number of teaching spaces is greater than 21, then the school has lost curricular flexibility or scheduling flexibility or both.* If $\frac{N}{n}$ is greater than 21, the school cannot have $b\%$ greater than 10% unless r rises above 0.85 (loss of scheduling flexibility); the school cannot keep r below 0.85 except by allowing $b\%$ to fall below 10% (loss of curricular flexibility).

Clearly a school which has $\frac{N}{n}$ greater than 21 has a powerful argument for persuading the LEA to provide more accommodation (or else reduce the school's intake).

7.7 Worked example

You are the Head of the Laura Norder High School, an 11–16 school with 1440 pupils (N) and 80 full-time-equivalent teaching staff (T). The number of teaching spaces (including all sports facilities) is 65 (n). The curriculum you wish to provide for the next school year requires 528 curriculum units (x).

(a) What is the 'basic provision' of curriculum units for this number of pupils?
(b) What would be the bonus?
    What would be the relative bonus? Comment on the value.
(c) Use the nomogram to determine the necessary contact ratio (c). Comment on the value.
(d) Use the nomogram to determine the rooming fraction (r). Comment.
(e) An inspector suggests that your staff should have more class contact time. Suggest a reply.

Timetable test 3 - accommodation 93

(a) The basic provision = ⅓ × number of pupils = ⅓N = $\frac{1440}{3}$ = 480 cu's.
(b) The bonus = actual provision − basic provision
 = 528 − 480
 = 48 cu's

The relative bonus $b\% = \frac{\text{bonus cu's}}{\text{basic cu's}} \times 100\%$

$= \frac{48}{480} \times 100\%$

$= 10\%$

This is the lower limit, for curricular flexibility.

(c) The staffing ratio $\frac{N}{T} = \frac{1440}{80} = 18.0$. This is not generous.

Using the nomogram (top labels), with $\frac{N}{T} = 18.0$ and $b\% = 10\%$, gives $c = 0.73$. (Alternatively, one can use $x = 9cT$.)
(In a 40-period week this is an average of 29⅓ periods per week. In a 35-period week it is an average of 25⅔ periods per week.)
In earlier years this would have been considered rather low. Whether it is reasonable today depends on how much pastoral care and support for discipline is needed from Deputy Heads and Year Tutors or House Tutors.

(d) $\frac{N}{n} = \frac{1440}{65} = 22.2$

This is greater than 21 so the school must suffer a lack of flexibility.
Using the nomogram (bottom labels), with $\frac{N}{n} = 22.2$ and $b\% = 10\%$, gives $r = 0.90$. (Alternatively, one can use $x = 9rn$.)
This value is high, so all types of accommodation must be used at about 90%. The curriculum is being forced to conform to the building.

(e) If the school is an inner-city comprehensive, perhaps a split-site, then the value of c is not low. Under more favourable conditions, even if it is agreed that c ought to rise, it cannot do so without raising r. This will force the curriculum to conform even more closely to the accommodation and it will force even more compromises during scheduling.
The school clearly needs more accommodation in order to
 (i) reduce $\frac{N}{n}$ to less than 21
 (ii) reduce r to 0.85 or less, to allow better scheduling
 (iii) raise $b\%$ above 10% to allow better curricular provision
As a bare minimum, to get $\frac{N}{n} = 21$, the school needs $n = \frac{N}{21} = \frac{1440}{21} = 69$ rooms. That is, at least 4 more rooms. The types of room that are needed could be decided by looking at r for each type of accommodation.

7.8 Summary

The curricular provision in a school depends on the number of teaching spaces (n) and the rooming fraction (r).

$$r = \frac{\text{average usage of rooms (in periods)}}{\text{number of periods in the school week}}$$

= fraction of rooms occupied for teaching (on average)

$$= \frac{\text{number of periods provided on the timetable}}{\text{number of teaching spaces} \times \text{number of periods in a week}}$$

Number of curriculum units = $x = 9rn$

As r rises above 0.85, there are likely to be increasingly severe restrictions on the curriculum and the timetable.

If $\frac{N}{n} > 21$ then the school has lost curriculum flexibility or scheduling flexibility or both.

Values of r for different types of accommodation help to give an order of priority for scheduling.

Further formulae can be found in Appendix 2.

8 Other timetable checks

8.1 Introduction
8.2 Zarraga's Rule
8.3 Balancing the teaching power for lower school classes
8.4 Option pools for the Lower Sixth and the Upper Sixth
8.5 Minority subjects in the Sixth Form
8.6 Deciding priorities — fixed points, part-time teachers, split-site schools etc.
8.7 Summary

In the last three chapters we have seen how the data can be checked for impossibilities (i) in the staffing of departments, (ii) in the option pools and (iii) in the use of accommodation. With these impossibilities removed, a complete solution to the timetable may be possible without any further compromise. However this could be decided only by attempting to schedule the data. For the complicated timetables that are attempted in most large schools today, it is worthwhile looking further for ways of providing still more flexibility. In the first sections of this chapter we look at ways of providing this extra flexibility. A later section of the chapter is concerned with the problem of deciding priorities. This is an essential last step before going on to consider the scheduling stage in the next chapter.

96 *Timetabling*

8.2 Zarraga's Rule

One of the limitations on the timetable is the way in which the teacher teams of the upper school interact with the pure class activities which may be taking place in the lower school.

For example, consider a 4th Year team consisting of teachers 1, 2, 3 and 4.

4th Year team | 1 | 2 | 3 | 4 |

These four teachers are due to teach the 4th Year all at the *same* time, in *parallel*.

It may happen, by chance, that the Heads of Departments request the same four teachers to all teach the same lower school class, say 1A:

1A
| 1 |
| 2 |
| 3 |
| 4 |

In this case these four teachers are due to teach 1A at *different* times, *in series*.

This can lead to difficulties in scheduling. Suppose for example that after scheduling the 4th Year, you eventually come to schedule 1A and look for a teacher to take the class for period 1 on Monday. You may find that teacher 1 is not free because he is teaching in the 4th Year team. If you try then to schedule teacher 2 for period 1 on Monday, you will find that he is not free — he also is teaching in the 4th Year team. Similarly with teachers 3 and 4. If all the other teachers for 1A are not free because they have been scheduled for other classes then you are in difficulty. The class is available, a room is available, the time is available, but *none* of the teachers is free.

Clearly this situation is less likely to arise if the four teachers who are in parallel in the 4th Year are not put in series for the same lower school class. Unless there is a good educational reason against it, the four teachers should be allocated to four *different* 1st Year classes. For example, if 1A, 1B, 1C, 1D are four equal mixed ability classes then the members of the departments will not mind if you re-allocate like this:

I do not know who originated this idea but since it was first put to me by M.N. Zarraga of STAG, I think of it as Zarraga's Rule: *As far as possible, teachers who are members of the same teacher team in one part of the school should be allocated to different classes for pure class activity in another part of the school.*

Applying this rule to Lower School classes, consulting with Heads of Departments as necessary, can lead to a surprising increase in flexibility in the later stages of scheduling. The more heterogeneous the option pools, the more important it is to apply this rule.

To investigate the staffing of your classes in order to apply Zarraga's Rule, you should take each teacher team in turn (shown horizontally on your Curriculum Plan) and for each team compare it with all the pure class activities (shown vertically on your Curriculum Plan) to see if a team and a class have two or more teachers in common.

Alternatively, the computer program given in Appendix 13 can be used to find which classes and which teachers are involved.

8.3 Balancing the teaching power for lower school classes

While you are looking at possible teacher changes for lower school classes in the light of the previous section, it is also worthwhile looking at the quality of teaching to be provided to those classes. It is important (not only for justice but also to control disruption) that the strengths and weaknesses of the teaching staff should be distributed equitably.

This can be considered most easily by looking in the 'master' booklet (section 4.5). The master booklet shows the Curriculum Plan with the relevant staff initials entered next to each group of pupils. Looking down each column (that is, for each class) the group of teachers allocated to each class can be seen easily. In judging the relative strengths and weaknesses of these groups of teachers it may be helpful to allot a simple (and confidential) numerical value to each teacher. For example:

1 = probationary or weak teacher
2 = strong classroom control but routine teaching style
3 = adequate classroom control with good, lively teaching style
4 = excellent, above average teacher

In this way a total value can be found for each class and any imbalance corrected by interchanging teachers (and consulting with Heads of Departments as

98 *Timetabling*

necessary). Obviously these judgements must be made carefully, in the light of all that you have observed of these teachers and these classes.

Two other criteria may be considered at the same time:

1 It may be preferable for the ratios of old/young teachers to be uniform.
2 Similarly it may be preferable for the ratios of male/female teachers to be uniform.

As a further refinement you may wish to ensure that no class is allocated a group of teachers with weak health or a strong involvement with examination panels for which they might require several days' absence during the year.

8.4 Option pools for the Lower Sixth and Upper Sixth

If your school has a small Sixth Form then it may be possible to obtain further flexibility by looking at the grouping of the subjects provided for the Upper Sixth.

For the Lower Sixth year, your option pools will be determined by considering the requirements for careers and university entrance. In Sixth Forms of less than 100 students it is likely that not all the possible permutations of subjects will be chosen. For instance, it may be possible to choose Chemistry, French and Economics from your option pools but perhaps no-one has chosen to do so this year. When it comes to scheduling the Upper Sixth., you will know which permutations have been chosen and which have not. This may allow you to change the grouping of the subjects for the Upper Sixth timetable so that you have more flexibility at the scheduling stage.

The best way to see whether it is possible to modify the option pools is to draw up a Clash Table for the students in the present lower Sixth (see also section 2.6). This can be done manually or using the OPT1 computer program (Appendix 4).

For example, consider the simplified Clash Table shown in Figure 45.

	M	E	P	H	C	G	A	B	Ec	F
F		×		×		×				×
Ec	×	×	×			×			×	
B	×	×	×	×	×		×	×		
A		×		×			×	×		
G		×	×			×			×	×
C	×		×		×			×		
H		×		×			×	×		×
P	×		×		×	×		×	×	
E		×		×		×	×	×	×	×
M	×		×		×			×	×	

Figure 45

Other timetable checks 99

This Clash Table shows the ten most popular subjects at A-level (not including General Studies). These ten subjects account for three-quarters of the total entry at A-level. As before, the Clash Table is symmetrical about a diagonal. The crosses show where there is a clash for this particular group of students.

In this example the options in the Lower Sixth were:

>M *or* E
>P *or* H
>C *or* G *or* A
>B *or* Ec *or* F

Inspection of the Clash Table shows that the grouping of subjects could be changed (for some or all of the scheduled periods) if the change would help to schedule other classes in the school.

For example, from this Clash Table:

	M *or* H
with	P *or* E
or,	M *or* G *or* A
with	C *or* E
Alternatively,	C *or* A *or* Ec *or* F
with	G *or* B
	etc.

Having some flexibility in these 7th Year option pools allows the timetabler to put a lower priority on the scheduling of the 7th Year and so give a better quality to the scheduling of the main school.

8.5 Minority subjects in the Sixth Form

The importance attached to minority-time activities in the Sixth Form can have an important effect upon the scheduling.

Consider first the Sixth Form shown in the Schematic Diagram in Figure 46 (the subjects are the same as in the last section).

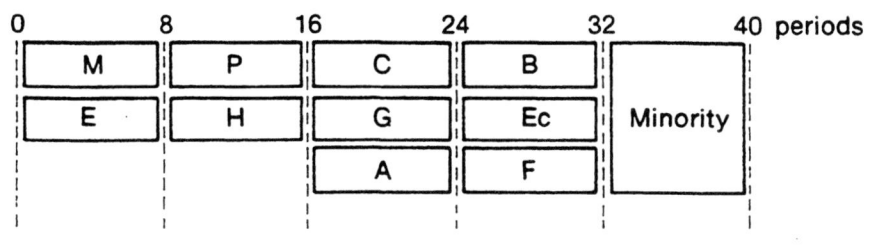

```
0        8        16       24       32       40 periods
┌──────┐┌──────┐┌──────┐┌──────┐┌──────────┐
│  M   ││  P   ││  C   ││  B   ││          │
└──────┘└──────┘└──────┘└──────┘│          │
┌──────┐┌──────┐┌──────┐┌──────┐│ Minority │
│  E   ││  H   ││  G   ││  Ec  ││          │
└──────┘└──────┘└──────┘└──────┘└──────────┘
                ┌──────┐┌──────┐
                │  A   ││  F   │
                └──────┘└──────┘
```

Figure 46

In this school a high priority is placed on minority subjects. The timetable is arranged so that all the A-level students have access to the same minority

100   *Timetabling*

subjects. This policy forces the subjects in each option pool to be timetabled together and to have the same period-breakdown.

Now consider an alternative scheme:

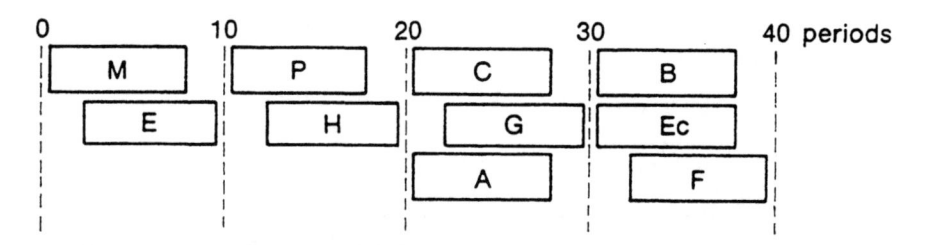

Figure 47

In this school the minority subjects have been given a lower priority. They will be timetabled into the gaps between the main blocks. This means that students taking different A-level will have access to different minority subjects. This policy allows the subjects in each pool to spread over a greater number of periods (10 periods for each pool in the diagram). This has two timetabling advantages:

1   It will be easier to fit this scheme against the 4th Year and 5th Year teacher teams (on average, fewer resources are needed in each period).
2   It allows subjects within the same pool to have different period-breakdowns. In this example, if required, H could be scheduled as 4 doubles while P is scheduled as 2 doubles and one quadruple:

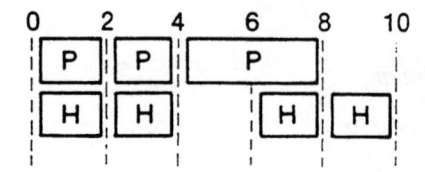

Figure 48

It is possible to vary the amount of spread allowed. This is an advantage if some pools are more difficult to schedule than others. For example: two 'easy' pools kept to 8 periods each and two other 'difficult' pools allowed to spread over 12 periods each.

Other permutations are possible. For example: two of the option pools allowed to spread over 10 periods each, two pools kept to only 8 periods each, leaving 4 periods for common activities (e.g. General Studies, Games).

Of course, the decision about the importance of minority subjects should be taken as a matter of policy (bearing in mind the advantages to the Sixth Form and to the main school), rather than merely as a matter of scheduling expediency.

8.6 Deciding priorities — fixed points, part-time teachers, split-site schools etc.

When you eventually arrive at the scheduling stage and look at the virgin timetable model, it is important to have an order of priority for fitting the various items on to the timetable. Initially it is easier to look at priorities and constraints under seven separate headings before combining them into one overall order of priority.

1 Fixed points
These must be given the highest priority. Examples of fixed points include:

(a) *Fixed times for swimming*
For example, if the local swimming baths are available only on a Tuesday morning then the swimming lessons for the 1st Year must be scheduled for Tuesday mornings. It is essential to have the exact days and times well before scheduling begins.

(b) *Shared playing fields*
If your playing fields are shared with another school (or if the transport to sports facilities is available only at certain times) then Games will have a high priority. As before, it is essential to get agreement on exact times well before scheduling begins.

(c) *Linked courses at Colleges of Further Education*
Many schools arrange courses for 4th Year, 5th Year and 6th Year students at the local FE College. These are often strongly vocational courses in automobile engineering, building construction, audio-typing etc. One advantage of these courses is that their staffing does not count against the school's establishment.

There are disadvantages: for example, some pupils tend to get 'lost' on their way to the college unless there is adequate staff supervision. The restriction on the school timetable can be severe because of specific times dictated by the college, affecting large teacher teams in the 4th Year and 5th Year. There may also be a difficulty if the dates of the terms for school and college do not coincide.

(d) *Sixth Form consortia*
Urban 11-18 schools with small Sixth Forms sometimes group together into consortia to maintain provision of less-popular subjects. One member of a consortium will provide Latin, another Domestic Science etc.

As before it is essential to agree on days and times at an early stage. Difficulties arise if the schools are some distance apart or if the period-breakdowns of the school days are dissimilar. For example, if one school operates a 2-2-2-2 day while another school prefers a 2-2-3 day, it will usually be preferable to timetable shared subjects on mornings only.

(e) *TV and radio programmes*
Details of the programmes are published by the BBC and ITV companies during the Spring Term. The restriction for programmes has eased already for radio and should ease further for TV as more schools purchase colour cassette video-tape recorders with automatic timing and recording facilities.

(f) *Games periods*
Some schools like to restrict games for a whole year-group to the last two periods of a particular afternoon. The timetabler should know whether the double period should be at the end of a particular afternoon or whether any afternoon will do.

(g) *Management meetings*
Some schools restrict these to certain times.

(h) *Year-Tutors or House-Tutors*
Some schools may place a high priority on pastoral staff being free at particular times to meet with the Educational Welfare Officer. Other schools may require particular staff to be free after assembly on certain days or to be free last period before school detention takes place (in order to round up culprits).

2 Part-time teachers

Part-time teachers are often a serious constraint on the timetable and often must be given a high priority. For the timetabler, part-time teachers are usually a curse. Wherever possible part-time teachers should only be allowed to teach pure class activities. If a part-timer is allowed to become a member of a team then his or her 'part-time-ness' is transferred to the other members of the team. For example, if a part-timer is available only on Monday and Tuesday and is a member of the teams for some 4th Year and 5th Year options, then these teams must teach on Monday and Tuesday and so all the other classes taken by all the members of the teams will tend to be squeezed into Wednesday, Thursday and Friday. This effect tends to 'ricochet' round the timetable and can produce a serious skew to the timetables of some departments and some classes.

Obviously, if *two* part-timers are in the same teacher team then the team can teach only at times that are common to both part-timers.

The availability of part-time teachers should allow for the required period spread of the subject. For example, a part-time teacher of French who is available for only three afternoons will not allow the 5-single-periods-on-5-days that support good French teaching.

The availability of part-timers should be ascertained as early and as clearly as possible. The timetabler can hope that there will be some flexibility in the agreed time although, as the law now stands, it seems that part-time teachers can insist that they teach for exactly the same days and periods as they taught on the last timetable.

3 Split-site schools

Split-site or 'federal' schools are more difficult to timetable than single-site schools. One reason is that if the school has three laboratories in each building, there is a total of six but only three are available at any time to each population. A more serious difficulty is that a teacher cannot really be expected to teach a class in the upper school for period 1 and then teach a lower school class for period 2. Some schools apparently do expect this 'instant commuting' but I cannot think how they can justify it on educational grounds. Other schools solve this problem (and create another) by limiting commuting to only one or two teachers, thus emphasizing the split nature of the school.

With half or more of the staff commuting, the situation can be relieved by operating a 2-2-2-2 day (with morning and afternoon breaks long enough to allow commuting between buildings).

Care must be taken to ensure that each teacher is based clearly in one of the buildings — a member of staff teaching 16 periods in each building will have obvious difficulties. For the timetabler, a colleague who teaches 32 periods and is split 30-2 between buildings will cause no difficulty; a split of 24-8 will cause more difficulty to the timetabler as he tries to block the teacher into one building for a whole session. It is probably wise to direct Heads of Department to limit the split to 20-12, but the effect of this on the timetable will vary from department to department. For example, if Home Economics is always taught in half-day sessions then 20-12 or even 16-16 is easy to schedule. However for French, which should be scheduled with a lot of single periods, even 24-8 may cause severe difficulties for the timetabler and for the teacher (who may have to commute frequently).

If you work in a split-site school then the split for each teacher can be shown on the Staff Loading Chart, as explained in section 4.6. By inspecting this chart a list can be drawn up showing the order of priority for scheduling the members of staff who commute.

4 Teacher teams

By inspecting the Conflict Matrices (chapter 6) and the Curriculum Plan (section 4.3) one can draw up an order of priority for the scheduling of the teacher teams, whether these are teams for Mathematics, English and French sets, or teams for the option pools. A simple rule to apply is that the more teachers involved and the more periods for which they are due to be scheduled, the greater the difficulty. That is, the product of teachers multiplied by periods can be used to decide the order of priority (this corresponds roughly to the *area* of the item to be fitted to the timetable model, see chapter 9). Clearly the order of priority should be modified after considering other constraints that are mentioned in this chapter.

Remember to include the teacher teams needed for any management meetings or for any essential departmental meetings that are to be timetabled.

5 Rooms

Using the ideas developed in sections 7.2 and 7.3, the timetabler should calculate the rooming fraction for each type of teaching space. Clearly a Chemistry laboratory with $r = 94\%$ will have a higher priority than a Needlework room with $r = 60\%$. A list can be drawn showing the order of priority for different types of room.

6 Lesson length and spread

The timetabler should be aware of the lesson length required by each subject and the preferred spread of the periods throughout the week. For example: five singles of French on five days; a single period of PE and a double period of Games on different days; no more than three days (including the weekend) to elapse between Spanish lessons etc.

7 Other constraints and priorities

A variety of other factors may be considered. For example, the priority given to the Upper Sixth will depend upon the flexibility shown in the Clash Table (section 8.4).

It may be decided to give some priority to scheduling Mathematics and other academic lessons in the mornings for difficult classes in the 3rd Year or 4th Year. Cookery for the 4th Year may be preferred in the morning to allow the pupils to eat the results of their practical sessions.

It may be decided to give some priority to reducing the movement of younger pupils round the building between single periods by careful consideration of the sequence of lessons. It may be decided that a department which has suffered in previous years should have a higher priority this time.

When all these seven factors have been considered and an order of priority decided under each of the seven headings, then the timetabler can consider an *overall* order of priority.

Fixed points normally take precedence over everything else. Next in order of priority might be a part-time teacher who is a member of a large teacher team, commutes between the two sites of a split-site school and is teaching Physics (for which the rooming fraction is 92%). Considering other composite constraints like this, the timetabler can draw up lists of priority to help at the scheduling stage. It will usually be sufficient to draw up four lists under headings such as: 'extreme priority, 'high priority', 'important', 'lower priority but still needing consideration' etc.

8.7 Summary

This chapter has considered methods of introducing additional flexibility, particularly in the staffing of the lower school pure class activities and in the arrangement of the option groups in the Sixth Form. The chapter has also been concerned with deciding the priority to be attached to the various items that have to be fitted now that the scheduling stage has been reached.

9 Scheduling

9.1 Introduction
9.2 Six timetable models
9.3 Ten rules for scheduling
9.4 Worked example
9.5 Nine tactics and moves
9.6 Fitting a difficult item
9.7 Allowing for different period-breakdowns
9.8 Improving the quality
9.9 Rooming
9.10 Checking the timetable
9.11 Distributing the timetable
9.12 Assessing your timetable
9.13 Alternative timetable cycles
9.14 Block timetabling
9.15 Summary

At last we reach the stage of which most people think when we say 'timetabling'. At this stage we allocate particular activities to particular times of the week, and so produce a device which controls the movement of a large number of people, bell by bell, for many weeks. The final timetable is a very powerful device and its construction places a heavy responsibility on the timetabler and on his ability to remember all the requests, preferences, whims and habits of his colleagues, and to judge fairly their relative merits for staff, pupils and the school as a whole.

Clearly we wish to obtain a timetable of the highest quality, a timetable which is enabling rather than restrictive. We do not wish to include any of the compromises that were listed in section 5.1, particularly as compromises made early in the scheduling stage may tend to avalanche further compromises at a later stage.

Obviously the construction needs to be done in a logical manner. The number of permutations is too great for any other method. Indeed, even for the smallest school, if just one year-group were to be scheduled in a random manner, the number of ways of doing this would greatly exceed the number of atoms in the universe!

Logic, however, means different things in different schools. In one school in the north of England, 'logic' consists of the Head of Mathematics being allowed to schedule his Sixth Form Maths on the timetable board, followed by the Head of English who schedules his Sixth Form groups and so on, down a pecking order of departments until the Sixth Form timetable is finished. Then the Head of Maths has first chance at the 5th Year timetable, followed by other departments in order, until that year group is completed. It is not clear at what

106 Timetabling

stage in this process violence or nervous breakdowns occur. Other teachers report 'do-it-yourself' methods, bartering in the staffroom: '2A haven't had any science this week, I'll swap one period of 4D for two periods of 2A this afternoon'.

Some people think of scheduling as a process of completing a jigsaw puzzle, but it is not as simple as that — when you buy a jigsaw at least you know that it has a solution! With a timetable there may not be a solution — or, more likely, there will be many solutions, depending on the compromises that you make. Our job is to get the best of those solutions.

Even when the timetable is viewed as a jigsaw puzzle, it must be thought of as a kind of 5-dimensional jigsaw, because there are five main variables to be considered. These are:

— the **class** of pupils to be scheduled
— the **subject** they will be taught
— the **teacher** who takes the class
— the **room** in which the lesson takes place
— the **time** at which the lesson takes place

In order to keep control over these variables, we must build up the timetable on some kind of 'model'.

9.2 Six timetable models

Your timetable model should include all of the five main variables. A good model will also show clearly other variables such as the grouping of classes and the length of lessons. When using the model, two important factors are security and flexibility in use. These factors, as well as cost and portability, are discussed later in this section.

All the timetable models used in schools have two physical dimensions — the length and width of the sheet of paper or plastic board or whatever is used. Two of the five main variables are shown on these two axes. The two variables that are usually shown are the first and last in the list given earlier — the *classes* of pupils and the *times* of the school week. Some timetables show classes vertically and time horizontally, but, as we shall see later, the better method (because of the way our eyes move when reading) is to have the *classes horizontally* and *time vertically*. The classes should run from the Sixth Form at the left to the 1st Year at the right. The periods should run from Monday-period-1 at the top down to the last period in the school week at the bottom.

Figure 49 shows part of such a timetable for a school operating an 8-period day.

The different timetable models that are available each use the same basic grid but have different ways of representing the information. Figure 50 compares six common timetable models.

One, two or three stars are given under each of four headings. The more stars the better, but note that the categories have varying importance. By far the most

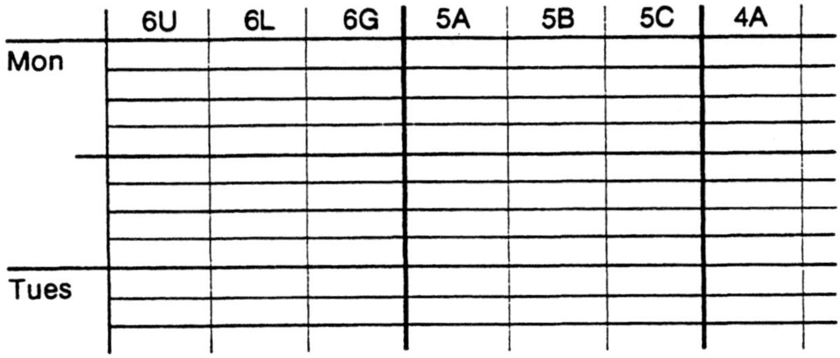

Figure 49

Timetable model	Flexible?	Secure?	Portable?	Cost?
1 Pencil, paper, rubber	★	★★★	★★★	★★★
2 Prograph–plastic pegs and board	★	★★	★	★
3 Small cards and pigeon-holes	★	★★	★	★★
4 Large cards, pins on softboard	★★	★★	★	★★
5 Large cards, card base, gravity	★★★	★	(★★★)	★★★
6 Magnetic plastic and tinplate base	★★★	★★	★★★	★★

Figure 50

important is the first — we must have a model which is *flexible* in use if we are to obtain a high quality timetable.

Each of these models is discussed in turn.

1 Pencil, paper, rubber
If you teach in a two- or three-form entry grammar school then this may be the model for you. You will need a large rubber eraser and tough paper. It is useful to develop a strong left wrist so that you can use the rubber without changing hands each time. This model is secure (the information will not fall off the model), portable (for carrying home or to departmental meetings etc.) and cheap. The final version can be copied on a commercial xerox machine (at a photocopying agency) to provide staffroom copies etc.

Unfortunately, this model is not sufficiently flexible for use in large schools where there are large teacher teams. Each time an activity is moved to another period, the information has to be erased and copied again — with large teacher teams this becomes unbearable. Complicated 'musical chairs' moves cannot be attempted easily and if such a move fails then it is very tedious restoring the original position. Clearly a better model would allow the physical movement of information without the need to erase it. All the other models allow this.

2 The Prograph board

This consists of a large plastic board honeycombed with thousands of small pigeon-holes (each about 7 mm × 7 mm). Into these pigeon-holes fit small plastic pegs. For each class and for each period there are normally three pegs to be fitted:

a coloured peg for the subject, with an abbreviation of the subject name marked on the end of the peg

a white peg for the teacher, with the teacher's number marked on the end of the peg

a green peg for the room with the room number marked on the end

This is one of the commonest models in use but it has some severe disadvantages. It is by far the most expensive of the models listed, costing several hundred pounds for most schools (a school of 1000 pupils needs over 6000 pegs and about 30 sq. ft of board). It is not easily portable, being large and heavy and usually screwed to a wall.

It ought to be secure – a perspex sheet is provided to fit over the front to prevent pegs coming out. In practice some unhappy events have occurred. One headmaster took home a Prograph board on the back seat of his car to complete his timetable over the weekend. Duly completed he brought it back to school on Monday morning. Unfortunately he had forgotten to fit the front plastic sheet, there were some road-works on his route, the car jumped and in the school car-park he was seen scrabbling on the floor of his car, desperately picking up dozens of pegs.

In another school, a deputy head had completed about three-quarters of his timetable when he went home one night, leaving off the front perspex sheet. A cleaner came into his room to sweep up, nudged the board with the broom handle and knocked some of the Prograph pegs on to the floor. Being a kind and considerate cleaner, she picked up the pegs and fitted them into some empty spaces on the board – presumably where they looked the prettiest! It would have been ironic if this produced a better timetable than the one intended!

The greatest disadvantage of the Prograph method is that the information to be stored remains in a large number of small pieces. Moving one class for a single period means moving only two or three pegs but moving large teacher teams for double, triple or quadruple periods can mean moving a very large number of pegs, always with the possibility of dropping some, particularly if you have thick fingers and especially if the move does not work and you have to restore the original position. With the timetable model that I usually use, I have sometimes made 'musical chairs' moves involving six large cards – with the Prograph model this would have required the movement of 120 pegs! Also, when moving large numbers of pegs there is always the possibility of moving some members of a team but forgetting the others – a fatal mistake!

Other disadvantages of the Prograph board include an unpleasant effect on the eyes caused by the large number of regular holes, the difficulty of reading the details except from close to the board and the nuisance of having to remember each teacher's number.

An advantage of the Prograph board lies in the way it checks a timetable. If the feeder boards for staff and rooms (placed to the left and right of the main board) are used correctly, then a timetable which fits on to the board should run without any clashes when the new term starts. A Prograph board is sometimes useful for checking a timetable which has been constructed on another, more flexible model (see section 9.10).

3 *Small cards and pigeon-holes*

This commercial model is similar to the Prograph method, except that the three bits of information – subject, teacher, room – are written on to a small card. The cards fit into small slots on a large metal or plastic board.

This model is less expensive than the Prograph, slightly more portable but perhaps slightly less secure. Integrating the three bits of information on to one card (for each class and each period) is an improvement but for large teacher teams and multiple periods, the number of cards to be moved can be large.

The three remaining models are all variations on one theme.

4 *Large cards and pins on softboard*

This is an home-made model. A large piece of softboard is marked out in a grid and then fixed to a wall or used flat on a desk. Coloured cards are then pinned in position on the grid.

The big advantage of the card model is that the cards can be as large as you like and can integrate as much information as you like – you are not restricted to the situation in the previous model of 'one card for each class and each period'. This means that if a teacher team is to teach 4 classes in parallel, the card for this team is cut so that it is 4 classes in width. In this way moving one card moves the whole team and there is no possibility of moving only part of the team by mistake (unless you use a pair of scissors to cut the card).

Also, if the subject is intended to be taught for a single period the card will be cut so that it is only one period vertically; if it is intended to be a double period it will be cut larger to be two periods vertically. In this way multiple periods cannot be broken up into smaller periods (unless you use scissors).

Of course, colour should be used to give quick visual clues: the base colour for each card should indicate the subject area. Abbreviations for the subject, the teacher and the room-number are written on the card. Because the design of these larger cards is a common feature of this and the next two models, further details of the layout and labelling of the cards are given later in this section.

5 *Large cards on a card base*

This is very similar to the last model but instead of a softboard base, only card is used (a 22″ × 30″ card is large enough for a 7-form-entry 11–18 school). This base

110 Timetabling

card is laid horizontally during scheduling and only gravity is used to hold the coloured information cards in position. This means that it is very flexible in use (the cards can be moved to new positions very easily and quickly) but it is not very secure (unless you have a private room used only for scheduling at that time of year). Before completion it is not portable – the timetabler must work entirely at school or entirely at home. Once completed, the timetable is made secure by glueing down the coloured cards to the base card (e.g. using Copydex latex glue). It is then portable and easily carried to departmental meetings etc.

6 Magnetic plastic and tinplate base

I am quite sure that this is the best model — it combines excellent flexibility and portability with reasonable security and cost. The materials are sold by companies dealing in office supplies and display materials. It is made from sheets of coloured magnetic plastic which can be cut to size using scissors. The plastic is available in seven colours and extra stripes of colour can be added if necessary, using self-adhesive coloured plastic tape, available from the same suppliers. The plastic can be labelled using pencil, ball-point or felt-tip pens (either water-based or spirit-based inks, although the latter is not easily removed). Of course the magnetic 'cards' can be used again for next year's timetable. The magnetic attraction is surprisingly strong – turning the timetable model horizontally upside down and hitting the back of the board will not easily displace even the smallest magnetic 'cards'. At the same time the 'cards' are easily lifted and moved to another position.

The base is made of a thin sheet of steel on a card base (to stiffen it). The base can be bought ready-marked in a grid of rectangles (size: 1 in. horizontally and ½ in. vertically). A base of size 36 in. horizontally × 24 in. vertically (hinged at the centre to fold down to 18 in. × 24 in.) can easily accommodate a 7-form-entry 11–18 school and is easily portable, especially if a wire handle is passed through holes drilled at the top of the board. One commercial version of the base is covered in thin transparent plastic on which notes, reminders and other data can be written in pencil and later rubbed off or washed off. It is useful to have a second base of the same size to act as a feeder board, storing all the magnetic 'cards' before they are moved down on to the main board.

The final version can be mounted on the wall of your office and with the bright colours and clear staff initials, the details can be read quickly from a distance of several metres. As with the previous model, the final timetable can be copied by a large commercial xerox machine at a photocopying agency.

The coloured 'cards'

The design of the coloured 'cards' is a common feature of the last three models and is discussed here in more detail.

1. First consider their size. Vertically, along the columns, a distance of ½ in. for each period on the grid is convenient (a 40-period week is then 20 in. which fits comfortably on to a desk). The cards need to fit easily *within* the grid lines so that a single-period card should measure about 11 mm, a double-period

card about 23 mm and a quadruple-period card about 48 mm.

Horizontally, 1 in. for each lower school class on the grid is often convenient. For upper school bands or half-year-groups, a width of 2 in. or 3 in. on the grid is usually convenient, depending on the size of the teacher teams (a team of up to four or five teachers can fit into a width of 2 in.). The shape of the cards will vary depending on the banding or setting, and on the period-breakdown of the subject. Figure 51 shows three examples.

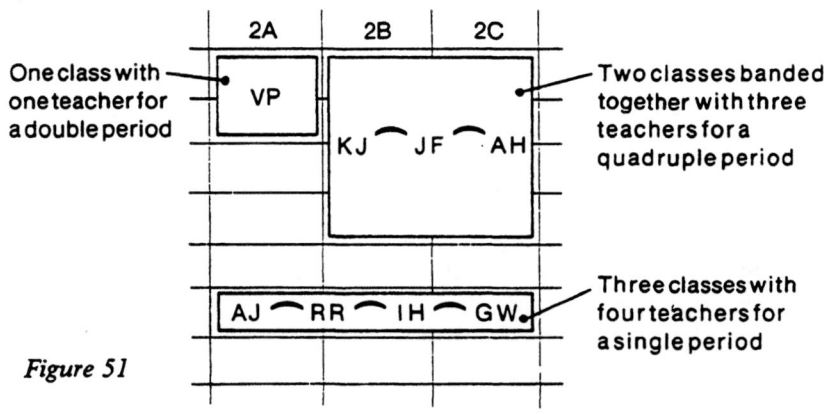

Figure 51

One class with one teacher for a double period

Two classes banded together with three teachers for a quadruple period

Three classes with four teachers for a single period

On the whole, the greater the *area* of the card, the greater the number of teacher-periods involved and so that higher the priority for fitting that card. That is, one of the rules of scheduling is: 'large cards first'.

2   Second, consider the colour of the cards. I use the following colour scheme:

green — English (language and literature)
red — Mathematics
brown — Languages (different languages can be shown by different colours of ink for the labels)
yellow — Science (different sciences can be distinguished by different colours of ink for the labels: e.g. green - Biology, red - Chemistry, blue - Physics)
blue — History, Geography etc. (again inks can be used to distinguish)
orange — creative/practical subjects such as Art, Craft, Home Economics, Commercial and Technical subjects
pink — Music (green labels); PE (red labels)

Curiously, other timetablers, who have developed colour schemes independently, have often chosen the same colours — is there a basic greenness about English?

3   Cutting a card for a homogeneous option pool is straightforward because only one colour is needed. For a heterogeneous option pool, more than one colour is needed if we wish to provide strong visual clues to help the timetabler. For example, if a heterogeneous pool consists of History, Physics and French then three colours — blue, yellow and brown — are needed if the

112 Timetabling

subjects are to be identified quickly during scheduling. This can be achieved by adding strips of colour to a card by using self-adhesive plastic tape, which is available in the same colours as the magnetic plastic, from the same suppliers. Tape of width $7/16$ in. is probably the most useful size.

4   The staff initials can be marked on the card in the same two-letter code that was used earlier in the Conflict Matrix. This can be done permanently in ball-point or spirit-based felt-tip pen; alternatively, if you feel you might wish to change the initials later, then pencil or (on magnetic plastic) water-based overhead projector felt-tip pens may be used. When marking staff initials, you may find it useful to give further visual clues to distinguish between staff by using different coloured inks to write the initials or to underline the initials.

5   In addition, the name of the subject can be written on the card — for example to distinguish between the different science courses. This helps others to read the timetable model during the year it will be in use.

6   Part-time teachers or others with particular restrictions should be marked with a large asterisk or else their initials should be ringed clearly.

7   It is worthwhile marking the name of the class in one corner of the card, in case the card becomes displaced sideways by accident.

The important thing is that *all the information should be immediately available* on the cards and there should be strong visual clues to help the timetabler as he moves the cards up and down the model. Figure 52 illustrates how all this information is integrated on to the card or piece of magnetic plastic.

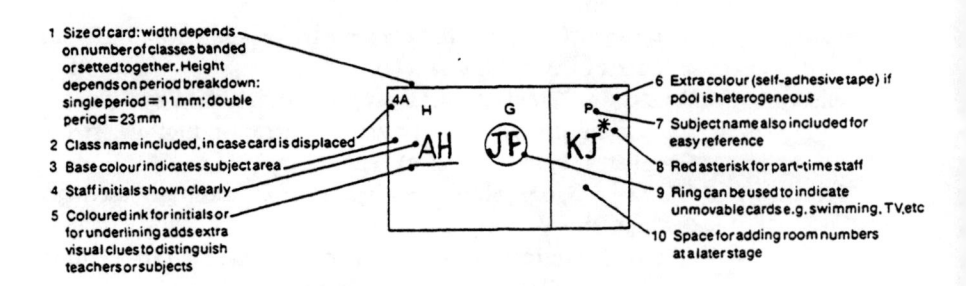

1   Size of card: width depends on number of classes banded or setted together. Height depends on period breakdown: single period = 11 mm; double period = 23 mm
2   Class name included, in case card is displaced
3   Base colour indicates subject area
4   Staff initials shown clearly
5   Coloured ink for initials or for underlining adds extra visual clues to distinguish teachers or subjects
6   Extra colour (self-adhesive tape) if pool is heterogeneous
7   Subject name also included for easy reference
8   Red asterisk for part-time staff
9   Ring can be used to indicate unmovable cards e.g. swimming, TV, etc
10 Space for adding room numbers at a later stage

Figure 52

Of the five variables listed earlier — class, subject, teacher, room, time — four of them are thus shown explicitly on the model. The exception is the room which is usually dealt with at a later stage. However, if your school has only one specialist room of a particular type and this room is to be used by more than one teacher, then the room number should be shown on the relevant cards to prevent double-assignment clashes.

Scheduling 113

The basic rules of the card model
It should be clear that since each card belongs to one class or one band of classes, the first major rule of the scheduling game is that *the cards may only move 'vertically'* and never 'horizontally'. That is, each card may move 'vertically' up and down the school week to different times, but the teachers on a card are scheduled for a particular class and so the card must not move sideways.

The second major rule of the timetabling game is that there *must not be a clash 'horizontally'*. This is, two cards having a teacher's initials in common cannot both be scheduled for the same time of the week — they cannot be allowed on the same 'horizontal' row of the model.

This means that as you bring down a card from the feeder board, your eyes are constantly scanning horizontally, as when reading a book, to see which times of the week are free for this particular card. This is where the visual clues provided by the colours are so important. If you are moving down a yellow card (science) then your eyes are rapidly scanning the rows, ignoring all other colours, looking only for yellow cards — and each time one is found, checking to see if the cards have a teacher in common (or in the case of certain specialist rooms marked on the cards, to see if they have a room in common).

It is best to cut out and label *all* the cards for the whole timetable before beginning any scheduling. Then all the cards should be arranged directly above the class to which they belong, on a 'feeder' board (again the magnetic model is particularly convenient as it allows a feeder board to be angled against a wall at the back of the desk on which the main board is laid). As the cards move down from the feeder board on to the main board (larger cards first), a bar-chart develops on the feeder board, showing which classes have fewest degrees of freedom. As we shall see later, this is very useful during the later stages of scheduling. Figure 53 shows a simplified picture of the timetable model.

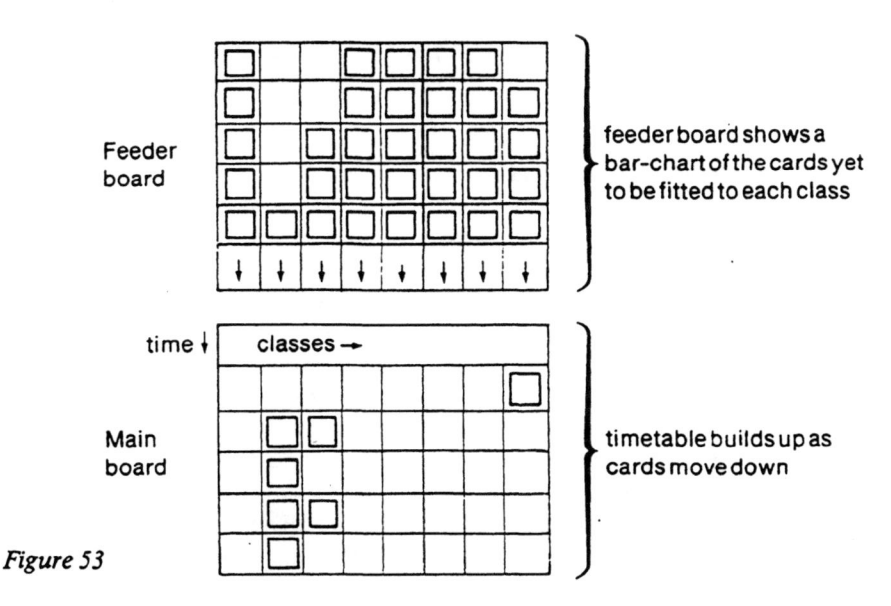

Figure 53

114   *Timetabling*

Some timetablers prefer to have extra boards — for teachers and for rooms — to the left and right of the main board so that they can keep a running check on the deployment of staff and accommodation. I prefer not to do this — the loss of flexibility, as the timetabler must constantly keep a check on the extra boards (particularly after a large 'musical chairs' move) seems to me to be too great a price. Instead I prefer to do occasional checks on the allocation of free periods and specialist rooms — perhaps at the 50% and 90% stages and of course upon completion of the main board.

9.3   Ten rules for scheduling

In an attempt to give some guidance for would-be timetablers, I include ten rules for scheduling:

1   Have all the information immediately available
It is vital to have all the information to hand and preferably built into the timetable model itself (as with the coloured card model). If you suddenly get an incredibly brilliant idea which is going to solve all your scheduling problems, but then find that you have to shuffle through piles of paper to check one item of information, you are likely to lose your way in a rising tide of frustration.

2   Link each teacher with a room where possible
Of the five main variables — class, subject, teacher, room, time — shown on the timetable model, the least explicit is the room. For this reason it helps if you can link a teacher to a room as much as possible. The staff will also prefer this — people like to work from a fixed base with known equipment and storage. Of course it is unlikely that you will be able to do this completely — most schools have more teachers than rooms.

As mentioned earlier, if you have only one specialist room of a certain type and two or more staff are due to use it, then you should show that room explicitly on the relevant cards.

3   Start with the worst constraint
The question of deciding priorities was discussed in section 8.6. After considering your priorities in the ways suggested in that section, you should be able to draw up lists of priorities under headings such as 'extreme priority', 'high priority', 'important', 'lower priority but still needing consideration'. These lists can then be clipped to the side of the main board or the feeder board.

In general the larger the *area* of the card (implying more teachers for more periods) and the more special markings on it (specifying part-time teachers, special restrictions or special subjects) then the greater the priority for it to be fitted early. It helps if the high priority cards are arranged at the bottom of the columns on the feeder board.

There will usually be some cards that are absolutely predetermined (e.g. swimming baths or links with a college) and these must be placed first. Thereafter, fitting the first large teacher-team on to the almost virgin timetable can be a dramatic moment. It can be a worrying time because, with too much freedom in placing the cards, the human timetabler cannot judge whether the placements are ideal or whether they somehow contain the seeds of later disaster. This is one area where a computer ought to be better than a human because the machine ought to be able to look further ahead — at perhaps six or more future stages, whereas a human can imagine only one, two or at most three future stages in the scheduling. This brings us to the fourth rule:

4 Look ahead to possible problems

Although we have a limited ability to look ahead it obviously makes sense, as you place each card, to consider how that card will affect other cards that are yet to be fitted. Scanning the feeder board or the lists of priorities will tell you which are the cards due to be placed soon. The timetabler soon develops the knack of looking at the card in his hand and always considering:

(a) the positions (times) that are possible because of what has been fitted already, *and*
(b) which of these positions looks best for other cards that are about to be fitted.

5 Consider carefully before saturating a particular period with a particular subject

I have mixed feelings about this rule because my instinct sometimes runs counter to the application of the principle of compatibility. As an example, imagine you are scheduling a school with six laboratories. Suppose that for Monday period 1 you have already placed cards that will need to use five of these six laboratories. Suppose further that you now need to bring on a card that requires just one laboratory. Clearly you could place that card on Monday period 1 because one laboratory is available. Indeed, it follows from the principle of compatibility that you should do this in order to minimize the number of free resources in that period. However, instinct tells me that, given alternatives, it would be better to place the card elsewhere and delay 'saturating' this particular period with this particular subject. Later, in dealing with the simpler pure-class activities of the lower school, I might find that a science class is forced into this period and then I would need a laboratory for it. At the half-timetable stage, trying to keep one of the labs free for each period seems a useful thing to do, if I know I will need single laboratories at a later stage. Applying the principle of compatibility more rigidly and saturating the period would have a stronger appeal when larger teacher teams were involved.

6 Bias the craft lessons towards the afternoon

Many timetablers would disagree with this suggestion but it is certainly worthwhile considering the best time of day for certain subjects particularly where a difficult class or a weak teacher is involved. On the whole it would seem best that subjects where the pupils are usually able to move around the room (e.g. Art, Craft, Games) should be timetabled at the end of the day. The same argument would suggest that subjects like Mathematics and Science should take place early in the day. I do not know of any research to support this. Another school of thought suggests that the first period after lunch may be a good time in inner-city schools because many children will then have broken their fast by eating for the first time since the previous evening. On the whole it is probable that the room and the direction of the wind have a greater effect on the pupils' behaviour.

7 Do not fill up a day with Craft, Games etc. – leave room in each day for Maths, English etc.
Unless you are conscious of this point you may find that you have given one class Art and Games on Tuesday morning followed by Craft all Tuesday afternoon. By squeezing Mathematics, Science, History etc. out of Tuesday you will necessarily squeeze them into the other four days of the week. Your pupils may not truant on Tuesdays but perhaps they will be more likely to absent themselves on other days.

8 Aim for an even spread in the columns (time) – with no clashes along the rows (classes)
Again the colours of the cards are a great help. As he places or replaces each card, the timetabler should scan 'vertically' up and down the column to see the time interval between similar cards. Of course the timetabler should already know the preferences of the different departments. Language teaching, which relies on the 'drip-feed' method, particularly in the lower school, will require an even spread throughout the week (preferably 5 single periods on 5 different days). Other subjects requiring regular practice, such as Mathematics, will need a similar consideration.

Sometimes the timetabler will have to judge between the requests of the staff and the requirements of the pupils. For example, some Mathematics departments are fond of double periods in the lower school. The attention span of undergraduates is said to be 20 minutes so the attention span of 12-year-olds must be rather shorter. This requires a determination by the teacher to provide a variety of experiences during the lesson — something not always in evidence in Maths lessons. Sometimes scheduling tactics can help here — for example, scheduling a double period across a break. This gives the pupils the benefit of a break halfway through the lesson without having to pack their bags (and the benefit that they return to work after the ideal revision interval of 10–15 minutes). It gives the teacher the benefit of being in one room for two periods and being able to develop a large topic if he or she wishes.

Science and Craft departments may sometimes ask for 'the last two periods in an afternoon followed by the first two periods on the next morning'. The timetabler will have to judge the advantages of these requests against the limitations imposed on the timetable.

The timetabler should check that a class does not have all the lessons in a certain subject during afternoons only (and certainly not always last period in the afternoon — such scheduling is given swift condemnation in the staffroom!).

Throughout this consideration of subject spread (up and down the columns), one overriding rule applies: there must be no clash along the rows. That is, no two cards carrying the same initials can ever be on the same row at the same time (because a teacher cannot teach in two places at the same time).

Continuing in this way and dealing with all the activities shown on the priority lists, the timetabler will gradually bring down more and more cards from the feeder board, meeting and solving problems as he goes along. He will probably schedule all of the Upper School and most of the Lower School in this way. However, when all of the main priorities have been dealt with, there may come a time when it is not clear which part should be tackled next. This is where rules 9 and 10 are useful:

9   Fill in first those classes which are nearest to completion

and

10   When filling in a class, concentrate first on the teacher whose personal timetable shows least freedom

A beginner might think that if some classes are 90% completed and others are only 50% completed, then it would be best to provide an even figure by concentrating first on the classes which are only 50% complete in order to bring them up to the 90% mark. This would be a mistake. A class which is only 50% completed (and so 50% empty) has plenty of flexibility, many *'degrees of freedom'*. Such a class can be left for a while. A class which is 90% completed (and so only 10% empty) has less flexibility, fewer ways of being completed, fewer degrees of freedom. This class must be timetabled sooner. Taking the extreme case, a class which has 39 of its 40 periods fitted has only one single period to be fitted and only one place to put it. This class should be tackled immediately by fitting the single period card into the empty gap or, if it causes a clash there, finding some 'musical chairs' solution (see section 9.5).

One of the beauties of the card models is that the boards show you immediately what is yet to be fitted for each class and which class is the tightest and has priority to be tackled first. In action, the timetabler regularly scans the 'bar-chart' displayed by the cards on the feeder board, seeing which class has priority now and which classes will have priority soon.

That is rule 9. Rule 10 helps in those cases where, having found which class is due to be tackled next, you find that there is more than one teacher involved and you cannot decide which teacher to concentrate on. The same principle applies: the teacher with the least flexibility, the fewest degrees of freedom, should be tackled first. Identifying this teacher is not as straightforward as identifying the class. It can be done by scanning the feeder board (or the main board, but by now this will be rather full) to count the number of unfitted periods for each of the teachers concerned. Knowing the number (and the number of free periods for each teacher) will allow you to decide who has the least flexibility and so the highest priority.

A simple guess is usually sufficient. However, if you wish, you can calculate the degree of freedom by:

$$\text{degree of freedom}, f = \frac{\text{number of places for fitting this teacher's (or class's) cards}}{\text{number of cards yet to be fitted for this teacher (or class)}}$$

For example, if you wish to fit in *two* double periods for a particular teacher and there are *six* places in the week where one could go, then $f = \frac{6}{2} = 3$. In practice there is no need to calculate this accurately, a 'guesstimate' is sufficient.

The value of f gives you a guide as to what to do:

(a) If f is much greater than unity there is plenty of flexibility and no need for the timetabler to do anything yet.
(b) As f decreases and tends towards a value of one, the timetabler should consider it more and more as its priority increases.
(c) If $f = 1$ the card should be fitted immediately. This might be considered the ideal time. The ideal timetable might be thought of as one where every card in turn had a value of $f = 1$, so that a timetable was just possible while at the same time the Heads of Department and the timetabler had asked for the most they could get from the timetable.
(d) If f is less than one then you are in trouble and must give priority to fitting this card by moving other cards.

In these paragraphs I have been assuming a kind of repulsive force as the cards on the feeder board force themselves off the feeder board and on to the main board. However, in the later stages of scheduling, when you are fitting pure class activities, you may find a slightly different situation. This is when the blank spaces on the main board exert a kind of attractive force, pulling particular cards off the feeder to particular positions on the main board. This change of emphasis arises because you may find that for a particular period in the week, the class is free and the room is free but only *one* of the staff is free and so must be fitted into that period. Sometimes you may find that *none* of the staff due to teach this class is free and then you must start 'musical chairs' moves with the cards in order to find someone who can take the class for that period. This change of emphasis, from feeder board cards to main board blanks, comes only in the later stages of scheduling and is more difficult to see for a human timetabler (although a computer could cope more easily, by scanning every period regularly). If you have applied Zarraga's Rule (section 8.2) then you should have less difficulty with this problem.

For convenience, the 10 scheduling rules are listed again here:

1. Have all the information immediately available.
2. Link each teacher with a room where possible.
3. Start with the worst constraint.
4. Look ahead to possible problems.
5. Consider carefully before saturating a particular period with a particular subject.

6 Bias the craft and similar lessons towards the afternoon.
7 Do not fill up a day with Craft, Games etc. — leave room in each day for Mathematics, English etc.
8 Aim for an even spread in the columns (time) — with no clashes along the rows (classes).

In later stages:

9 Fill in first those classes which are nearest to completion, and
10 When filling in a class, concentrate first on the teacher whose personal timetable shows least freedom.

9.4 Worked example

To illustrate some of the rules given in the last section consider the simple and artificial scheduling problem shown in Figure 54.

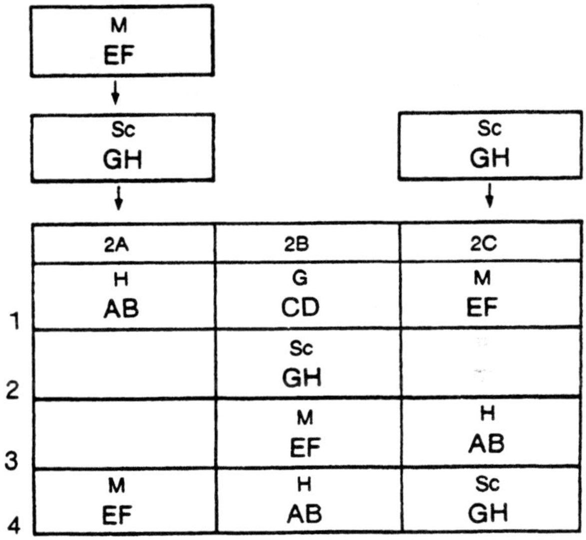

	2A	2B	2C
1	H AB	G CD	M EF
2		Sc GH	
3		M EF	H AB
4	M EF	H AB	Sc GH

Above the table:
- M EF ↓
- Sc GH ↓ (to 2A column)
- Sc GH ↓ (to 2C column)

Figure 54

The diagram shows three 2nd Year classes with their timetable partially completed and three activities yet to be placed. The problem is to fit all the activities into the time-frame shown, in such a way that the two Maths lessons for 2A are separated as much as possible and the two Science lessons for 2C are also separated as much as possible. You are urged to attempt this problem before reading the solution given below.

The first point to note is that there are only 4 teachers and 4 subjects involved in this simple problem. All the History is taught by teacher A B, all the Science by G H etc. The second point is that adding even a small amount of colour to the diagram makes it very much clearer to see the pattern. Thirdly you will find the problem becomes very much easier to solve if you use *movable* coloured cards rather than pencil and fixed paper.

120 *Timetabling*

Rules 1 and 2 already apply. Rules 3 and 4 do not help us much in this artificial example although we might guess that Science has a higher priority than Maths. Rule 8 reminds us of the basic rules — the cards may only move up and down columns; the cards must not clash along rows.

We must decide where to start. 2B is already completed (so we need not echo Hamlet's question: '2B or not 2B'). Rule 9 helps us to decide which class we should start with: 2C has less freedom and so is given the higher priority.

If the Science card for 2C is moved down to the empty space, it clashes with GH taking 2B. AB for 2C could move up to period 2 so that GH for 2C could go in period 3, but this would put the two Science cards next to each other — the opposite to what was requested. A better solution is to move down EF for 2C to period 2 (no clash) and then place GH for 2C in period 1 (so that the Science cards for 2C are separated as much as possible).

Turning now to 2A, we assume that the Science card has a higher priority than the Maths card and so move it first (rule 3). GH for 2A cannot go in period 2 (clashes with GH for 2B) but it can go in period 3 (no clashes).

Now we move down the Maths card. EF for 2A cannot go in period 2 (clashes with EF for 2C) but if AB for 2A is moved down to period 2 (no clashes) then EF for 2A can go in period 1 (no clashes and the Maths cards for 2A are separated as much as possible, as requested).

This gives the best solution with the Maths and Science each separated as much as possible. Other (poorer) solutions are possible. For example the whole of row 1 (i.e. period 1) can be interchanged with the whole of row 2 (period 2).

9.5 Nine tactics and moves

In the last example all the moves were very straightforward 'one-steps': a card simply moved into an empty space where it caused no clashes. On a real timetable model the moves are often more complicated. Some examples are given in this section.

Most of the moves are 'musical chairs' manoeuvres: the cards move round the timetable model until, hopefully, they all find a place to sit down.

In each of the following examples of tactical moves, it is supposed that the timetabler's attention is concentrated on the top left-hand corner of the diagram where teacher AB is shown to be scheduled for class 2A for period 1. The aim of each move is to free teacher AB for period 1 *or* to free class 2A for period 1 *or* to free both class and teacher for period 1.

1 A two-step to clear teacher AB from period 1
See Figure 55(a).

In this case a simple interchange, involving only class 2A, clears teacher AB from period 1 so that he may be used elsewhere for period 1.

This move depends on AB initially being free for period 4 and on teacher PQ initially being free for period 1 — otherwise they cannot move as shown. The timetabler must scan the full length of 2A's column to find periods where these conditions apply. When the two periods concerned are not on the same day, the move may mean that one of your constraints is broken — for example it could mean that you will now have two periods of French on the same day whereas previously they were well spread.

2 A two-step to clear class 2A for period 1
See Figure 55(b).

This move involves two classes, not necessarily adjacent to each other. The move relies on there being a symmetry about the positions of AB and the positions of the blanks for the two classes involved. In order to spot such a move, the timetabler need only look at cards for AB, and only those cards which lie on rows containing a blank for 2A.

As with all these moves, the result may be unsatisfactory, because it may spoil the period-spread that has been carefully built up with earlier placements.

3 A two-step to clear both teacher AB and class 2A for period 1
See Figure 55(c).

This useful move is quite easy to spot: the timetabler scans up and down the 2A column to find a suitable place for AB; if AB is teaching 2B at that time, the timetabler scans the 2B column to find a suitable place for AB to move to.

4 A three-step to clear teacher AB from period 1
See Figure 55(d).

The diagram is self-explanatory. Three teachers are involved but only one class. Of course the periods involved are not usually all on the same day (as shown in the diagram) but widely spread throughout the 35 or 40 periods of the week.

For all of these moves it is useful to mark possible positions on the model using coloured plastic pegs (e.g. Prograph pegs, Lego bricks or markers from Waddington's game of 'Risk'). When making a large move these pegs can also be used to mark the original positions in case the move does not work and you have to restore the original situation.

5 A three-step to clear class 2A for period 1
See Figure 55(e).

Three classes are involved but only one teacher. As before, the result may upset your period-spread for the subject taken by AB.

6 A three-step to clear both teacher AB and class 2A for period 1.
See Figure 55(f).

This move involves finding a vacant place for AB in another column at another time (like move 3 but extended by a further step). Sometimes it is easier to look at this move backwards, i.e. in reverse order.

122 *Timetabling*

(a) A 2-step to clear teacher AB from period 1

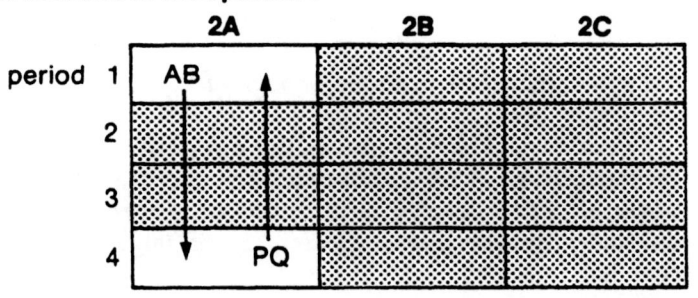

(b) A 2-step to clear class 2A for period 1

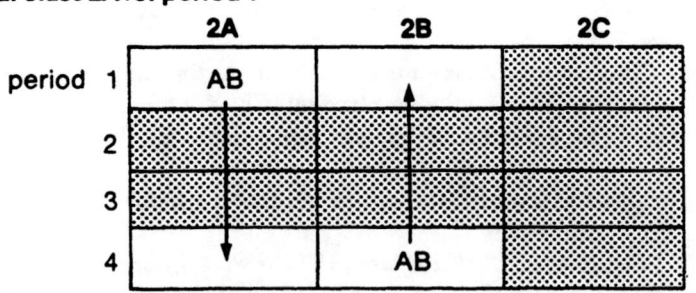

(c) A 2-step to clear both teacher AB and class 2A for period 1

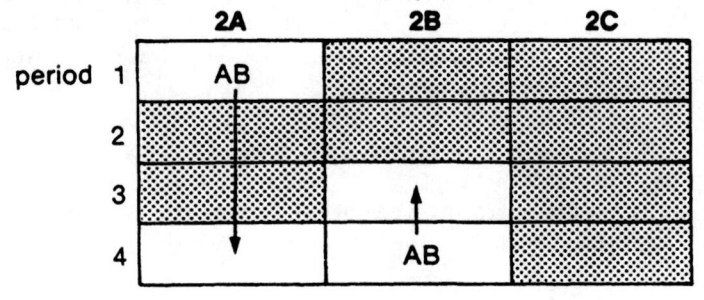

Figure 55

(d) A 3-step to clear teacher AB from period 1

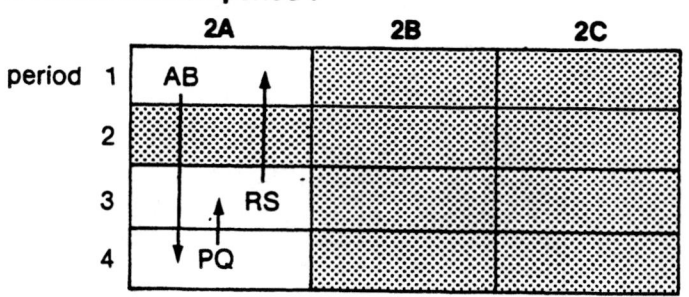

(e) A 3-step to clear class 2A for period 1

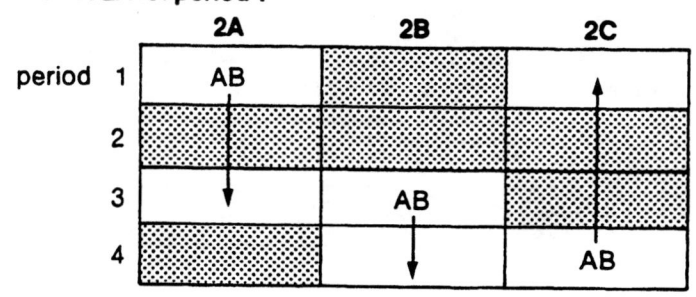

(f) A 3-step to clear both teacher AB and class 2A for period 1

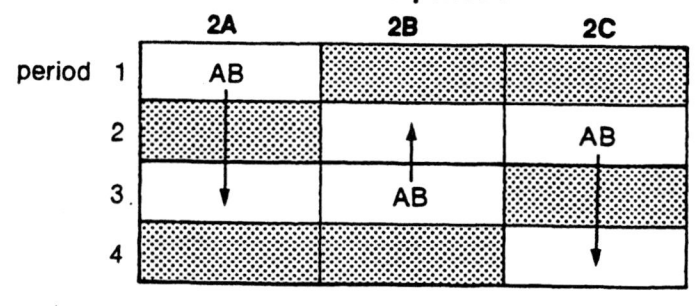

Figure 55

124 *Timetabling*

(g) A combination of two 2-steps to clear both AB and 2A for period 1

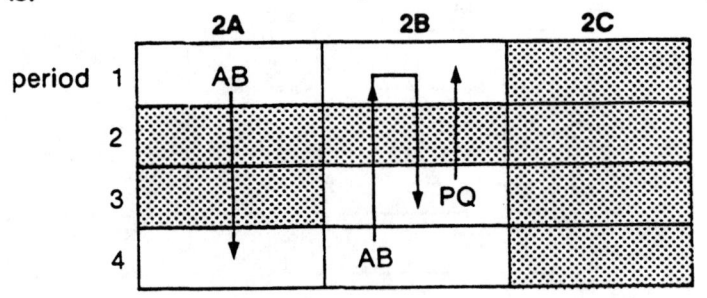

	2A	2B	2C
period 1	AB		
2			
3		PQ	
4		AB	

(h) A multiple 2-step or 'roll-over'

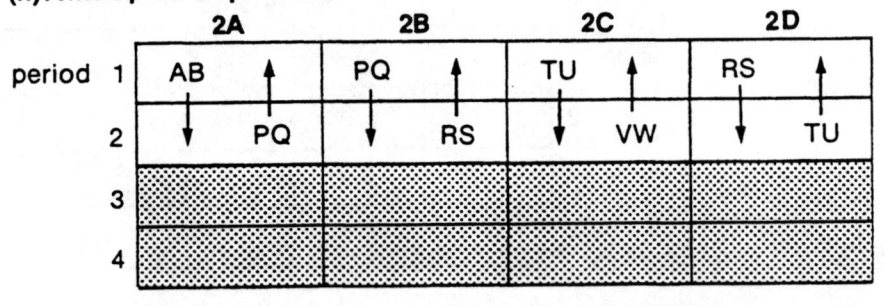

	2A	2B	2C	2D
period 1	AB	PQ	TU	RS
2	PQ	RS	VW	TU
3				
4				

(i) Interchanging teachers to clear class 2A for period 1

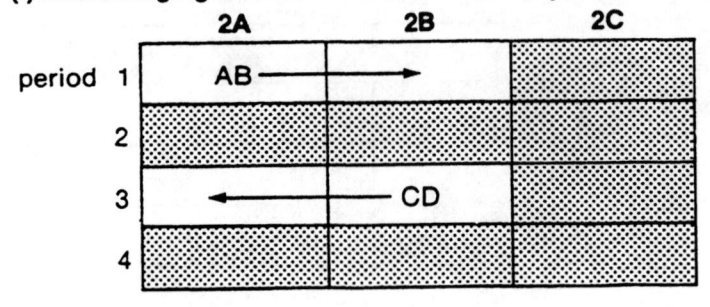

	2A	2B	2C
period 1	AB ———→		
2			
3	←——— CD		
4			

Figure 55

Obviously these steps can be extended to give more complicated moves. Four-step moves are not too difficult and moves up to six-step are possible when coloured pegs are used as markers. Where large cards are involved, a six-step movement transfers large amounts of information — sometimes the equivalent of over 100 Prograph pegs.

7 A combination of two two-steps to clear both AB and 2A for period 1
See Figure 55(g)

Obviously combinations of two or more moves can be made. This example is a combination of move 2 and move 1. Alternatively it can be seen as a combination of move 3 and a simple one-step. It can also be seen as a variation of move 6. It involves two classes and two teachers, the result being: AB with 2A period 4, AB with 2B period 3, PQ with 2B period 1.

8 A multiple two-step or 'roll-over'
See Figure 55(h).

In this example, teachers PQ, RS, TU are teaching for both of the periods shown, while teachers AB and VW are teaching for only one period each. By making the moves shown, AB will be scheduled to teach for period 2 instead of period 1.

This move is not the same as a total interchange of all of the row for period 1 with all of the row for period 2 (although, of course, this can be done). In this move only this set of interconnected teachers are interchanged, the rest of each row remaining unchanged.

This move relies on the last member of the chain reaction (in this case VW) being able to move. Because the move usually involves two adjacent periods (for example, the two halves of a double period) it is usually quite easy to see this move and to deal with large numbers of cards, for as many as a dozen classes.

A similar move can be used to clear a class. For example, if VW were missing from the diagram, the same set of moves could be used to clear class 2C for period 1.

There are two situations when a 'roll-over' move is particularly useful:
(a) At the rooming stage, when you wish to get AB into a specialist room which is available for period 2 but not for period 1.
(b) At the final polishing stage when you are trying to improve the quality of your timetable. This move may allow you to get a better sequence of events or a better traffic flow round the building (see also section 9.8). In this case the move can be used even if 'AB' and 'VW' are the same teacher, so forming a closed circuit.

9 Interchanging teachers to clear class 2A for period 1
See Figure 55(i).

This is a more extreme remedy. Suppose, in the example shown, that AB and CD are both Geography teachers. It may be acceptable to exchange classes, as shown, particularly if the classes are in the lower school and similar or equal in age, ability and number of periods.

126 *Timetabling*

If you make an exchange like this then:
(a) Remember that all the periods of that subject for both classes must be exchanged or else you will have a split class.
(b) Remember to re-label the class names on all the cards involved.
(c) Tell the Head of Department why it has happened.

You are more likely to need to make this move if you have not applied Zarraga's rule (section 8.2). In the example shown in the diagram, one might suppose that the move had to be made because none of 2B's teachers were available to take the class for period 1.

9.6 Fitting a difficult item

As a guide to finding a solution in difficult circumstances, consider the following steps, in order:

1 *Find a time in the week when the class is free for the required number of periods.* Then:
(a) Are the teachers (and rooms) free or able to be freed by moves like numbers 1, 3, 4, 6, 7, 8, in the last section?
(b) What constraints are violated by these moves — for example, does it give two periods of French on the same day, or PE and Games on the same day?

2 *Find a time in the week when the required teachers (and rooms) are free for the required number of periods.* Then:
(a) Are the classes free or able to be freed by moves like numbers 2, 3, 5, 6, 7, 8 in the last section?
(b) When looking to fit a double period, a good place to begin is where there is already a single blank on the main board. Then you can try to find a way of making that single blank grow into a double blank. A variation on this method is to find a single period already fitted which can grow into a double period (displacing another card if necessary), thus leaving only a single period to be fitted.
(c) Consider what constraints have been violated (see 1(b) above).

3 *Find a time in the week when as many as possible of the required classes and teachers (and rooms) are free.* Then:
(a) Can the remaining classes and teachers (and rooms) be freed by moves like those given in the last section?
(b) As in 1(b) above.

4 If there is still no solution, can a solution be found by:
(a) *Splitting multiples into smaller amounts of time?*
   e.g. a double becomes two single periods.
(b) *Grouping periods into larger multiples?* e.g. two single periods become a double period (a good place to look is where one single is already fitted — see 2(b) above).

5   If there is still no solution, *find a time when the class(es) are free or can be made free*. Then:
    Can suitable teachers (and rooms) be allocated by changing the specification of resources and using moves like number 9 in the last section?

6   If there is still no solution then you will have to consider changing the *curricular* structure — for example, breaking up a parallel setting arrangement.

9.7   Allowing for different period-breakdowns

A difficulty sometimes arises when two activities are in parallel on the curriculum, but require a different period-breakdown when they are scheduled.

Consider an example. Suppose a school decides to introduce a second foreign language, Spanish, for 4 periods per week, to two classes in the 2nd Year, as an alternative to Craft and Domestic Science.

Part of the Curriculum Plan might appear as in Figure 56.

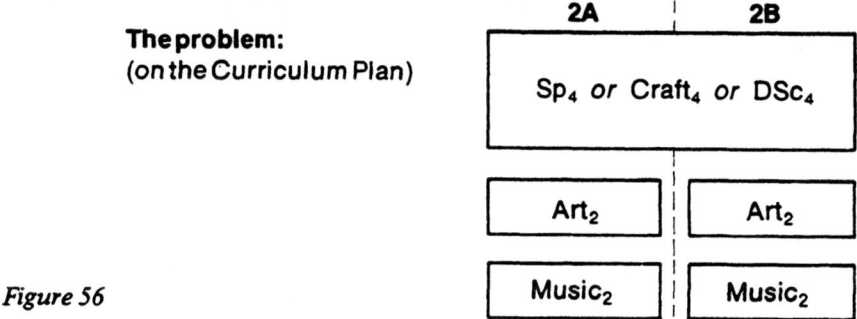

The problem:
(on the Curriculum Plan)

2A	2B
Sp_4 or $Craft_4$ or DSc_4	
Art_2	Art_2
$Music_2$	$Music_2$

Figure 56

The difficulty arises because Spanish requires 4 single periods while Craft and Domestic Science prefer one quadruple period.

A possible scheduling solution is shown in Figure 57:

A solution
(on the timetable model)

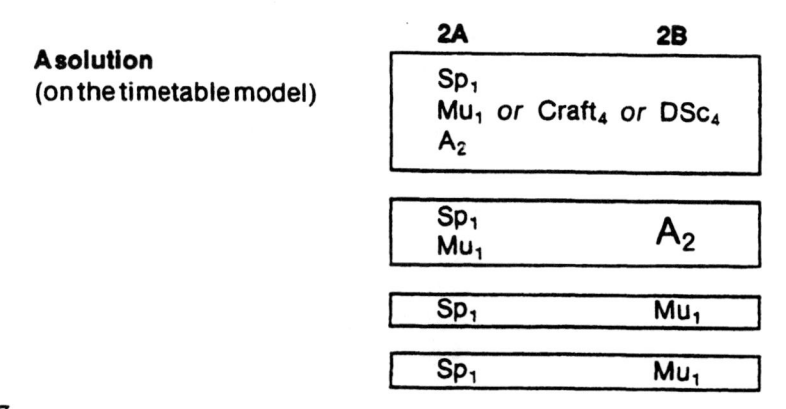

2A	2B
Sp_1 Mu_1 or $Craft_4$ or DSc_4 A_2	
Sp_1 Mu_1	A_2
Sp_1	Mu_1
Sp_1	Mu_1

Figure 57

This solution requires that:
(a) half the population of 2A and 2B takes Spanish
(b) the Music department agrees to single periods

9.8 Improving the quality

Timetabling is essentially about the deployment of human beings. The timetabler needs to think constantly about the effect of his actions on people — both pupils and staff. Merely satisfying the arithmetical demands of the data to produce a workable timetable is not sufficient. We should provide a high quality, enabling timetable that will allow staff and pupils to give of their best.

When looking at the quality of your timetable, you may wish to consider the following aspects:

(a) There should be a good period spread, particularly in subjects like French and Mathematics. Hopefully the completed timetable will already show that the periods for each subject are distributed well, but if there are any flaws it is workwhile spending some time in trying to improve matters. Straightforward two-step moves (like moves 1, 2, 3, in section 9.5) are the first things to look for.

(b) While making these moves it is worthwhile keeping a look-out for other situations such as 'French for period 1 followed by Spanish for period 2'. There will be less confusion if such similar subjects are separated by at least a break or a single period.

(c) The 'free' periods for the staff should be well distributed. The importance attached to this will vary from school to school but it is worth considering, especially for those in weaker health or those who are frequent commuters in split-site schools. Again two-step moves provide the most likely solutions. The number of staff free in any period should be as even as possible — this will be important for the person responsible for arranging cover for staff absences.

(d) The timing of lessons can have a strong effect on some classes of pupils. For example, Maths lessons which always occur late in the afternoon for a class of less able pupils can have disastrous consequences. Scanning up and down the columns should show up any imbalances like this.

You may then wish to consider block exchanges — for example, exchanging the whole of one double period (across the entire timetable) for another double period. Eight-period days with equal morning and afternoon sessions have a clear advantage here — for example, you might exchange the whole of Tuesday morning for the whole of Tuesday afternoon. The 2-2-2-2 school day has a further advantage: in theory any quarter of a day can be exchanged for any other quarter. In practice there may be difficulties with any exchange: fixed points for TV, swimming etc. will prevent an exchange of those periods.

A good sense of judgement is needed before any exchange: improving the timetable for one class almost always means the opposite for another class.

(e) The sequence of two single periods can be important. For example, consider

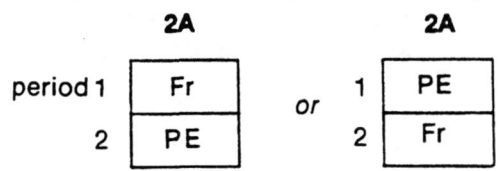

	2A
period 1	Fr
2	PE

or

	2A
1	PE
2	Fr

The first is clearly the better arrangement. In the second the pupils are likely to arrive at the French lesson hot, damp, late and possibly volatile.

(f) As a further example of the importance of the sequence of two lessons, consider the following simple case study.

Mr M, a Mathematics teacher, is weak; the pupils leave his lessons in some disorder, feeling very lively, perhaps frustrated at his poorly structured lessons.

Mr G, a Geography teacher, is middle-aged, has good discipline but requires standard situations, promotes a rather inflexible classroom atmosphere.

If you were to schedule Maths for period 3 followed immediately by Geography for period 4 then the pupils are likely to have a poor Maths lesson followed by a lesson where Mr G reacts against the lively mood of the pupils as they arrive boisterously at his classroom. In turn, the pupils are likely to react against his rather inflexible manner and a poor atmosphere results. If, instead, you were to interchange the two lessons then the pupils would probably have a good Geography lesson followed by a Maths lesson as good as before (or perhaps better, if some of Mr G's calmer influence carries over to period 4).

After two or three timetables, most of these considerations will come naturally to the concerned timetabler. Knowing the school well and observing it in action, he or she will instinctively feel doubtful about some combinations of teacher, class, room, time of day, day of week, traffic route and previous or following lesson.

9.9 Rooming

With the exception of some specialist rooms, the allocation of rooms is usually left until the feeder board is empty and all the cards have been fitted to the main board (and inspected for quality).

The ideal rooming allocation would give each teacher his preferred room and put each class into one particular room for all its periods in that subject. Whether you can do this depends on the value of the rooming fraction (and how closely the number of pupils divided by the number of teaching spaces approaches 21, see chapter 7). If you cannot allocate a particular class the same room for all its lessons in a particular subject, it should always be possible to fit the lessons into a maximum of two rooms. It would be quite wrong for a class to have its five French periods in five different rooms. Learning (as well as teaching) is partly a matter of habit, and pupils need the security of the same room, same desk, same walls, same teacher to support their learning habits. Perhaps the ideal timetable would also ensure the same time of day for every French lesson.

If possible, the timetabler should delegate some of the rooming to the relevant Heads of Departments. For example, the Heads of the Science and Craft departments can certainly be expected to allocate their specialist rooms. Delegating in this way will not only lighten your load, but also will give other members of staff a greater understanding of your problems and perhaps a greater appreciation of your efforts.

Obviously specialist rooms are allocated before considering general classrooms. When allocating rooms, I find coloured markers are a great help. I lay a sheet of paper to the right of the main board and place on top of it columns of coloured plastic or card markers, one colour to each room that I am considering and one marker to each period. Then the markers are gradually moved off the paper on to the main board. The rule for moving the markers is that they can *only move sideways, along a row*. That is, each marker belongs to a particular period and must not move to another period. Scanning the columns on the paper tells me which rooms are available for each period; scanning the columns on the main board tell me how consistently I am allocating a particular class-subject to the same room. Where there are alternatives it is worthwhile considering how they will affect the traffic-flow round the building. When finally determined the room number should be written on each card. A note should be made of the rooms left free for each period of the week.

Some timetablers prefer to build up the class timetable on a 'card' model (because of its flexibility) and then transfer the details to a Prograph board before using the room pegs to allocate rooms. The final state of the Prograph board shows which rooms are free and which staff are free for each period of the week.

9.10 Checking the timetable

When you have finally completed the scheduling and apparently fitted all the information correctly on to the model, it is wise not to heave too large a sigh of relief until you have checked it. This is the first stage in the scheduling process when I think it is really useful to have a partner or an assistant (at most earlier stages a second person can be a hindrance — except when they supply drinks of coffee or something stronger).

The most likely and most serious error is that you may have scheduled a teacher *twice* on the same row — that is, you have scheduled a teacher to be with two classes at the same time.

For my first two timetables I transferred the information from my card model to a Prograph board in order to check it. A Prograph *ought* to check it perfectly, providing the staff and room pegs are moved *only* along horizontal rows without any deviation. This is not always easy to ensure because of the small size of the holes and their repetitious layout.

Nowadays I check the timetable on the 'card' model and, so far, have not made a single double-booking error. I check my magnetic plastic model by laying a metre rule horizontally just below the row that I am inspecting. The rule helps to guide my eyes as they scan left and right along the row, checking cards of the same colour for the same initials. Although I have not yet made a double-booking error, I always check very carefully because of Murphy's Law: 'if something can go wrong, it will, and at the worst possible time'.

The method of checking the timetable at one school is remarkable. Late in the summer term, all the staff and pupils are given copies of the new timetable and then the school bells are rung every five minutes. Each five minutes represents a full period on the new timetable, which the pupils and staff try to follow, bell after bell, so that a full school week is simulated in about three hours! This is followed by a staff meeting to discuss the new timetable!

9.11 Distributing the timetable

Custom varies from school to school. Some schools like to have large copies of the master timetable hanging in the staffroom, Head's room, school office, main corridor etc. For three of the timetable models (paper, cardboard and magnetic plastic) it is possible to get large or small xerox copies produced at a photocopying bureau.

An alternative method (or a supplement) is to provide each teacher with a Timetable Booklet. This consists of one page for each year group. The pages are laid out in a grid like the master timetable (with classes horizontally and time vertically). The horizontal lines of the grid are shown only at breaks and lunches, with double lines at the end of each day.

A simple code gives the information in each rectangle of the grid:

E   AJ   12   indicates a *single* period of English with teacher AJ in room 12.

$\begin{array}{c} E \\ AJ\ 12 \end{array}$ indicates a *double* period of English with teacher AJ in room 12.

If two (or more) classes are banded or setted together for some lessons, the appropriate vertical line is deleted for those periods in the timetable booklet. If lessons cross a break (e.g. cookery) the appropriate horizontal line is deleted. A year-group of up to 7-form-entry will fit comfortably on to one page of A4 paper.

A further valuable feature of such a booklet is the inclusion of a *homework* timetable for each class. The homework timetables for the whole of a 7-form-entry school can be shown on two sides of A4 paper.

Some timetablers copy out each teacher's individual timetable for distribution. This can be a lengthy and tedious task. I prefer to provide each teacher with a copy of the Timetable Booklet and a number of timetable blanks. Each teacher is requested to extract his or her personal timetable from the booklet and provide a sufficient number of copies (for the Head, for the Deputy or whoever arranges cover for staff absence, for the school office so that secretaries can locate staff quickly etc.). This method not only spreads out the burden of copying timetables

132 *Timetabling*

but it also encourages staff to look at the timetable as a whole and become aware of other features apart from their own personal timetable.

One of the advantages of timetabling by computer (see chapter 10) is that the machine can be used secretarially to print individual timetables. It is possible to program a small microcomputer to accept the data from a manual timetable model and then use this data to print out individual staff or class or room timetables (see Appendix 15).

9.12 Assessing your timetable

Many timetablers are easily tempted to ignore this topic, partly because it is a difficult thing to do satisfactorily. However, it should be attempted, preferably during the first half-term of its operation. Inevitably the result will be a matter of opinion.

One way is to ask each department to provide comments on good and bad features. A second way is to inspect each teacher's personal timetable for poor distribution etc. Another way is to walk the corridors, particularly at bell times, observing the movement of pupils and feeling the atmosphere. A fourth way is to analyse the main timetable board by counting the number of unsatisfactory features.

Among the criteria that you might consider are essential for a quality timetable are the following:

1 The timetable should enable, support and project the school's educational philosophy. It should comply fully with the required setting and option structures.
2 There should be a good distribution of subjects throughout the school week. Academic subjects should not appear consistently late in the day. Each teacher's timetable should be well distributed. (See also the list in section 9.8.)
3 Staff timetables should be as close as possible to those requested by the Head of Department, in terms of classes, period-breakdown and rooms requested. No class should have two teachers for the same subject unless this was planned.
4 There should be optimal use of the school's resources, particularly specialist rooms.
5 All constraints imposed by part-time teachers and fixed points (e.g. linked courses) should be observed absolutely.

If you wish to assess how tight your scheduling is, and if you are a gambling person, there is a game you might like to play. Challenge anyone to (a) throw a coin on to your model (laid horizontally), and then (b) find a way of moving the card marked by the coin without breaking any of your timetabling constraints. If he can do so, you owe him the value of the coin (and vice versa). If you lose more than once, you might be forced to decide that you are not asking enough of your timetable and could probably afford to aim for more setting in some subjects.

9.13 Alternative timetable cycles

Throughout the previous sections we have assumed a standard 5-day 'rectangular' week. However it is worth noting that other arrangements are possible.

The commonest alternative to the standard week is a 6-day cycle. This is usually 7 periods × 6 days = 42 periods or 8 periods × 6 days = 48 periods. These arrangements are usually introduced when schools wish to bring further subjects on to the curriculum without being able to decide where the periods should come from. In practice the pupils are usually quick to adapt although they may be more likely to have an excuse for forgetting their books. The staff usually find it more difficult to adapt to the new system and are more likely to be late for their lessons.

A 10-day cycle seems a better prospect. In scheduling, most of the items may be the same for both weeks of the cycle and only a few of the items may alternate. For example, a class may have Careers one week and Religious Education the other week.

Most timetables are 'rectangular' in shape. That is, all the classes have the same number of periods in a day. A few schools have deviated from the rectangular arrangement by introducing an extended day, whereby some year-groups on some days begin earlier or stay later. Such an arrangement can greatly increase flexibility and ease the scheduling task by reducing the number of resources that are required simultaneously.

A modification of the same idea leads some schools to adopt a staggered lunch break. This might require half the school to work a 4–lunch–4 day while the other half operates a 5–lunch–3 day. These arrangements may cause some complications for the timetabler but they allow the school to make more efficient use of its limited resources.

9.14 Block Timetabling

Block timetabling or 'faculty' timetabling or 'consistent blocking' is an attractive idea. In essence the school timetabler decides the basic structure of the timetable but the details of the schedule are left to individual faculties. This method is feasible only where the school is organized into true faculties or where it is easy to form natural ad hoc 'faculties' for the purpose of timetabling.

The school timetabler's model looks like a simplified class timetable. Instead of classes the horizontal axis is usually divided into half-year-groups. The time axis is usually divided into 20 (double) periods at this stage. Each card on the model shows only the name of the faculty with no details of particular subjects or teachers. The cards are adjusted using the usual rules and bearing in mind the total number of periods required by each faculty and the total number of staff available in each faculty. Usually the blocking is consistent in the sense that Maths and Science (grading pupils by similar criteria) are paired together for a year group. Similarly English and Humanities are usually paired together.

The result of this blocking may show, for example, that on Monday period 1 (a 70-minute period) the Maths and Science 'faculties' each have half the 1st Year and half the 4th Year. This information is then passed to the faculty timetabler (or to a faculty meeting) to decide the details of which teacher takes which group in which room. If they wished, the Maths and Science faculties could agree to exchange the two halves of the 1st Year after 35 minutes on Monday morning so that the pupils have a single period of each subject.

Among advantages claimed for this method are: the teachers at the chalkface can have a greater say in determining the timetable that rules their days; the faculty can decide whether to employ mixed-ability teaching, team-teaching or setting by ability; departmental meetings are more easily arranged; cover for absent staff becomes a responsibility of the faculty.

Although these ideas may seem attractive, in practice it may be impossible to implement such a scheme because of the difficulties in forming natural 'faculties', whether because of staffing or because of accommodation. A further difficulty arises if any of the option pools are heterogeneous — in the 4th Year, 5th Year or in the Sixth Form.

For more details on block timetabling see the bibliography.

9.15 Summary

One of the most important factors in developing a good quality timetable is the choice of a good model — one which suits you and is flexible in use. Although guides to rules and tactics have been given in this chapter, it is practice which gives a timetabler the skill and fluency in manoeuvring the pieces of the model. However, quality is what really matters and this can only be obtained by a timetabler who, in addition to having the skill, also knows well the teachers (and their preferences, foibles and failings) and knows the school and regularly observes every part of it in action.

10 Computer timetabling

10.1 Introduction
10.2 The Nor-Data system
10.3 The SPL system
10.4 The Oxford school timetabling system
10.5 The future

There is a story about a Deputy Head who spends a whole day typing his timetable data into a computer. The computer whirrs and flashes its lights and eventually types out, as its solution, the single word 'No'. 'No what?' types the Deputy Head in a fit of rage at the idiot machine. The machine hesitates and then slowly types out 'No *sir*'.

The story illustrates a common reaction — part fear, part admiration — towards computers. And yet the idea of computer timetabling is certainly an attractive one. Computer can count and compare numbers a million times faster than humans, so why not let them do the job for us?

The construction of timetables requires the handling of large amounts of data, something computers should be able to manage better than humans. Computers should be able to reduce the work load for senior staff so that they are available for their more human functions of pastoral care for both pupils and staff. Computers should be able to save us time by dealing with the secretarial problems of producing staff and class timetables.

'Computers should be able to ... ' Unfortunately, at the time of writing, they have not yet fulfilled their promise. At the beginning of the 1970's it seemed that the timetabling problem would soon be solved by the computer; at the beginning of the 1980s we can see that this has not yet happened, even though computers have become much cheaper and much more common. True, many schools do obtain a timetable 'by computer', but it cannot be said that the timetabling problem has yet been solved entirely successfully.

The reasons for this are to do with the difference between an electronic computer and the 'computer between your ears'. An electronic computer is extremely fast and extremely stupid. It can only do what it is told; it can only deal with the program instructions and the data that it is given and nothing more. By contrast, your brain is very slow, but very good at making judgements. Since the timetable is a device for controlling and directing humans, many of the decisions made in its construction are human judgements. The brain of a good timetabler contains a wealth of information on which those human judgements are based.

136 Timetabling

The depth of human information that can be given to a computer can be shown by two examples. 'We have a problem with the bus queues at the end of afternoon school and this is giving us a bad name in the community and so the Deputy Head ought to go and supervise the pupils except on Thursdays when he can round up culprits for detention' becomes, for the computer, 'DH not period 8'. 'Mr J. Bentham has a wooden leg and should only teach on the ground floor' becomes, for the computer, 'JB not rooms 31–50'. By contrast the human timetabler might aim for these conditions, but for the greater good of the greater number he might occasionally ask Mr Bentham to teach upstairs. The machine cannot do that — its rules are fixed.

Similarly, if in scheduling you are faced with the choice of fitting Mr Smith (suffering his male menopause, hates Monday mornings, usually late to classes after registration, likes the Sixth Form but too fond of sending 4C pupils to the Deputy Head etc.) *or* of fitting Miss Jones (just out of her probationary year, overanxious, marks meticulously but absent rather too many days, not sure how to handle teenage boys when they try to be matey etc. etc.) then you cannot decide who is to have priority on the timetable without knowing the real Mr Smith and Miss Jones, the classes, the subjects, the time of day, the lessons which precede and follow etc. Much of this information is information that you don't know that you know, until you find yourself using it. It is difficult to see how this information could be given to a machine (even assuming that the program could handle it), unless or until the computer evolves into something akin to a humanoid. Since the science fiction of today has a habit of becoming the science faction of tomorrow, we may well see this in due course.

For the present, it seems to me that the computer and the human brain each have something to offer the other. The computer can deal very quickly with the straightforward parts; the human can judge better for the difficult parts. The ideal is some kind of symbiotic relationship. The machine processes the quantities; the human ensures the quality.

One thing that has been learned during the last ten years of computer timetabling is the inadequacy of the 'one-shot' approach. Early users of the systems expected to put their data into the machine and within minutes receive a complete timetable. With 9–13 middle schools containing no option schemes, this was possible. With 11–16 comprehensive schools, containing the complicated option schemes that we had come to expect, the best that might be expected was a 95% fit. Even this would not have been bad if the unfitted 5% (the 'kick-outs') were only simple pure-class activities. Often they were not, often they contained large teacher-teams in the 4th Year and 5th Year and this required the dismantling of large sections of the timetable in order to fit them.

The more modern approach is iterative. The machine is asked to place only the first 100 activities and then stop. The human timetabler inspects this partial timetable, fitting in any kick-outs by making such compromises as are necessary. The machine is told of these adjustments and then asked to fit the next 100 activities, and so on. In this way any large kick-outs are fitted without having to dismantle large sections of the timetable. When fitting kick-outs or looking at the quality of the timetable at each step, I strongly urge users to copy the computer print-out on to their usual manual model (magnetic plastic, Prograph etc.). This is the only way you can see the true quality of the timetable — rows of numbers on a computer print-out do not allow you to see the pattern of the events.

Using this iterative approach, many schools now produce a timetable using a computer. The state of the art is such that a computer timetable is likely to be better than a manual timetable produced by a moderate or poor timetabler. Experienced and competent timetablers can also benefit from using a computer. I find that the time spent in scheduling still covers the same number of weeks. However, instead of the constant intense effort of manual timetabling, there is more variation — periods of routine (filling in the data tables, waiting for a 'run' to come back from the machine) which allow me to recuperate in order to really attack a problem when it arrives. The cost of the running time on a mainframe computer (once the program has been bought) is currently about £300 for a 7-form-entry school. This is a small fraction of a teacher's salary. The cost should fall dramatically once a program becomes available for a school-based microcomputer.

It is not the purpose of this chapter to provide a full guide to computer timetabling — prospective users should refer to the bibliography or obtain the relevant user's manual. However, the next three sections give very brief outlines of the three main systems — the Nor-Data, the SPL and the Oxford systems.

10.2 The Nor-Data system

This system originated in Norway in 1966 and was developed by Dr Harald Michalsen. The system can be purchased from the Royal Institute of Public Administration. It is used extensively in Scandinavia, and in the United Kingdom by more than twenty local authorities. It seems to be the best system available for the sort of curricula that we have come to expect in the UK. I have used it for the last four years.

After all the usual timetable checks have been completed (as explained in chapters 5, 6, 7, 8) the information is transferred to data tables. Figure 58 illustrates part of one of these tables.

				I	O	E	N	G		
Class	Periods		T		Rm	D		
2 A		6	E	L	1	4	2	
Parallel	2	B	M	M	1	5		

Figure 58

The example shows the specification for English which will be referred to in later print-outs as activity number 10. The specification states that 2B should be taught in parallel with 2A; that the two teachers are EL (to be in room 14) and MM (to be in room 15). These room numbers can refer to actual rooms or to types of room. This table also specifies that there should be six periods of English in the school week and that these should include two double periods (and therefore two single periods also). There are also ways of specifying that the system may break up the double periods or combine the single periods if you wish to give it extra flexibility. Other data tables allow the user to specify the days or periods that part-timers or other staff are not available. When completed the tables are converted into punched cards which are fed into the machine. Absolutely no knowledge of computers or programming is required.

The program has three main parts, each of which can be iterated. The Forprogram-part-1 checks the data for errors (e.g. in the period totals for classes and teachers). If this is clear the Forprogram-part-2 is used to look for timetabling impossibilities. If any are found, action should be taken before moving to the Mainprogram which does the scheduling. This program can be steered to particular areas of the curriculum if the user wishes; other areas can be suppressed for some runs so that they are used only as background information and not scheduled until a later run.

This very brief outline cannot do justice to the system—the user's guide runs to over sixty pages and timetablers are usually given a week's training course initially. Most schools find that their timetables benefit simply because the timetablers, in order to complete the data tables, are forced to think more carefully about what they are doing.

Dr Michalsen is said to be working on a version of the Nor-Data system which is suitable for a school-based microcomputer.

10.3 The SPL system

This system was developed in New Zealand by Dr Charles Kent of Systems and Programs Ltd. It is marketed in the UK by the National Computing Centre. About twenty local authorities in the UK use the system.

I have used the system only once, in 1973, when it provided nothing more valuable than several hundred metres of computer paper, so my opinions are clearly biased. The system has been enhanced in the years since then, but a 1978 report by LAMSAC (see the bibliography) found it less successful than the Nor-Data system.

The basis of the SPL system (like the Nor-Data system or a manual timetable) is that the program begins with a blank timetable and proceeds to fill it in by calculating a degree of freedom for each item, selecting the item with the least degree of freedom and searching for positions to place it. For each position that it found, the results of placing it there are calculated and the position of least damage is chosen. Although this heuristic method is the basis, other, more rigorous, mathematical methods are used to support it. Further details of the system can be found by reference to the bibliography.

10.4 The Oxford school timetabling system

This system was developed by Dr M. Dempster of Oxford Systems Associates. The basic method of this system is different from the other two. Essentially it begins with a full timetable! It can be shown mathematically that a timetable solution can always be found, and easily, providing that all special requirements are ignored. This system initially ignores all special requirements such as fixed times, setting, period spread, period-breakdown, special rooms etc., and produces a full 'timetable'. It then proceeds to move towards the required timetable by interchanging elements of the simple 'timetable'. A particular point of interest is that the system is intended to be interactive — this is, the user will be able to communicate with the machine while it is making the interchanges and so influence the machine with human judgements.

10.5 The future

The disadvantages of computer timetabling at present are the cost, the queuing-time with a mainframe computer and the lack of direct human influence on the program during a run. The advantages of a computer are its speed, its memory and its ability to look farther ahead than a human.

In my day-dreams I think of a program written for a microcomputer that could be used in school or at home, whenever I needed it. The computer would be placed side by side with my magnetic plastic model so that the best features of both were used. Initially the machine would be given the data that is shown on each card. Naturally it would apply and display the various timetable checks (as do the programs in the appendices) so that the data could be amended where necessary. Thereafter the program would be interactive. At each stage the machine would tell me the cards with the fewest degrees of freedom, but the one to consider first would be my choice. The computer would tell me which positions were feasible for that card together with the consequences of using each position, but the final choice would be mine. I would then be able to tell the machine of my decision to place card 143 on Monday morning periods 1 and 2 by typing (or, eventually, speaking) a phrase such as '143M12'. The scheduling would proceed by my asking the computer a series of 'what if ... ?' questions. Of course, once the timetable was completed the machine would print out staff, class and room timetables. Throughout the school year it would also help me to decide who should cover for absent colleagues by providing at the beginning of each day a listing of names, weighted by factors such as previous use for cover, number of free periods, extra responsibilities etc.

Such a system would surely give us the best of both man and machine. I look forward to the day when we have it. Of course, by then the demands on our timetables may have changed — perhaps our pupils will be following individualized learning programmes, American-style, or perhaps our schools will have become convinced of the benefits of a common-core curriculum, without the complicated option schemes that cause such difficulty today.

Appendix 1

A flowchart for curriculum planning and timetabling

Bold boxes = policy decisions for Head or Management Team
Other boxes = calculations, operations for Director of Studies, Timetabler

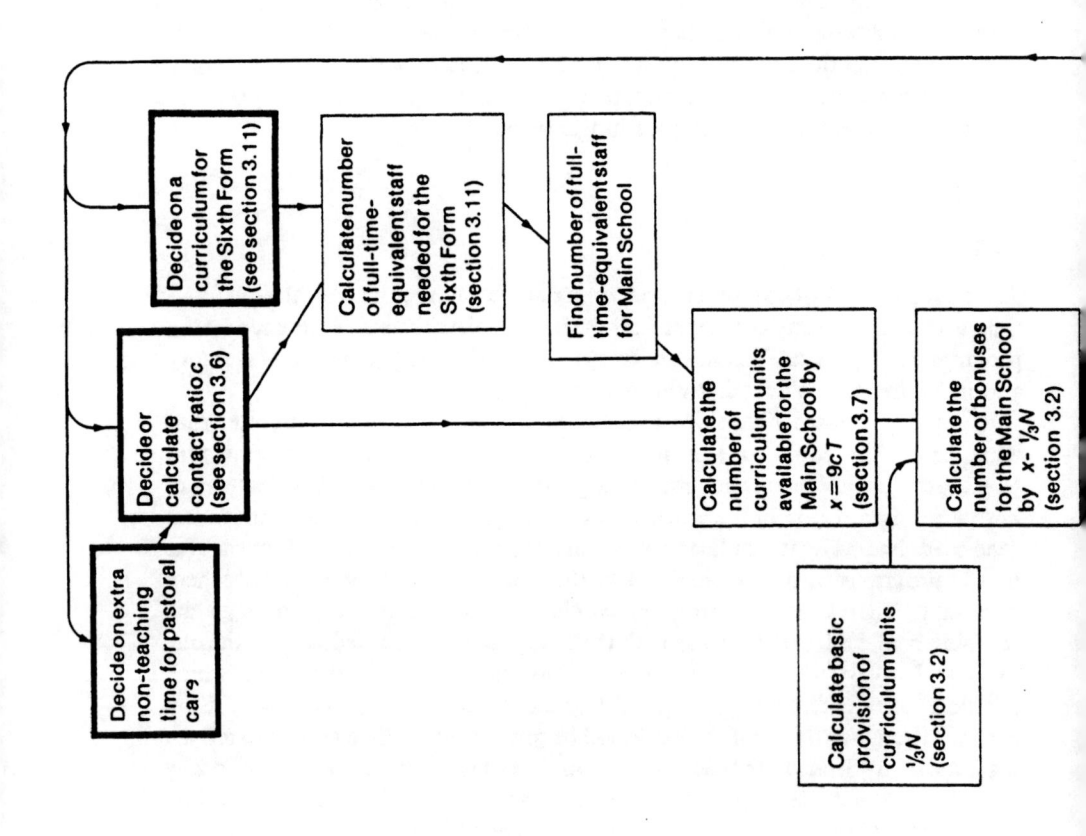

```
┌──────────────────┐     ┌──────────────┐     ┌──────────────┐
│ **Decide on a**  │────▶│ Calculate    │────▶│ Find number  │
│ **curriculum for**│    │ number of    │     │ of full-     │
│ **the Sixth Form**│    │ full-time-   │     │ time-        │
│ **(see section** │     │ equivalent   │     │ equivalent   │
│ **3.11)**        │     │ staff needed │     │ staff for    │
│                  │     │ for the      │     │ Main School  │
│                  │     │ Sixth Form   │     │              │
│                  │     │ (section     │     │              │
│                  │     │ 3.11)        │     │              │
└──────────────────┘     └──────────────┘     └──────────────┘
                                                     │
┌──────────────────┐                                 ▼
│ **Decide or**    │                          ┌──────────────┐     ┌──────────────┐
│ **calculate**    │─────────────────────────▶│ Calculate the│────▶│ Calculate the│
│ **contact ratio c**│                        │ number of    │     │ number of    │
│ **(see section 3.6)**│                      │ curriculum   │     │ bonuses for  │
│                  │                          │ units        │     │ the Main     │
│                  │                          │ available for│     │ School by    │
│                  │                          │ the Main     │     │ $x - \tfrac{1}{3}N$ │
│                  │                          │ School by    │     │ (section 3.2)│
│                  │                          │ $x = 9cT$    │     │              │
└──────────────────┘                          │ (section 3.7)│     └──────────────┘
                                              └──────────────┘
┌──────────────────┐                                 ▲
│ **Decide on extra**│                               │
│ **non-teaching** │                          ┌──────────────┐
│ **time for pastoral**│                      │ Calculate    │
│ **care**         │                          │ basic        │
│                  │                          │ provision of │
│                  │                          │ curriculum   │
│                  │                          │ units        │
│                  │                          │ $\tfrac{1}{3}N$ │
│                  │                          │ (section 3.2)│
└──────────────────┘                          └──────────────┘
```

*The events on these two pages might not take place every year –
perhaps in alternate years or when there is a major change in
curriculum, intake or staffing*

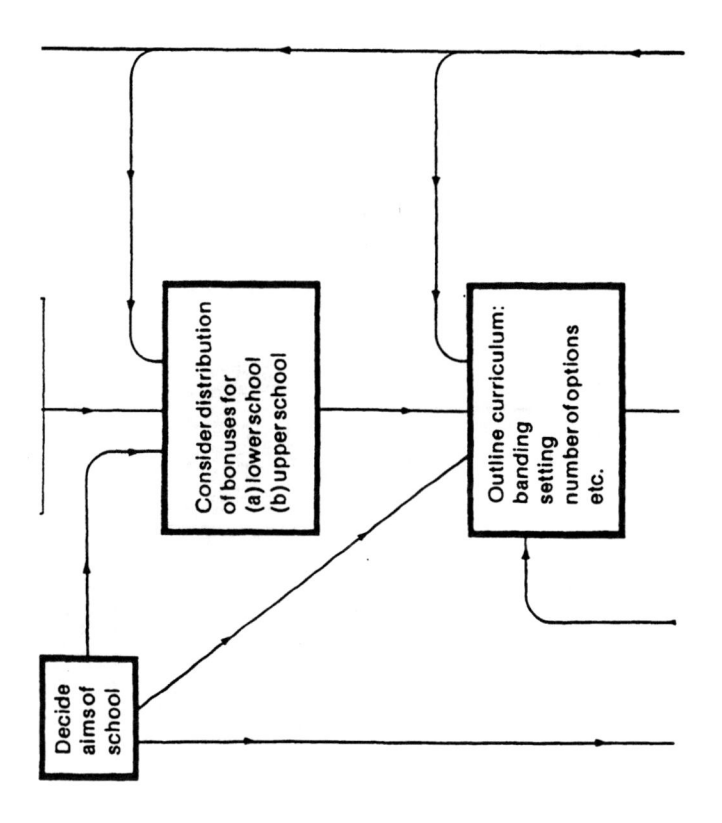

Appendix 1 141

- Consider distribution of bonuses for (a) lower school (b) upper school
- Outline curriculum: banding setting number of options etc.
- Decide aims of school

142 *Timetabling*

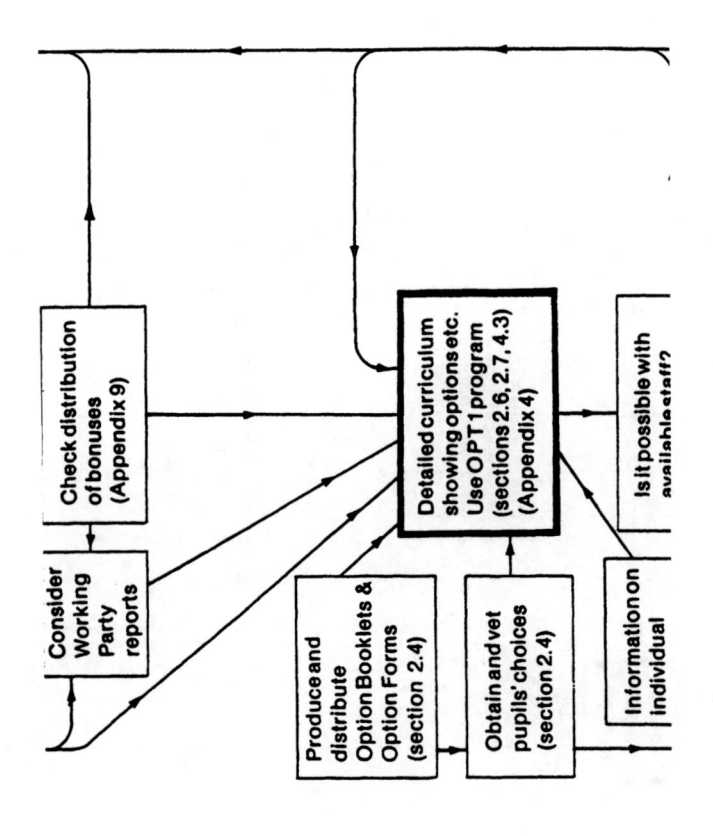

- Check distribution of bonuses (Appendix 9)
- Consider Working Party reports
- Produce and distribute Option Booklets & Option Forms (section 2.4)
- Obtain and vet pupils' choices (section 2.4)
- **Detailed curriculum showing options etc. Use OPT 1 program (sections 2.6, 2.7, 4.3) (Appendix 4)**
- Is it possible with available staff?
- Information on individual

Spring Term

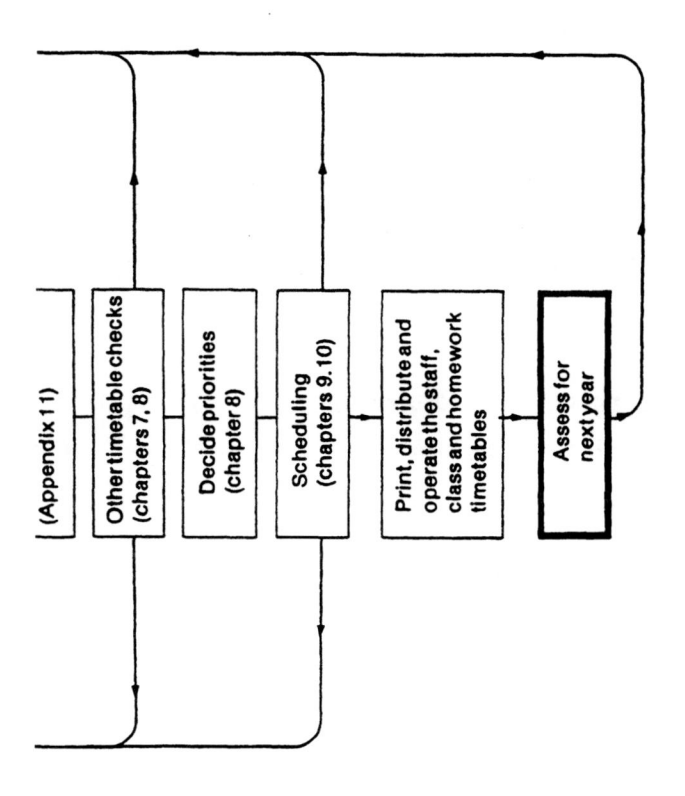

Appendix 1 143

- (Appendix 11)
- Other timetable checks (chapters 7, 8)
- Decide priorities (chapter 8)
- Scheduling (chapters 9, 10)
- Print, distribute and operate the staff, class and homework timetables
- **Assess for next year**

Summer term

Appendix 2
21 Curriculum formulae

Symbols:

N = number of pupils
T = number of staff
n = number of teaching spaces
} these are determined by the LEA

c = contact ratio
r = rooming fraction
x = number of curriculum units
$b\%$ = relative bonus
} these are determined by the school

These formulae apply to the main school only; if you have a Sixth Form, see section 3.11

A. T.I. Davies (1969) proposed:

Since x curriculum units are provided for N pupils, each of whom studies 9 cu's,

$$\text{the average class size} = \frac{9}{x} \text{ of } N = \frac{9N}{x} \qquad (1)$$

If a class has zero bonus, then x = basic cu's = $\frac{N}{3}$. Substituting in (1),

$$\text{the average class size for zero bonus} = \frac{9N}{N/3} = 27$$

Also, since the effective number of teachers is cT, for N pupils, we can say:

$$\text{the average class size} = \frac{N}{cT} \qquad (2)$$

Equating (1) and (2) and eliminating N, we get the *Staffing Equation* or 'First Law':

$$x = 9cT \qquad (3)$$

$$\text{The number of bonuses} = x - \frac{N}{3} = 9cT - \frac{N}{3} \qquad (4)$$

21 Curriculum formulae

The relative bonus $b\% = \left(\dfrac{x - \dfrac{N}{3}}{\dfrac{N}{3}}\right) \times 100\% = \dfrac{(3x - N)}{N} \times 100\%$ \hfill (5)

From (4) and (5): number of bonuses $= \dfrac{b\% \times N}{300}$ \hfill (6)

From (3) and (5): $b = \dfrac{(27cT - N)}{N} \times 100$

Rearranging we get. $\dfrac{N}{T} = \dfrac{2700c}{100+b}$ \hfill (7)

This is the equation I used in drawing up the nomogram (for the top labels).

B. I.B. Butterworth (1975) proposed:

$$\text{rooming fraction } r = \frac{\text{average number of teaching spaces in use } (cT)}{\text{total number of teaching spaces } (n)}$$

That is: $r = \dfrac{cT}{n}$ \hfill (8)

Eliminating c from equations (7) and (8), we get:

$\dfrac{N}{n} = \dfrac{2700r}{100+b}$ \hfill (9)

This is the equation which connects the bottom labels on the nomogram.

C. However, we can take the ideas of Davies and Butterworth several steps further, as follows:

Eliminating T from (3) and (8) we get the *Rooming Equation* or 'Second Law':

$x = 9rn$ \hfill (10)

From (3) and (10), it is sometimes useful to think of the timetable as requiring:

average number of staff teaching at any time		average number of classes at any time		average number of rooms used at any time	
cT	=	$x/9$	=	rn	(11)

146   Appendix 2

For curricular flexibility, b should be not less than 10% (see section 3.8).

From (5) : $\left(\dfrac{3x - N}{N}\right) \times 100\% \geqslant 10\%$

hence: $x \geqslant 0.367 N$ \hfill (12)

This gives the minimum number of curriculum units required for a main school of N pupils.

From (3) and (12): $9cT \geqslant 0.367 N$
$$\therefore c \geqslant 0.0407 \, \dfrac{N}{T} \qquad (13)$$

This gives a minimum value of c (once the LEA decides the staffing ratio). c cannot continue to decrease indefinitely unless the staffing ratio improves.

For *timetabling* flexibility, r should be not greater than about 0.85 (see chapter 7).

From (10): $\dfrac{x}{9n} \leqslant 0.85$

$$\therefore x \leqslant 7.7n \qquad (14)$$

This gives a preferred maximum value for the number of curriculum units in the school or in a department requiring specialist rooms.

From (3) and (14) : $9cT \leqslant 7.7n$
$$\therefore c \leqslant \dfrac{0.85n}{T} \qquad (15)$$

This gives a preferred maximum value for the contact ratio.

Changing the subject to T:

$$T \leqslant \dfrac{0.85n}{c} \qquad (16)$$

This can be used to calculate the 'maximum' size of a specialist department.

21 Curriculum formulae 147

For both curricular flexibility *and* timetabling flexibility, we combine (12) and (14):

$$0.367N \leqslant x \leqslant 7.7n \tag{17}$$

This gives the range of values which x can take.

Also, from (13) and (15):

$$0.0407\frac{N}{T} \leqslant c \leqslant \frac{0.85n}{T} \tag{18}$$

This gives the range of values which c can take.

Equating the upper and lower limits in either (17) or (18), we get Johnson's rule of thumb:

$$\frac{N}{n} < 21 \tag{19}$$

If the number of pupils divided by the number of teaching spaces is greater than 21, then the school has lost curricular flexibility ($b < 10\%$) or timetabling flexibility ($r > 0.85$) or both.

If a 9-13 middle school or the lower school of a split-site complex has a curriculum which is only a 'basic' provision of $\frac{N}{3}$ then from (14) we get, for that building:

$$\frac{N}{n} < 23 \tag{20}$$

This implies a correspondingly lower value of $\frac{N}{n}$ for the upper school building.

Finally, although it is not very useful, we can combine N, n, T, c, r, b into one equation. The best version, from (7) and (8) is:

$$\frac{Nn}{T^2} = \frac{2700c^2}{r(100+b)} \tag{21}$$

The left-hand side of this equation is determined by the LEA: the variables in the right-hand side are determined by the school. The value of each side of the equation is usually in the range 16 ± 2.

Appendix 3

Using the computer programs

The programs on the following pages were written for a small microcomputer. Specifically they were written for a PET-8, preferably (but not necessarily) with a Commodore printer attached. They were designed to run on either the 8K or larger machines (with either the old or the new ROM-set).

For the most part the programs are written in a 'portable' BASIC so that they may be used on other microcomputers. However, owners of 380Z, TRS80, Apple or 6800 machines will have to change some or all of the print routines.

PET owners may type in the programs from the listings given on the following pages and then 'SAVE' them on tape. However if you wish to eliminate this task, ready-to-run cassettes can be supplied, as follows:

OPT1 — Draw Clash Table and write a tape
OPT2 — Fit choices against Option Pools
OPT3 — Edit the tape
OPT4 — Print option group lists
OPT5 — Print option group lists
OPT6 — Print pupils' option timetables

£15 per set of six†

TT1 — Staff Deployment Analysis*
TT2 — Combing Chart
TT3 — Conflict Matrix
TT4 — Zarraga's Rule
TT5 — Timetable Memory
TT6 — Timetable Printout

£15 per set of six

†Please state whether old or new ROM versions required.
*Please state whether 8K or better (13K) version required.

Cheques with order, please, to   Chris Johnson
                                    120A Urmston Lane
                                    Stretford
                                    Manchester M32 9BQ

Other programs are available: Marks (to calculate and order your examination marks) and Reading Ages (to find the reading ages of your textbooks and worksheets, quickly).

At the time of writing the programs are being modified and taped for other machines, particularly the 380Z, Tandy, and Apple machines.

The options programs

Although the later programs are self-contained, the first six (OPT1 — OPT6) are interconnected and have certain features in common.

OPT1 prints a Clash Table of the pupils' choices (see section 2.6). It also produces a data tape of the information about pupils. This data tape is used in the other five programs.

OPT2 compares the pupils' choices with a proposed option scheme and prints the resulting group sizes. It also shows which pupils will not fit the scheme and what is needed in order to fit them (see section 2.8). The data tape from OPT1 can be used so that the program can be run without supervision and several option schemes investigated.

OPT3 is used to edit the data tape, for at least two reasons:
  (a) To change some pupils to their reserve choices in order to run OPT2 again to see if there is a better fit.
  (b) Once the option scheme is decided, to change the data tape to show the final decision for each pupil so that the data tape can be used with OPT4, OPT5, OPT6.

OPT4 is used to print lists for (photocopying and) providing to members of staff.

OPT5 is used, less conveniently, when the number of pupils is too large for OPT4 on your machine.

OPT6 is used after the timetable is finished, to provide a slip of paper for each pupil showing each of their final options subjects together with the teacher, room and time of the week (for giving out to pupils at the start of the new school year).

The route through these programs is normally:
OPT1; OPT2; (OPT3 then OPT2 perhaps several times); OPT3; OPT4 or OPT5; OPT6.

If you offer more than 18 subjects to any group of pupils and you have only an 8K machine with the old ROM-set, the route is slightly different: OPT3 is used after OPT1 (for details see Appendix 4).

In all the OPT programs subjects are referred to by a one-letter code of your own choice. The following is only a suggestion:

A	Art	J		S	Science
B	Biology	K	(Metalwork)	T	Technical Drawing
C	Chemistry	L	Eng. Literature	U	
D	German	M	Music	V	
E	Economics (Home)	N	Needlework	W	Woodwork
F	French	O		X	
G	Geography	P	Physics	Y	(Typing)
H	History	Q		Z	Dummy subject
I		R	RE		(+ any graphics symbols)

Appendix 4

OPT1 — Drawing a Clash Table and writing a data tape

Relevant sections

2. 6, 8.4

Input

From keyboard; pupils' choices in order of preference using one-letter code; preferably with pupils' names also.

You will need

A blank tape and all the pupils' Options Forms. If you cannot use OPT4 (run the first part of OPT4 to find out) and so must use OPT5, the forms should be in alphabetical order and separated into boys/girls if you want your group lists the same way.

Output

A Clash Table and a data tape to use in the other OPT programs.

Time required

About 15 minutes for 30 pupils

* *

Entering the information

Most of the steps are explained on the screen but the following hints should be helpful:

Remember to press 'return' after each entry.
The most useful format is probably:
B JOHNSON KEITH HGPCA
G JOHNSON ANN FHBAM
The boy/girl prefix can be omitted (but see OPT4/OPT5).
Type a space between each part of the entry.
Remember to give the subjects in order of preference, most wanted subject first.
Remember to enter the surnames in alphabetical order if you cannot use OPT4.
Remember to spell names like Stephen/Steven carefully because staff are likely to use the final lists for reports etc.

OPT1 – Drawing a Clash Table and writing a data tape   151

You can include careers information after the forename if you wish (this may help you after using OPT2, but it will probably have to be deleted by OPT3 before using OPT4/5 and OPT6).

You can include the new form name after the forename if you know it (but make sure the subjects always come last).

Include all the names, even those of absent pupils, adding dummy subjects as necessary e.g. XXXXX. (Do not include the dummy subject in the list for the Clash Table).

If you wish to reserve space on the tape for new pupils or pupils who may be promoted or demoted to the group later, include sufficient extras such as:
G NOBODY1 XXXXX
You will be able to use OPT3 later to alter this as you wish.

After each entry and 'return' nothing appears to happen for about 20 seconds until it draws the new Clash Table. With care, the beginning of the next entry can be made, slowly, during these 20 seconds — but after the Table is drawn, check the data on the screen carefully before pressing 'return'.

After every 20 entries, the data is written on to the data tape. (Just follow the screen instructions).

After your final pupil has been entered, enter EOF (for 'end of file') and press return. The remaining data is written on to the tape and then the Clash Table is printed on the printer (if attached).

If the Table scrolls off the screen, you can see it again by typing GOTO 700 ('return') (but do not enter any more data).

If you have more than 18 subjects

With more than 18 subjects there is some difficulty in fitting the display on to the screen.

If you enter 19 subjects then the 18th and 19th subjects will overlap if the number of pupils choosing them is more than nine.

If you enter 20 subjects then the 6th/7th, 13th/14th and 19th/20th overlap likewise. 21 subjects is too many for an 8K machine with the old ROM-set. Larger numbers can be used with a machine having a new ROM-set and an 80-column printer (then change line 1630 so that '37' is a larger number, up to 77).

An alternative way is as follows:

When you have more than 18 subjects, enter the 17 subjects that are probably the most popular as usual, but for all the other subjects enter a single dummy subject (e.g. Z). Use the same dummy name (Z) for all subjects after the seventeenth. Z must be included in the list for the Clash Table. The 17 subjects are then shown correctly on the printout. The Z row and column show the totals for the subjects covered by the dummy. Then go through all the forms containing a subject in the dummy and separate the Z totals into separate subjects (i.e. separate the Z row upwards into two or more rows and separate the Z column sideways into two or more columns). Then you must use OPT3 to update the tape to show real subjects, instead of the dummies, before going to OPT2.

152 *Appendix 4*

The listing
The following special symbols appear in the lines shown:

'clear'	lines 10, 105, 400, 698, 1800
'cursor down'	lines 30, 50, 60, 75, 130, 200, 230, 260, 370, 430, 460, 490 495, 498, 1000, 1010, 1100
'cursor up'	lines 770, 1125, 1135
'reverse field'	lines 495, 1000
'reverse field off'	line 495

```
10 PRINT"⌑        OPTIONS CLASH TABLE (OPT1)"
15 PRINT"                                     "
20 PRINT"       (C)1979 KEITH JOHNSON"
30 PRINT"▨THIS PROGRAM ANALYSES THE PUPILS'"
35 PRINT"CHOICES TO HELP YOU TO DECIDE THE"
40 PRINT"SUBJECTS FOR THE OPTION POOLS."
50 PRINT"▨(FOR MORE DETAILS,SEE KEITH JOHNSON'S"
55 PRINT"BOOK, PUBLISHED BY HUTCHINSON LTD)"
60 PRINT"▨▨▨▨DO YOU INTEND TO RECORD A DATA TAPE"
65 PRINT"(AT THE SAME TIME) TO SAVE TIME WHEN"
70 PRINT"USING LATER PROGRAMS?"
75 PRINT"▨PLEASE ENTER 'YES' OR 'NO'"
80 INPUT Q$
85 IF Q$="NO" THEN 100
90 IF Q$="YES" THEN GOSUB 1000:GOTO 100
95 GOTO 75
100 GOSUB 1800
105 PRINT"⌑PLEASE GIVE THE NUMBER OF SUBJECTS"
110 PRINT"(SUBJECTS,NOT TEACHING GROUPS) OFFERED"
120 PRINT"TO THIS GROUP OF PUPILS:"
130 PRINT"▨FOR DISPLAY ON THE SCREEN,"
132 PRINT"THE LIMIT IS 18 SUBJECTS."
134 PRINT"(FOR 19 OR MORE SEE THE BOOK)"
140 INPUT N:H=INT(N/2)
150 DIM A$(H,N):DIM B$(H+1,N):DIM N$(N)
200 PRINT"▨▨▨NOW ENTER A ONE-LETTER CODE FOR"
210 PRINT"EACH OF THESE SUBJECTS"
230 PRINT"▨ENTER THEM ONE AT A TIME"
240 PRINT"(EACH FOLLOWED BY A 'RETURN')"
260 PRINT"▨USE A ONE-LETTER CODE FOR EACH"
270 PRINT"SUBJECT   E.G.  H  FOR HISTORY"
300 FOR I=1 TO N
310 IF I>H GOTO 340
320 INPUT A$(I,0)
330 A$(0,I)=A$(I,0):GOTO 360
340 INPUT B$(I-H,0)
350 A$(0,I)=B$(I-H,0)
360 NEXT I
370 PRINT"▨▨HOW MANY OF THESE SUBJECTS DOES"
380 PRINT"EACH PUPIL CHOOSE?"
390 INPUT M
400 PRINT"⌑NOW,FOR EACH PUPIL IN TURN,"
410 PRINT"AND USING THE SAME ONE-LETTER CODE,"
420 PRINT"ENTER THEIR CHOICES AS SHOWN BELOW."
425 PRINT"(";M;"SUBJECTS PER PUPIL)"
430 PRINT"▨AFTER A FEW SECONDS THE PROGRAM WILL"
440 PRINT"DRAW A CLASH TABLE AND WAIT FOR THE"
450 PRINT"NEXT ENTRY."
460 PRINT"▨E.G.   IF I HAD ASKED FOR HISTORY,ART,"
470 PRINT"        PHYSICS,CHEMISTRY & GEOGRAPHY"
```

OPT1 - Drawing a Clash Table and writing a data tape

```
475 PRINT"       (IN THAT ORDER OF PREFERENCE)"
480 PRINT"      THEN YOU WOULD ENTER:"
490 PRINT"XB JOHNSON KEITH HAPCG    ('RETURN')"
492 PRINT"(PREFIX  B=BOY  G=GIRL  IS OPTIONAL)"
495 PRINT"XQXNOTE■:■AFTER THE LAST PUPIL■,■ENTER■:"
498 PRINT"X      EOF    ('RETURN')X"
500 IF Q$="NO" THEN 505
504 IF P=20 THEN GOSUB 1200
505 GOSUB 1100
506 IF Z=2 THEN GOSUB 1200
508 X$=RIGHT$(D$,M)
510 FOR I=1 TO N
520 FOR J=1 TO M
530 IF I>H GOTO 550
540 IF A$(I,0)=MID$(X$,J,1) THEN N$(I)="1"
545 GOTO560
550 IF B$(I-H,0)=MID$(X$,J,1) THEN N$(I)="1"
560 NEXT J
570 NEXT I
600 FOR I=1 TO N
610 FOR J=1 TO N
620 IF I>H GOTO 640
630 IF N$(I)="1" AND N$(J)="1" THEN A$(I,J)=STR$(VAL(A$(I,J))+1)
635 GOTO 650
640 IF N$(I)="1" AND N$(J)="1" THEN B$(I-H,J)=STR$(VAL(B$(I-H,J))+1)
650 NEXT J
660 NEXT I
698 PRINT"J"
700 FOR I=N TO 0 STEP -1
710 FOR J=N TO 0 STEP -1
720 X=(INT(J*(37/N)))
730 IF I=0 THEN X=X+1
740 IF I>H GOTO 760
750 PRINT TAB(X);A$(I,J):GOTO 770
760 PRINT TAB(X);B$(I-H,J)
770 PRINT"II"
780 NEXT J
785 PRINT:IF N<11 THEN PRINT
790 NEXT I
800 FOR I=1 TO N
810 N$(I)=""
820 NEXT I
900 GOTO 500
1000 PRINT"XXINSERT AND REWIND A BLANK TAPE ON WHICH TO RECORD THE DATA
1010 PRINT"XXENTER: 1  IF USING THE MAIN TAPE UNIT"
1020 PRINT"X        2  IF USING THE SECOND UNIT"
1030 INPUT S
1040 IF S=1 THEN R=122:Q=2
1050 IF S=2 THEN R=58:Q=3
1060 DIM L$(20)
1080 WF$=STR$(1)
1090 P=0:Z=1
1095 RETURN
1100 PRINT"ENTER NEXT DATA NOW:X"
1110 INPUT D$
1140 IF LEFT$(D$,3)="EOF" THEN Z=2
1150 IF Q$="NO" THEN 1180
1160 P=P+1
1170 L$(P)=D$
1180 RETURN
1200 POKE 243,R
1210 POKE 244,Q
1215 IF Q$="NO" THEN 1330
1220 PRINT"WRITING DATA ON TAPE NOW"
1230 OPEN 1,S,Z,WF$
```

```
1240 IF P=0 THEN 1310
1250 FOR I=1 TO P
1260 F$=L$(I)
1270 T2=TI
1280 PRINT#1,F$
1290 IF TI-T2>120 THEN GOSUB 1360
1300 NEXT I
1310 WF$=STR$(VAL(WF$)+1)
1320 CLOSE 1
1330 IF Z=2 THEN 1350
1340 GOTO 1090
1350 GOSUB 1600:PRINT"COMPLETED":END
1360 POKE 59411,53
1370 T2=TI
1380 IF TI-T2<6 THEN 1380
1390 POKE 59411,61
1400 RETURN
1600 IF P$="NO" THEN 1695
1603 CR$=CHR$(141)
1605 OPEN 1,4
1610 FOR I=N TO 0 STEP -1
1620 FOR J=N TO 0 STEP -1
1630 X=(INT(J*(37/N)))
1640 IF I=0 THEN X=X+1
1650 IF I>H THEN 1670
1655 IF A$(I,J)="" THEN 1680
1660 PRINT#1,TAB(X)A$(I,J)CR$;
1665 GOTO 1680
1670 IF B$(I-H,J)="" THEN 1680
1675 PRINT#1,TAB(X)B$(I-H,J)CR$;
1680 NEXT J:PRINT#1:NEXT I
1690 CLOSE 1
1695 RETURN
1800 PRINT":HAVE YOU GOT A PRINTER ATTACHED
1810 PRINT"PLEASE ANSWER  YES  OR  NO"
1820 INPUT P$
1830 IF P$="YES" OR P$="NO" THEN 1850
1840 GOTO 1810
1850 RETURN


        ** OPT1 **
        FOR PETS WITH NEW ROMS
        (LARGE KEYBOARD & EXTERNAL CASSETTE)
        CHANGE THE FOLLOWING LINE NUMBERS:
1200 GOTO 1215
        DELETE LINES 1040,1050,1210
```

Appendix 5

OPT2 — Fitting the pupils' choices to the option pools

Input

From the keyboard or, better, from the data tape produced by OPT1 (and perhaps updated by OPT3).

You will need

The data tape and a proposed option scheme (devised after inspecting the Clash Table shown by OPT1).

Output

Display (on the screen and a printer), with a layout as shown in section 2.8, showing:
(a) the pools
(b) the number of pupils fitted to each subject
(c) the number of pupils requesting each subject but not fitted
(d) the percentage of pupils fully fitted
(e) the percentage satisfaction (calculated by total number of individual choices fitted, divided by total number of individual requests)
(f) each pupil's choices in his preferences order and in the order in which they are fitted to the pools, with underlining to show which choices have not been fitted and which pools would have to be modified for this pupil to have his choices fitted

These displays are shown in section 2.8.

With a printer attached, there is a choice between printing details of all the pupils or just the unfitted pupils.

Time required

About 10 minutes for 30 pupils (but once running the system does not need supervising).

* *

Entering the information

All the steps are explained on the screen but the following should be helpful:
When entering information about the pools, it is the number of different *subjects* (not teaching groups) in a given pool that is required (e.g. three History groups in the same pool are counted as just one).

156 Appendix 5

Use exactly the same one-letter codes for subjects as in OPT1 (and OPT3).

The number of pupils choosing each subject is found from the diagonal of the OPT1 Clash Table (if a given subject is in more than one pool, give the same number each time the subject is entered).

When a pool has fewer subjects than the maximum, finish off that pool and move to the next pool by typing comma ('return').

If the display scrolls off the screen before you can inspect it (or perhaps copy it manually), you can press 'stop' and then later continue by typing CONT ('return'). Alternatively, slow down the screen display by pressing 'RVS'. At the very end of the program the display can also be shown again by typing GOTO5.

Because of the way the '% satisfaction' is calculated, 90% is not very good, whereas 93% is much better.

This program does not try to equalize numbers in the groups. For example, if pool 1 contains History and Geography, and so also does pool 2, then you will have to equalize the numbers by swapping pupils between the two pools.

When you have run this program several times with different possible options schemes and found the one that appears best (from all points of view) then it may be advisable to update the data tape for the unfitted pupils (using OPT3). After changing the subjects for these unfitted pupils to include their reserve choices, you can then run OPT2 again to see if there is an improvement.

There is a choice between printing out (1) only the unfitted pupils, or (2) all the pupils. (Both methods print out the pool numbers.) Although the first alternative is satisfactory for trial runs, the final run with the preferred option scheme should show *all* the pupils. This is so that the printout can be used, with OPT3, to change the order of subjects for each pupil on the tape, before using the tape with OPT4, 5, 6. (For OPT4, 5, 6 the tape must have, for each pupil, the subjects in the correct pool order — i.e. the subject in the first pool pool first, followed by the subject in the second pool, etc.)

If you are using very large option schemes (e.g. five pools each containing more than 7 different subjects) then, on an 8K machine, you may have to delete or simplify some of the lines containing remarks or explanations.

If entering the data manually, end with EOF comma EOF ('return'). With a data tape it will end automatically (just leave it switched on while you go and teach!).

The listing
The following special symbols appear in the lines named:

'clear'	lines 100, 1000, 1012, 1030, 1300
'cursor down'	lines 604, 1004, 1006, 1015, 1026, 1070, 1084, 1220, 1330, 1340, 1460, 1465, 2000, 2003, 2004, 2005, 3200, 3230, 3800
'cursor up'	lines 85, 160, 3170, 3360, 3500
'reverse field'	line 2000

OPT2 – Fitting the pupils' choices to the option pools 157

```
1 GOTO 1000
5 L=0
7 FOR I=1 TO P
10 IF S$(I)=" " THEN Z(P+I)=17+I:L=L+1
15 S$=S$+S$(I)
20 NEXT I
25 N2=N2+1
27 IF L=0 THEN N1=N1+1
28 N9=INT(((N1*100)/N2)+.5)
30 GOSUB 3000
35 GOSUB 100
40 IF V=2 THEN GOSUB 3300:GOTO 65
45 IF V=1 AND L>0 THEN GOSUB 3300
65 PRINT A$
70 PRINT"      ";X$;TAB(18);S$
75 PRINT.
77 IF L=0 GOTO 95
80 FOR I=(2*P) TO 1 STEP -1
85 PRINT TAB(Z(I));"T"
90 NEXT I
95 RETURN
100 PRINT"J":FOR I=1 TO P
110 PRINT"POOL ";I
115 N3=0
120 FOR J=1 TO Q
125 IF P$(I,J)="" GOTO 167
130 X=J-1
140 IF J>4 THEN X=J-5
150 IF J>8 THEN X=J-9
155 IF J=5 OR J=9 THEN PRINT
160 PRINT TAB(10*X);P$(I,J);STR$(R(I,J));"(";STR$(R(I,J)-N(I,J));")T"
167 N3=N3+R(I,J)
170 NEXT J
180 PRINT:PRINT"                              ("N3")"
190 NEXT I
191 IF N2=0 THEN 195
193 PRINT"     "N1"PUPILS FITTED OUT OF"N2"("N9"%)"
194 PRINT"             ("S"% SATISFACTION)"
195 RETURN
200 S$(I1)=P$(I1,J1)
210 Y$(K)="0"
220 Z(K)=0
230 R(I1,J1)=R(I1,J1)+1
260 FOR I=1 TO P
270 FOR J=1 TO Q
280 IF P$(I,J)=Q$(I1,J1) AND I<>I1 THEN N(I,J)=N(I,J)-1
290 NEXT J
300 NEXT I
310 FOR J=1 TO Q
320 Q$(I1,J)=""
330 NEXT J
340 K=0:F=0
350 RETURN
400 T(I1,K)=K:T(I2,K)=K
410 FOR I=1 TO P
420 F1=0
430 FOR J=1 TO K
440 IF T(I,J)<=K THEN F1=F1+1:J3=J
450 NEXT J
460 IF F1=1 THEN GOTO 480
470 GOTO 520
480 FOR J=1 TO P
490 IF T(J,J3)<9 THEN T(J,J3)=(K+1)
500 NEXT J
510 I=0
```

```
520 NEXT I
530 FOR Y=1 TO P
540 IF T(Y,K)=K THEN GOSUB 200:Y=P
550 NEXT Y
560 RETURN
600 PRINT"REMEMBER TO MAKE YOUR FINAL ENTRY:"
603 PRINT"EOF   COMMA   EOF  ('RETURN')"
604 PRINT"XNOW BEGIN:"
605 PRINT"ENTER PUPIL'S NAME,"P"CHOICES"
610 INPUT A$,X$
612 IF A$="EOF" THEN GOSUB 3100:GOSUB 3400:GOSUB 3700:END
615 IF LEN(X$)<>P GOTO 605
620 GOTO 680
680 GOTO 700
700 FOR I=1 TO P
710 FOR J=1 TO Q
715 Q$(I,J)=P$(I,J)
720 NEXT J
725 FOR J=1 TO P
730 T(I,J)=9
740 NEXT J
750 S$(I)=" "
760 Z(I)=I+3
770 Z(P+I)=0
780 Y$(I)=MID$(X$,I,1)
785 NEXT I
790 S$=""
795 K=0:F=0
800 IF K=P GOTO 930
805 K=K+1:D=0
810 FOR I=1 TO P
820 FOR J=1 TO Q
830 IF Q$(I,J)=Y$(K) GOTO 850
840 GOTO 870
850 D=D+1:I2=I:J2=J
860 IF D=1 THEN I1=I:J1=J
870 NEXT J
880 NEXT I
890 IF D>1 THEN GOSUB 400:GOTO 800
900 IF D=1 THEN GOSUB 200:GOTO 800
910 F=F+1
920 IF K<P GOTO 800
930 IF F=P THEN GOSUB 5:ON A GOTO 605,2015
940 FOR I=1 TO P
950 IF Q$(I1,J1)=Y$(I) THEN K=I
960 NEXT I
970 GOSUB 200
980 GOTO 800
1000 PRINT"⊐           OPT2-OPTION POOLS"
1002 PRINT"  ‾‾‾‾‾‾‾‾‾‾‾‾‾‾‾‾‾‾‾‾‾‾‾‾‾‾ "
1003 PRINT"        (C)1979 KEITH JOHNSON"
1004 PRINT"XXXTO CHECK YOUR PUPILS' CHOICES"
1005 PRINT"AGAINST A PROPOSED OPTION SCHEME"
1006 PRINT"XXXARE YOU USING A PRINTER?"
1008 PRINT"ENTER Y OR N"
1009 INPUT V$:IF V$="Y" THEN GOSUB 3200:GOTO 1012
1010 IF V$<>"N" THEN 1008
1012 PRINT"⊐ENTER THE NUMBER OF OPTION POOLS"
1013 PRINT"(THE MAXIMUM IS 8)
1014 INPUT P
1015 PRINT"XXXENTER THE MAXIMUM NUMBER OF SUBJECTS"
1016 PRINT"(NOT TEACHING GROUPS) IN ANY POOL"
1026 PRINT"X(E.G: H,H,H,G,G,E IS COUNTED AS 3)"
1028 INPUT Q
1030 PRINT"⊐NOW ENTER THE PROPOSED POOLS:"
1034 PRINT"-USE A ONE-LETTER CODE(AS IN OPT1)"
1038 PRINT"-DO NOT ENTER ANY SUBJECT TWICE IN THE"
```

OPT2 – Fitting the pupils' choices to the option pools

```
1040 PRINT" SAME POOL"
1044 PRINT" (E.G. H,H,H,G,G,E BECOMES H,G,E)"
1070 PRINT"XFOR EACH POOL ENTER:"
1072 PRINT"1ST SUBJECT:CODE,COMMA,NUMBER OF PUPILS"
1074 PRINT"CHOOSING THAT SUBJECT ('RETURN')"
1076 PRINT"2ND SUBJECT:  DITTO  ETC"
1084 PRINT"XNB:IF THE NUMBER OF SUBJECTS IN A POOL"
1086 PRINT"— IS LESS THAN THE MAXIMUM,THEN FINISH"
1088 PRINT"   THE POOL WITH A   COMMA ('RETURN')"
1091 DIM P$(P,Q),Q$(P,Q),N(P,Q),R(P,Q),Z(2*P)
1095 CR$=CHR$(141)
1100 FOR I=1 TO P
1110 PRINT"OPTION POOL "I
1120 FOR J=1 TO Q
1130 INPUT P$(I,J),N(I,J)
1140 IF P$(I,J)="" THEN J=Q
1150 NEXT J:NEXT I
1210 GOSUB 100
1220 PRINT"XFOR A FULL EXPLANATION OF THE OUTPUT,"
1230 PRINT"SEE KEITH JOHNSON'S BOOK ON"
1240 PRINT"'TIMETABLING' (HUTCHINSON LTD)"
1290 GOSUB 3800
1300 PRINT"JTHE NEXT STEP IS TO ENTER THE PUPILS'"
1305 PRINT"NAMES & CHOICES(IN ORDER OF PREFERENCE,"
1310 PRINT"MOST WANTED SUBJECT FIRST)"
1330 PRINT"XE.G.(FOR MANUAL ENTRY)"
1335 PRINT"JOHNSON (COMMA) HGPCA  ('RETURN')"
1340 PRINT"XOR,MUCH BETTER,USE DATA TAPE FROM OPT1"
1460 PRINT"XXIS THE DATA TO BE ENTERED FROM:"
1465 PRINT"X1   THE KEYBOARD?"
1467 PRINT"2   A DATA TAPE(FROM OPT1)?"
1470 INPUT A
1480 IF A<1 OR A>2 THEN 1460
1490 ON A GOTO 600,2000
2000 PRINT"XXXXINSERT AND REWIND THE DATA TAPE"
2003 PRINT"XWHEN YOU ARE READY,ENTER:"
2004 PRINT"X 1  IF USING THE MAIN TAPE UNIT"
2005 PRINT"X 2  IF USING THE SECOND TAPE UNIT"
2006 INPUT T
2008 IF T=1 OR T=2 THEN 2010
2009 GOTO 2003
2010 OPEN 2,T,0
2015 INPUT#2,Y$
2020 IF ST=64 OR ST=128 THEN 2070
2025 IF Y$="EOF" THEN 2070
2030 X$=RIGHT$(Y$,P)
2040 L1=LEN(Y$)
2050 A$=LEFT$(Y$,(L1-P))
2060 GOTO 700
2070 CLOSE 2
2080 IF Y$="EOF" THEN 2095
2090 GOTO 2010
2095 IF V$="Y" THEN:GOSUB 3400
2096 GOSUB 3100:GOSUB 3700:END
3000 IF L=1 THEN N4=N4+1
3010 IF L=2 THEN N5=N5+1
3020 IF L=3 THEN N6=N6+1
3030 IF L=4 THEN N7=N7+1
3040 S1=((N1*P)+(N4*(P-1))+(N5*(P-2))+(N6*(P-3))+(N7*(P-4)))/(N2*P)
3050 S=(INT((S1*1000)+.5))/10
3060 RETURN
3100 PRINT"       PUPILS    SUBJECTS FITTED"
3130 PRINT TAB(10);N1,P
3140 PRINT TAB(10);N4,P-1
3150 PRINT TAB(10);N5,P-2
3160 PRINT TAB(10);N6,P-3
```

Appendix 5

```
3170 PRINT"□":RETURN
3200 PRINT"▓TYPE  1  OR  2  TO PRINT DETAILS OF:"
3230 PRINT"▓1  UNFITTED PUPILS ONLY"
3240 PRINT"2   ALL THE PUPILS"
3270 INPUT V
3290 RETURN
3300 OPEN 1,4
3310 PRINT#1
3320 PRINT#1,A$
3330 PRINT#1,"     ";X$;TAB(14-LEN(X$));S$
3340 IF L=0 THEN 3380
3350 FOR I=1 TO (2*P)
3355 IF Z(I)=0 THEN 3370
3360 PRINT#1,TAB(Z(I))"-"CR$;
3370 NEXT I
3380 CLOSE 1
3390 RETURN
3400 OPEN 1,4
3405 PRINT#1:PRINT#1:PRINT#1
3410 FOR I=1 TO P
3420 PRINT#1,"POOL";I
3430 N3=0
3440 FOR J=1 TO Q
3450 IF P$(I,J)="" GOTO 3520
3460 X=J-1
3470 IF J>4 THEN X=J-5
3480 IF J>8 THEN X=J-9
3490 IF J=5 OR J=9 THEN PRINT#1
3500 PRINT#1,TAB(10*X);P$(I,J);STR$(R(I,J));
     "(";STR$(R(I,J)-N(I,J));")"CR$;
3520 N3=N3+R(I,J)
3530 NEXT J
3540 PRINT#1:PRINT#1,"                                    ("N3")"
3550 NEXT I
3560 PRINT#1,"    "N1"PUPILS FITTED OUT OF"N2"("N9"%)"
3570 PRINT#1,"            ("S"%SATISFACTION)"
3580 PRINT#1
3590 PRINT#1,"STUDENTS      SUBJECTS FITTED"
3600 PRINT#1,N1,P
3610 PRINT#1,N4,P-1
3620 PRINT#1,N5,P-2
3630 PRINT#1,N6,P-3
3640 CLOSE 1
3650 RETURN
3700 PRINT"PRESS ANY KEY TO REPEAT DISPLAY"
3710 PRINT"USE 'RVS' OR 'STOP'& CONT IF YOU WISH"
3720 GOSUB 3810
3730 GOSUB 100:GOSUB 3100:GOTO 3700
3740 RETURN
3800 PRINT"▓PRESS ANY KEY WHEN READY"
3810 GET X$:IF X$="" THEN 3810
3820 RETURN
READY.


        ** OPT2 **
        FOR PETS WITH NEW ROMS
        (LARGE KEYBOARD & EXTERNAL CASSETTE)
        CHANGE THE FOLLOWING LINE NUMBERS:
2012 U=0
2015 IF U=20 THEN 2070
2020 INPUT#2,Y$
2022 U=U+1
```

Also see additional improvements on p. 217

Appendix 6
OPT3 — Editing the data tape

You will need

The data tape from OPT1 and a second, blank, tape (clearly labelled).

Input

Either (a) for the pupils whose data you wish to change, their reserve choices or their new choices;

or (b) after you have decided the final option scheme, you will need the final output from OPT2 in order to put the pupils' subjects into the correct pool order (see below).

Output

A new data tape with the pupils' choices updated (and, if necessary, their names altered also).

* *

Entering the information

All the steps are explained on the screen but the following may be helpful:

Label both cassettes very carefully. Do not confuse them with the program tape! Make sure they are both fully rewound.

You can choose to change (1) names of pupils as well as subjects
(2) subjects only

Clearly option (2) is quicker, but you will need to use option (1) if

(a) you have spelt any names incorrectly (e.g. Tracey/Tracy; Stephen/Steven), *or*
(b) if you included names such as G NOBODY1 when using OPT1 (in order to reserve space on the tape) so that you can now change these to real names for pupils who have been promoted or demoted to this group.

The names and subjects are taken from the original data tape and shown on the screen in groups of twenty, each line being numbered. Enter the number of the line you wish to edit.

162 *Appendix 6*

With option (1) you must re-type the whole line (names and subjects).
With option (2) you just re-type the subjects.

For either option, if you have decided on your final option scheme (using OPT2) and now wish to move to OPT4 (or OPT5) and OPT6, *you must enter the subjects, for all the pupils, in the correct pool order* — i.e. the subject in the first pool first, followed by the subject in the second pool etc. — by using the output from OPT2 which shows (at the right-hand side) the pool order for each individual pupil (any gaps, which are underlined, being filled by interviewing the pupils as necessary). (See also sections 2.8, 2.9.)

When you have updated one group of twenty pupil, enter an = sign. Follow the instructions carefully to write the edited data on to the new tape.
Then follow the instructions to look at the next group of pupils.

When you have finished, make sure that you take the correct data tape 2 to use in the next program (which may be OPT2 again or may be OPT4, OPT5 or OPT6).

The listing

The following special symbols appear in the lines named:

'clear'	lines 1, 320, 670, 700
'cursor down'	lines 5, 10, 60, 90, 130, 170, 175, 180, 450, 900
'cursor up'	lines 435 (nine times)
'cursor right'	lines 450, 1040

```
1 PRINT"◻    OPT3-FOR EDITING THE DATA TAPE"
2 PRINT"                                    "
4 PRINT"     (C)KEITH JOHNSON 1979"
5 PRINT"▩▩FOR FULL DETAILS SEE THE BOOK"
6 PRINT"'TIMETABLING' (HUTCHINSON LTD)"
10 PRINT"▩▩YOU WILL NEED:"
20 PRINT"1) DATA TAPE 1 (FROM OPT1)"
30 PRINT"   AND"
40 PRINT"2) AN EMPTY TAPE 2 ON WHICH THE"
50 PRINT"   EDITED VERSION WILL BE BUILT UP"
60 PRINT"▩LABEL THESE TWO CASSETTES CLEARLY:"
70 PRINT"  'ORIGINAL 1' AND"
80 PRINT"  'NEW TAPE 2'"
90 PRINT"▩REWIND BOTH TAPES"
100 PRINT"                                 "
110 DIM L$(22):Z=1:WF$=STR$(1)
115 Z$="
120 PRINT"ENTER: 1  IF USING THE MAIN TAPE UNIT"
130 PRINT"▩       2  IF USING THE SECOND TAPE UNIT"
140 INPUT Y
150 IF Y=1 THEN R=122:Q=2
160 IF Y=2 THEN R=58:Q=3
165 IF Y=0 OR Y>2 THEN 120
170 PRINT"▩▩TYPE  1  OR  2  AS FOLLOWS:"
175 PRINT"▩WILL YOU NEED TO CHANGE:"
180 PRINT"▩ 1  NAMES AS WELL AS SUBJECTS?"
185 PRINT"  2  SUBJECTS ONLY?"
190 INPUT A
```

OPT3 - Editing the data tape

```
195 IF A<1 OR A>2 THEN 170
197 IF A=2 THEN GOSUB 900
200 PRINT"PUT ORIGINAL 1 IN CASSETTE RECORDER":PRINT
210 PRINT"PRESS ANY KEY WHEN READY"
220 GET A$:IF A$="" THEN 220
230 OPEN 1,Y,0
240 P=1
250 INPUT#1,Y$
260 IF ST=64 OR ST=128 THEN 310
270 IF Y$="EOF" THEN Z=2:GOTO 310
280 L$(P)=Y$
290 P=P+1
300 GOTO 250
310 CLOSE 1
320 PRINT"☐"
330 FOR I=1 TO (P-1)
340 PRINT I;L$(I)
350 NEXT I
400 PRINT"ENTER THE NUMBER OF THE LINE YOU WISH    TO EDIT"
410 PRINT"IF YOU DO NOT WISH TO CHANGE ANY THEN    ENTER '='"
420 INPUT N$
430 IF N$="=" THEN 500
435 PRINT"↑↑↑↑↑↑":PRINTZ$:PRINTZ$:PRINT"↑↑"
440 N=VAL(N$)
445 IF A=2 THEN GOSUB 1000:GOTO 320
450 PRINT "▮▮▮";L$(N)
460 PRINT"RE-TYPE THE CORRECT VERSION IN FULL:"
470 INPUT L$(N)
480 GOTO 320
500 PRINT
510 PRINT"REMOVE ORIGINAL 1 (WITHOUT TOUCHING THE TAPE)"
520 PRINT"PUT IN NEW TAPE 2 (WITHOUT TOUCHING THE TAPE)"
530 PRINT"PRESS ANY KEY WHEN READY"
540 GET A$:IF A$="" THEN 540
550 POKE 243,R
560 POKE 244,Q
570 OPEN 1,Y,Z,WF$
575 IF Z=2 THEN L$(P)="EOF"
580 FOR I=1 TO P
590 Y$=L$(I)
600 T2=TI
610 PRINT#1,Y$
620 IFTI-T2>120 THEN GOSUB 800
630 NEXT I
640 WF$=STR$(VAL(WF$)+1)
650 CLOSE 1
660 IF Z=2 THEN 700
670 PRINT"☐REMOVE NEW TAPE 2 (WITHOUT TOUCHING THE TAPE)"
680 FOR I=1 TO.P:L$(I)="":NEXT I
690 GOTO 200
700 PRINT"☐NEW TAPE 2 IS NOW COMPLETE"
710 END
800 POKE 59411,53
810 T2=TI
820 IF TI-T2<6 THEN 820
830 POKE 59411,61
840 RETURN
900 PRINT"▓▓HOW MANY SUBJECTS HAS EACH PUPIL CHOSEN?"
910 INPUT B
920 RETURN
1000 L=LEN(L$(N))
1010 B$=RIGHT$(L$(N),B)
1020 A$=LEFT$(L$(N),(L-B))
1030 PRINT"FOR       ";A$
1040 PRINT"▮▮";B$
1050 PRINT"RETYPE CORRECT SUBJECTS (& IN CORRECT"
```

Appendix 6

```
1060 PRINT"ORDER IF READY TO GO TO OPT4,5 OR 6
1070 INPUT B$
1080 L$(N)=A$+B$
1090 RETURN


        ** OPT3 **
        FOR PETS WITH NEW ROMS
        (LARGE KEYBOARD & EXTERNAL CASSETTE)
        CHANGE THE FOLLOWING LINE NUMBERS:
250 IF ST=64 THEN 310
260 INPUT#1,Y$
580 FOR I=1 TO P+Z-2
    REM DELETE LINES 150,160,550,560
```

Appendix 7
OPT4 — Printing option group lists

Relevant section

2.10

Input

The data tape from OPT1 after it has been updated by OPT3 (using the output from OPT2) so that the tape now has the pupils' choices in the correct pool order (i.e. subject in first pool first, subject in second pool second, etc.).

If you wish the group lists to include the name of the teacher, the room and the times of the lessons then you will need this information also (from the completed timetable).

Output

Printed group lists (ready for photocopying) for each of the option groups. The lists are headed with any information you give about the teacher, room, timetable, etc. The names are automatically sorted into alphabetical order before printing. Girls and boys can be printed separately if you wish (and if you coded them with G and B in OPT1).

★ ★

Entering the information

All the steps are explained on the screen but the following should be helpful:

The program begins by calculating the number of entries that your machine can handle. If it cannot cope with all the names on your data tape, you will have to use OPT5 instead.
An 8K machine can handle about 100 entries of the length of
B   JOHNSON   KEITH   HFPBA
A 16K machine should cope with any size of school.

Even if you do not have a printer, you should still find the program useful for extracting the lists and putting them in alphabetical order (so they can be typed from the screen).

166 *Appendix 7*

Please note that the correct lists will not be produced unless you have used OPT3 to ensure that each pupil has the correct number of subjects and in the correct pool order.

When all the lists have been printed they can be repeated by typing the letter 'R'. However, it is much kinder to your printer to print one set of lists and then get them photocopied.

The listing
The following special symbols appear in the lines named:

'clear'	lines 10, 200, 300
'cursor down'	lines 10, 40, 50, 100, 150, 170, 175, 210, 240, 320, 400, 410 440, 450, 460, 490, 510, 600, 610, 620, 1400
'reverse field'	lines 460, 600
'reverse field off'	line 460

```
10 PRINT"◧▓▓     OPT4-PRINTING OPTION LISTS"
20 PRINT"      ─────────────────────────────"
30 PRINT"       (C)1979 KEITH JOHNSON"
40 PRINT"▓▓▓FOR USE AFTER OPT1,2,3"
50 PRINT"▓FOR MORE DETAILS,SEE THE BOOK"
60 PRINT"'TIMETABLING' (HUTCHINSON LTD)"
100 PRINT"▓▓TO SEE ROUGHLY HOW MANY PUPILS"
110 PRINT"THIS MACHINE WILL DEAL WITH,"
120 PRINT"TYPE IN A TYPICAL ENTRY (AS IT"
125 PRINT"APPEARS ON THE TAPE FROM OPT1,OPT3)"
130 INPUT N$:L=LEN(N$):F=FRE(0)
140 N=INT(((F-1000)/(L*1.2))/10)*10
150 PRINT"▓THIS MACHINE WILL PROBABLY DEAL WITH"
160 PRINT"ABOUT"N"ENTRIES"
170 PRINT"▓IF THIS IS NOT ENOUGH,USE OPT5 INSTEAD"
175 PRINT"▓▓▓HAVE YOU GOT A PRINTER CONNECTED?"
180 PRINT"PLEASE ENTER  YES  OR  NO"
185 INPUT T$
190 IF T$="NO" THEN N=1:GOTO200
195 IF T$<>"YES" THEN 180
200 PRINT"◧PLEASE TYPE A NUMBER  1  OR  2:"
210 PRINT"▓ 1 -NAMES ON THE DATA TAPE ARE PRECEDED"
220 PRINT"      BY  B OR G  TO DISTINGUISH SEXES"
230 PRINT"      FOR SEPARATE LISTS"
240 PRINT"▓ 2 -NAMES ARE NOT PRECEDED BY SUCH A"
250 PRINT"      A CODE OR YOU DO NOT WANT SEPARATE"
260 PRINT"      LISTS"
270 INPUT L
280 IF L=1 THEN GOSUB 1200
290 IF L=2 THEN G=0:GOSUB 1300
295 IF L<1 OR L>2 THEN 200
300 PRINT"◧HOW MANY SUBJECTS HAS EACH PUPIL CHOSEN?"
310 INPUT P
320 PRINT"▓WHAT IS THE MAXIMUM NUMBER OF SUBJECTS"
330 PRINT"(NOT TEACHING GROUPS) IN ANY POOL?"
340 INPUT Q
350 DIM B$(B),P$(P,Q),Q$(P,Q)
360 IF G<>0 THEN DIM G$(G)
400 PRINT"▓NOW ENTER INFORMATION ABOUT EACH POOL:"
```

OPT4 – Printing option group lists

```
410 PRINT"XFOR EACH SUBJECT IN EACH POOL,GIVE:"
420 PRINT"ONE-LETTER CODE (COMMA) FULL NAME AND"
430 PRINT"ANYTHING ELSE YOU WISH TO BE PRINTED"
440 PRINT"XE.G."
450 PRINT"XH,HISTORY MR CLARKE MON1&2+WED5&6 RM9"
460 PRINT"XXXNOTE█: IF THE NUMBER OF SUBJECTS IN ANY"
470 PRINT"POOL IS LESS THAN THE MAXIMUM,END THE"
480 PRINT"POOL WITH A     COMMA ('RETURN')"
490 PRINT"XBEGIN NOW:"
500 FOR I=1 TO P
510 PRINT"XOPTION POOL"I
520 FOR J=1 TO Q
530 PRINT"SUBJECT"J
540 INPUT P$(I,J),Q$(I,J)
550 IF P$(I,J)="" THEN J=Q
555 P$(I,J)=RIGHT$(P$(I,J),1)
560 NEXT J:NEXT I
600 PRINT"XXXNOW INSERT AND REWIND THE DATA TAPE"
610 PRINT"XXENTER: 1  IF USING THE MAIN TAPE UNIT"
620 PRINT"X        2  IF USING THE SECOND UNIT"
630 INPUT Y
640 IF Y=0 OR Y>2 THEN 610
700 I=0:J=0:K=0
710 OPEN 1,Y,0
720 INPUT#1,N$
740 IF ST=64 OR ST=128 THEN 780
750 IF N$="EOF" THEN 780
760 IF L=1 THEN GOSUB 1500:GOTO 720
770 K=K+1:B$(K)=N$:GOTO 720
780 CLOSE 1
790 IF N$="EOF" THEN 800
795 GOTO 710
800 FOR I=1 TO B-1
810 F=0
820 FOR J=1 TO B-I
830 IF B$(J)<=B$(J+1) THEN 880
840 T$=B$(J)
850 B$(J)=B$(J+1)
860 B$(J+1)=T$
870 F=1
880 NEXT J
890 IF F=0 THEN I=B-1
895 NEXT I
900 IF G=0 THEN 1000
910 FOR I=1 TO G-1
920 F=0
930 FOR J=1 TO G-I
940 IF G$(J)<=G$(J+1) THEN 985
950 T$=G$(J)
960 G$(J)=G$(J+1)
970 G$(J+1)=T$
980 F=1
985 NEXT J
990 IF F=0 THEN I=G-1
995 NEXT I
1000 FOR I=1 TO P
1010 GOSUB 1600
1020 FOR J=1 TO Q
1030 IF P$(I,J)="" THEN J=Q:GOTO 1140
1040 GOSUB 1700
1050 FOR K=1 TO B
1060 T$=RIGHT$(B$(K),P)
1070 IF MID$(T$,I,1)=P$(I,J)THEN F=LEN(B$(K)):T$=LEFT$(B$(K),(F-P))
     GOSUB 1800
1080 NEXT K
1090 IF G=0 THEN 1140
```

168 Appendix 7

```
1095 GOSUB 1900
1100 FOR K=1 TO G
1110 T$=RIGHT$(G$(K),P)
1120 IF MID$(T$,I,1)=P$(I,J)THEN F=LEN(G$(K)):T$=LEFT$(G$(K),(F-P))
     GOSUB 1800
1130 NEXT K
1140 NEXT J
1150 NEXT I
1160 PRINT"COMPLETED"
1170 PRINT"TYPE  R  FOR REPEAT OR PRESS 'STOP'"
1180 GET T$:IFT$="" THEN 1180
1190 IF T$="R" THEN 1000
1195 GOTO 1170
1200 GOSUB 1400
1210 INPUT "BOYS";B
1220 GOSUB 1400
1230 INPUT "GIRLS";G
1240 RETURN
1300 GOSUB 1400
1310 INPUT "PUPILS";B
1320 RETURN
1400 PRINT"XGIVE A NUMBER EQUAL TO OR"
1410 PRINT"GREATER THAN THE NUMBER OF"
1420 RETURN
1500 F=LEN(N$)
1510 IF LEFT$(N$,1)="B" THEN I=I+1:B$(I)=RIGHT$(N$,(F-2)):RETURN
1520 IF LEFT$(N$,1)="G" THEN J=J+1:G$(J)=RIGHT$(N$,(F-2)):RETURN
1530 PRINT"NAMES NOT CODED B OR G":END
1600 PRINT:PRINT:PRINT:PRINT:PRINT:PRINT
1610 IF N=1 THEN 1650
1620 OPEN 1,4
1630 PRINT#1:PRINT#1:PRINT#1:PRINT#1
1640 CLOSE 1
1650 RETURN
1700 PRINT:PRINT
1710 PRINT Q$(I,J)
1720 PRINT
1730 IF N=1 THEN 1790
1740 OPEN 1,4
1750 PRINT#1:PRINT#1
1760 PRINT#1,Q$(I,J)
1770 PRINT#1
1780 CLOSE 1
1790 RETURN
1800 PRINT T$
1810 IF N=1 THEN 1850
1820 OPEN 1,4
1830 PRINT#1,T$
1840 CLOSE 1
1850 RETURN
1900 PRINT
1910 IF N=1 THEN 1950
1920 OPEN 1,4
1930 PRINT#1
1940 CLOSE 1
1950 RETURN


          ** OPT4 **
          FOR PETS WITH NEW ROMS
          (LARGE KEYBOARD & EXTERNAL CASSETTE)
          CHANGE THE FOLLOWING LINE NUMBERS:
 720 IF ST=64 THEN 780
 740 INPUT#1,N$
```

Also see additional improvements on p. 217

Appendix 8

OPT5 — Printing option group lists

Relevant section
2.10

Input

As for OPT4

Output

Printed group lists (ready for photocopying) for each of the option groups. The group lists are headed with any information you give about the teacher, room, timetable, etc.

The names are printed in the same order as on the data tape (so they will be in alphabetical order only if you entered them that way into OPT1).

* *

Entering the information

All the steps are explained on the screen but the following should be helpful:

Use OPT4 if you possibly can (OPT4 sorts names alphabetically; it needs only one run of the data tape; it separates boys' and girls' names if you wish).

With this program the data tape has to be run once for each group to be printed.

Please note that the correct lists will not be produced unless you have used OPT3 to ensure that each pupil on the tape has the correct number of subjects in the correct pool order.

If the names on the data tape are preceded by B or G you can choose to have this code deleted or it can be included in the print-out. This program does not separate boys and girls into separate lists.

Appendix 8

The listing
The following special symbols appear in the lines named:

'clear'	lines 10, 200, 500, 600
'cursor down'	lines 10, 40, 50, 100, 175, 200, 220, 230, 250, 300, 310, 400, 410 500, 510, 525, 560, 570, 580, 600
'reverse field'	lines 300, 400

```
10 PRINT"↺◼◼       OPT5-PRINTING OPTION LISTS"
20 PRINT"                                     "
30 PRINT"         (C)1979 KEITH JOHNSON"
40 PRINT"◼◼◼FOR USE AFTER OPT1,2,3"
50 PRINT"◼FOR MORE DETAILS,SEE THE BOOK"
60 PRINT"'TIMETABLING' (HUTCHINSON LTD)"
100 PRINT"◼◼◼YOU SHOULD TRY OPT4 FIRST AND USE"
110 PRINT"THIS PROGRAM ONLY IF YOUR NUMBERS"
120 PRINT"ARE TOO LARGE FOR OPT4."
175 PRINT"◼◼◼◼HAVE YOU GOT A PRINTER CONNECTED?"
180 PRINT"PLEASE ENTER  YES   OR   NO"
185 INPUT T$
190 IF T$="NO" THEN D=1:GOTO 200
195 IF T$<>"YES" THEN 180
200 PRINT"↺◼◼HOW MANY SUBJECTS HAS EACH PUPIL CHOSEN?"
210 INPUT P
220 PRINT"◼PLEASE ENTER A NUMBER   1   OR   2:"
230 PRINT"◼ 1 -NAMES ON THE DATA TAPE ARE PRECEDED"
240 PRINT"     BY  B OR G   WHICH IS TO BE REMOVED"
250 PRINT"◼ 2 -NAMES ARE NOT PRECEDED BY SUCH A"
260 PRINT"       CODE OR YOU WANT TO KEEP THE CODE"
270 PRINT"       IN THE PRINT-OUT"
280 INPUT F
290 IF F<1 OR F>2 THEN 220
300 PRINT"◼◼◼NOW INSERT AND RE-WIND THE DATA TAPE"
310 PRINT"◼◼ENTER: 1   IF USING THE MAIN TAPE UNIT"
320 PRINT"         2   IF USING THE SECOND TAPE UNIT"
330 INPUT Y
340 IF Y=0 OR Y>2 THEN 310
370 GOTO 500
400 PRINT"◼◼◼NOW REWIND THE DATA TAPE"
410 PRINT"◼PRESS ANY KEY WHEN READY"
420 GET A$:IF A$="" THEN 420
500 PRINT"↺YOU MUST RUN THE TAPE THROUGH ONCE FOR"
505 PRINT"EACH GROUP THAT YOU WISH TO PRINT."
510 PRINT"◼FOR THE GROUP THAT YOU WISH TO PRINT"
515 PRINT"ON THIS RUN OF THE TAPE,GIVE:"
520 PRINT"          "
525 PRINT"◼THE POOL NUMBER (COMMA)"
530 PRINT"THE ONE-LETTER CODE (COMMA)"
540 PRINT"THE FULL NAME AND ANYTHING ELSE YOU"
550 PRINT"WISH TO BE PRINTED ('RETURN')"
560 PRINT"◼E.G."
570 PRINT"◼2,H,HISTORY MR CLARKE MON1&2+WED5&6 RM9"
580 PRINT"◼BEGIN NOW:"
590 INPUT N,P$,Q$
600 PRINT"↺"Q$"◼"
610 IF D=1 THEN 700
620 OPEN 1,4
630 PRINT#1:PRINT#1:PRINT#1:PRINT#1
```

OPT5 Printing option group lists

```
640 PRINT#1,Q$
650 PRINT#1
660 CLOSE 1
700 OPEN 2,Y,0
710 INPUT#2,N$
720 IF ST=64 OR ST=128 THEN 770
730 IF N$="EOF" THEN 770
740 Y$=RIGHT$(N$,P)
750 IF MID$(Y$,N,1)=P$ THEN GOSUB 800
760 GOTO 710
770 CLOSE 2
780 IF N$="EOF" THEN 400
790 GOTO 700
800 L=LEN(N$)
805 IF F=1 THEN N$=RIGHT$(N$,(L-2)):L=L-2
810 N$=LEFT$(N$,(L-P))
820 PRINTN$
830 IF D=1 THEN 870
840 OPEN 1,4
850 PRINT#1,N$
860 CLOSE 1
870 RETURN


        ** OPT5 **
        FOR PETS WITH NEW ROMS
        (LARGE KEYBOARD & EXTERNAL CASSETTE)
        CHANGE/ADD THE FOLLOWING LINE NUMBERS:
720 IF ST=64 THEN Z=1
755 IF Z=1 THEN 770
775 Z=0
```

Appendix 9

OPT6 — Printing pupils' option timetables

Input

The data tape from OPT1 updated by OPT3 so that the pupils' choices are in correct pool order (i.e. the same tape as used in OPT4 or OPT5).

You will also need information, from the completed timetable, about the name of the teacher, the room and the times of the lessons.

Output

A list, *for each pupil,* showing his final options; teachers, rooms and the times of the week for each lesson.

* *

Entering the information

All the steps are explained on the screen.

This program is not very useful if you do not have a printer.

Information about the subjects in the pools should be entered in the same way as for OPT2 and OPT4.

The print-out can be cut into strips (using a guillotine) so that each pupil can be given his or her timetable on the first day of term.

Form tutors may also find it useful to have a copy of the print-out during the next two years, in order to check that their pupils' school reports are completed. Similarly the Director of Studies and the Registrar may find the print-out useful for locating pupils quickly.

Sample output

```
BINKS MARGARET
  1   CHEMISTRY MR WRIGHT MON1&2+WED3&4 RM33
  2   HISTORY MR CLARKE TUES1&2+THURS5&6 RM9
  3   PHYSICS MR PALMER .MON5&6+WED1&2 RM32
  4   FRENCH MRS MURRAY TUES3&4+FRI1&2 RM8
  5   ART MRS BINNS WED5&6+FRI3&4 RM20
```

OPT6 – Printing pupils' option timetables

The listing
The following special symbols appear on the lines named:

'clear'	lines 10, 200, 300
'cursor down'	lines 10, 40, 50, 100, 160, 210, 240, 320, 400, 410, 440, 450 460, 490, 510, 600, 610, 620, 770, 900
'reverse field'	lines 460, 600
'reverse field off'	line 460

```
10 PRINT"        OPT6-PRINTING OPTION TIMETABLES"
20 PRINT"      ┌                              "
30 PRINT"        (C)1979 KEITH JOHNSON"
40 PRINT"   FOR USE AFTER OPT1,2,3 AND 4 OR 5."
50 PRINT" FOR MORE DETAILS,SEE THE BOOK"
60 PRINT"'TIMETABLING' (HUTCHINSON LTD)"
100 PRINT"   HAVE YOU GOT A PRINTER CONNECTED?"
110 PRINT"PLEASE ENTER  YES  OR  NO"
120 INPUT T$
130 IF T$="YES" THEN 200
140 IF T$="NO" THEN N=1:GOTO 160
150 GOTO 110
160 PRINT"  THEN YOU MAY NOT FIND THIS VERY USEFUL!":
    FOR I=1 TO 2000:NEXT
200 PRINT"  PLEASE TYPE A NUMBER  1  OR  2:"
210 PRINT"  1 -NAMES ON THE DATA TAPE ARE PRECEDED"
220 PRINT"      BY  B OR G  WHICH IS TO BE REMOVED"
240 PRINT"  2 -NAMES ARE NOT PRECEDED BY SUCH A"
250 PRINT"     CODE OR YOU WANT TO KEEP THE CODE"
260 PRINT"     IN THE PRINT-OUT"
270 INPUT F
280 IF F<1 OR F>2 THEN 200
300 PRINT"  HOW MANY SUBJECTS HAS EACH PUPIL CHOSEN?"
310 INPUT P
320 PRINT"  WHAT IS THE MAXIMUM NUMBER OF SUBJECTS"
330 PRINT"(NOT TEACHING GROUPS) IN ANY POOL?"
340 INPUT Q
400 PRINT"  NOW ENTER INFORMATION ABOUT EACH POOL:"
410 PRINT"  FOR EACH SUBJECT IN EACH POOL,GIVE:"
420 PRINT"ONE-LETTER CODE (COMMA) FULL NAME AND"
430 PRINT"ANYTHING ELSE YOU WISH TO BE PRINTED"
440 PRINT"  E.G."
450 PRINT"  H,HISTORY MR CLARKE MON1&2+WED5&6 RM9"
460 PRINT"   NOTE : IF THE NUMBER OF SUBJECTS IN ANY"
470 PRINT"POOL IS LESS THAN THE MAXIMUM,END THE"
480 PRINT"POOL WITH A    COMMA ('RETURN')"
490 PRINT"  BEGIN NOW:"
500 FOR I=1 TO P
510 PRINT"  OPTION POOL"I
520 FOR J=1 TO Q
530 PRINT"SUBJECT"J
540 INPUT P$(I,J),Q$(I,J)
550 IF P$(I,J)="" THEN J=Q
555 P$(I,J)=RIGHT$(P$(I,J),1)
560 NEXT J:NEXT I
600 PRINT"   NOW INSERT AND REWIND THE DATA TAPE"
610 PRINT"  ENTER: 1  IF USING THE MAIN TAPE UNIT"
620 PRINT"         2  IF USING THE SECOND TAPE UNIT"
630 INPUT Y
```

174 Appendix 9

```
640 IF Y=0 OR Y>2 THEN 610
700 OPEN 2,Y,0
710 INPUT#2,N$
720 IF ST=64 OR ST=128 THEN 760
730 IF N$="EOF" THEN 760
740 GOSUB 800
750 GOTO 710
760 CLOSE 2
770 IF N$="EOF" THEN PRINT "XXPRINTING COMPLETED":END
780 GOTO 700
800 L=LEN(N$)
810 IF F=1 THEN N$=RIGHT$(N$,(L-2)):L=L-2
820 S$=RIGHT$(N$,P)
830 N$=LEFT$(N$,(L-P))
840 GOSUB 900
850 FOR I=1 TO P
860 FOR J=1 TO Q
870 IF MID$(S$,I,1)=P$(I,J) THEN GOSUB 1000
880 NEXT J:NEXT I
890 RETURN
900 PRINT"XXXX"N$
910 IF N=1 THEN 960
920 OPEN 1,4
930 PRINT#1:PRINT#1:PRINT#1
940 PRINT#1,N$
950 CLOSE 1
960 RETURN
1000 PRINT Q$(I,J)
1010 IF N=1 THEN 1050
1020 OPEN 1,4
1030 PRINT#1,I;" ";Q$(I,J)
1040 CLOSE 1
1050 J=Q
1060 RETURN


        ** OPT6 **
        FOR PETS WITH NEW ROMS
        (LARGE KEYBOARD & EXTERNAL CASSETTE)
        CHANGE/ADD THE FOLLOWING LINE NUMBERS:
 720 IF ST=64 THEN Z=1
 745 IF Z=1 THEN 760
 765 Z=0
```

Appendix 10

TT1 — Staff deployment analysis

Input

From the keyboard

You will need

The Curriculum Plan for each year-group; the number of full-time-equivalent staff, not including the Head, but including part-timers (e.g. from the Staff Loading Chart); the total number of teaching spaces (not just rooms, see section 7.1); from your timetable, the average number of teaching spaces required in each period by the Sixth Form (if you have one); the number of pupils in each form or band.

Output

With an 8K PET the display is on the screen only.
With a 16K PET or a 32K PET the display is on the screen and on a printer if connected.

A 'Menu' is displayed:
1. Contact Ratio
2. Relative Bonus
3. Rooming
4. Staffing of Main School and Sixth Form
5. Pupils, periods, staff for years 1-5
6. Bonuses for years 1-5 numerically
7. Bonuses for years 1-5 graphically
8. Bonuses across any year-group (numerically)
9. Bonuses across any year-group (graphically)
10. Print 1-9 on a printer (16K or 32K PET only)

You can choose from the menu the display that you require, in any order. A great deal of information is displayed, as shown below:

176 *Appendix 10*

LAURA NORDER HIGH SCHOOL   27TH SEPTEMBER

CONTACT RATIO (C)

C= .731
AVERAGE LOAD= 29.2   PERIODS/WEEK

C(MIN) FOR B% = 10% IS   .655
C(MAX) FOR R = 0.85 IS   .68

AT ANY TIME:
    AVERAGE NO. OF STAFF TEACHING,
    AVERAGE NO. OF CLASSES TAUGHT,
    AVERAGE NO. OF ROOMS IN USE IS: 53

RELATIVE BONUS (B%)

B%= 22.2 %

ITS VALUE SHOULD BE > 10% FOR CURRICULAR FLEXIBILITY.
IT IS RARELY > 25%

FOR THE MAIN SCHOOL:
TOTAL NO. OF BONUSES= 75.7

TOTAL NO. OF CURRICULUM UNITS = 415.8
MIN. VALUE OF THIS (FOR B% > 10%) IS   373
MAX. VALUE OF THIS (FOR R < 0.85) IS   390

ROOMING

YOUR OVERALL ROOMING FRACTION (R) IS .9
IF R RISES ABOVE 0.85 THERE WILL BE A LOSS OF TIMETABLING
FLEXIBILITY.

YOUR VALUE OF : NO. OF PUPILS
                 ─────────────────────
                 NO. OF TEACHING SPACES   = 20

IF THIS FIGURE EXCEEDS 21 YOU WILL LOSE CURRICULAR FLEXIBILITY
OR TIMETABLING FLEXIBILITY, OR BOTH!
ON THIS BASIS YOUR MAXIMUM CAPACITY (FOR THE MAIN SCHOOL)
IS ABOUT 1060 PUPILS

STAFFING

TOTAL FULL-TIME-EQUIVALENT (FTE) STAFFING IS 72

FULL-TIME-EQUIVALENT STAFF FOR SIXTH FORM= 8.8
STAFFING RATIO FOR THE SIXTH FORM= 1: 11
MOST LEA'S STAFF SIXTH FORMS AT 1:11

FULL-TIME-EQUIVALENT STAFF FOR THE MAIN SCHOOL IS 63.2
AVERAGE STAFFING RATIO FOR THE MAIN SCHOOL = 1: 16.1

TT1 – Staff deployment analysis

YEAR	NUMBER OF PUPILS	NUMBER OF PERIODS	NUMBER OF FTE STAFF
1	200	402	13.7
2	207	329	11.2
3	204	333	11.3
4	198	391	13.3
5	211	393	13.4
TOTALS: 5	1020	1848	63.2

YEAR	CU'S	BONUSES	AVE. SIZE OF GROUP
1	90	+ 24	19.8
2	74	+ 5	25.1
3	75	+ 7	24.4
4	88	+ 22	20.2
5	88	+ 18	21.4
TOTALS: 5	415	+ 75	22.0

GRAPHICALLY:

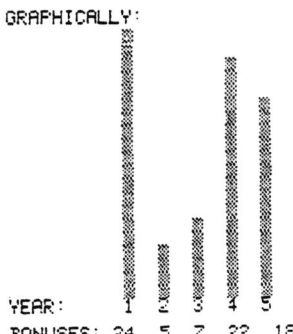

```
YEAR:     1  2  3  4  5
BONUSES: 24  5  7 22 18
```

YEAR/GROUP	CU'S	BONUSES	AVE. SIZE OF GROUP
1A	90	+ 24	19.8
TOTALS: 1	90	+ 24	19.8

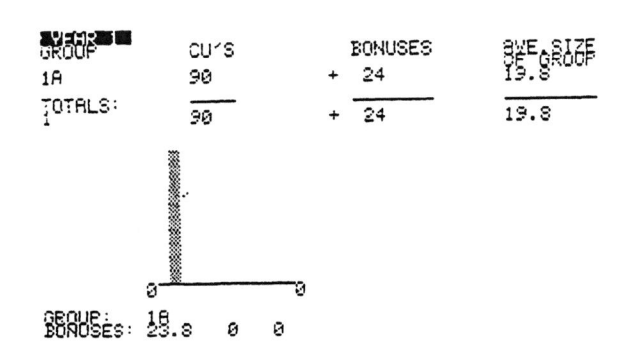

```
GROUP:     1A
BONUSES: 19.8   0   0
```

178 *Appendix 10*

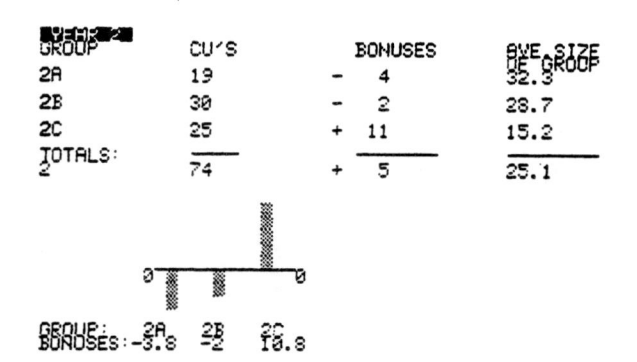

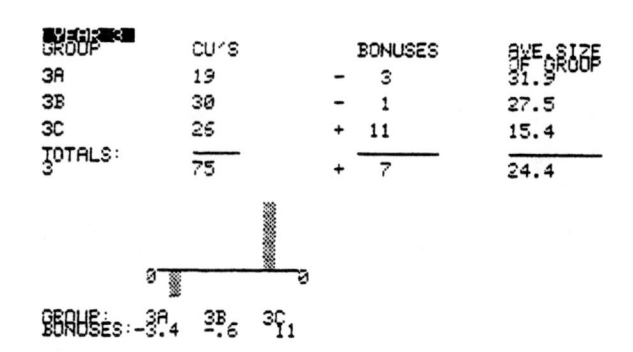

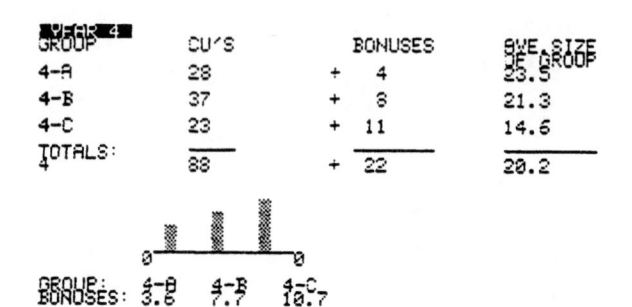

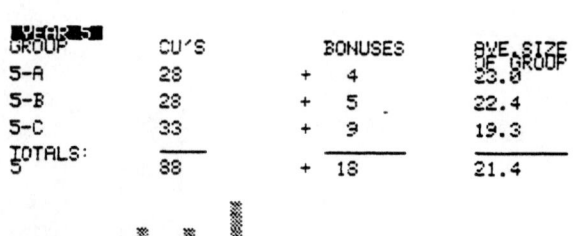

YEAR 2

GROUP	CU'S	BONUSES	AVE. SIZE OF GROUP
2A	19	− 4	32.3
2B	30	− 2	28.7
2C	25	+ 11	15.2
TOTALS: 2	74	+ 5	25.1

GROUP: 2A   2B   2C
BONUSES: -3.8   -.2   10.8

YEAR 3

GROUP	CU'S	BONUSES	AVE. SIZE OF GROUP
3A	19	− 3	31.9
3B	30	− 1	27.5
3C	26	+ 11	15.4
TOTALS: 3	75	+ 7	24.4

GROUP: 3A   3B   3C
BONUSES: -3.4   -.6   11.1

YEAR 4

GROUP	CU'S	BONUSES	AVE. SIZE OF GROUP
4-A	28	+ 4	23.5
4-B	37	+ 8	21.3
4-C	23	+ 11	14.6
TOTALS: 4	88	+ 22	20.2

GROUP: 4-A   4-B   4-C
BONUSES: 3.6   7.7   10.7

YEAR 5

GROUP	CU'S	BONUSES	AVE. SIZE OF GROUP
5-A	28	+ 4	23.0
5-B	28	+ 5	22.4
5-C	33	+ 9	19.3
TOTALS: 5	88	+ 18	21.4

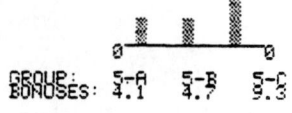

GROUP: 5-A   5-B   5-C
BONUSES: 4.1   4.7   9.3

TT1 - Staff deployment analysis 179

Time required
About 15 minutes if a printer is connected.

★ ★

Entering the information
As usual the steps are explained on the screen (rather briefly in the 8K version)

If you do not know the number of teaching spaces, or do not wish to consider rooming, enter the number as 0.

The program asks for a number equal to or greater than the number of groupings in any year-group. The maximum is 12 for an 8K PET but you are unlikely to need that many. For example: if your 4th Year (and also your 5th Year) is grouped in two half-years; if your 2nd Year (and 3rd Year) are grouped as three bands; but your 1st Year is taught as 8 separate forms and you wish to enter them as 8 distinct groups, then the number to enter is 8. If, instead, you chose to enter the 1st Year as one group then the number would be 3 (because of the 3 bands in the 2nd Year).

If you have a large number of these sub-groups in any year-group then you may find that you get an 'out-of-memory-error' on an 8K PET. In this case you will have to remove or shorten some of the lines of text to provide more memory space.

For each of these groups you enter three items of information, separated by commas and ending with an = sign. The 3 items are:
name of group *comma* number of pupils *comma* number of periods =
e.g. 1A, 32, 44 =
Alternatively the number of periods can be added up automatically by the machine as you work your way down the Curriculum Plan. The numbers must be separated by + signs.
e.g. 4U, 94, 18+18+4+8+16+20+12+18+4+2+1+6=
Using this method, the total length must not exceed 79 characters (just under 2 lines on the screen)

If you have a situation where a year-group is divided into 3 bands for most of the week, but there are some occasions when there is a team of teachers across two or more bands (e.g. for Maths sets) then you should consider the year-group as 3 bands and decide (approximately) what is the share of the Maths periods for each band (by counting the number of Maths periods and considering the number of pupils in each band)

If any year-group has fewer sub-groupings than the number you entered earlier, then you can move to the next year-group by entering

either =, =, =   'return'
or = three 'return's

Appendix 10

If your school has a 'withdrawal unit' for disturbed or disturbing pupils then you should:

either (a) spread the number of periods for which it is staffed across all the (relevant bands in all the) year groups;

or (b) subtract the staffing of the unit from your total (remembering that for one teacher to be present in the unit all week requires the equivalent of about 1.3 staff (see section 3.6).

The listing
This is shown in two parts.
The first part will *just* run on an 8K PET.
The second part shows the extras which give a much improved version for running on a 16K or 32K PET with a printer attached.
The following special symbols appear in the lines named:

'clear'	lines 100, 300, 650, 700, 1400, 1560, 3120
'home'	line 2970
'cursor down'	lines 130, 150, 170, 200, 220, 360, 400, 570, 600, 670, 730, 750, 770, 780, 810, 880, 1020, 1045, 1180, 1440, 1470, 1490, 1510, 1540, 1600, 1700, 2010, 2020, 2040, 2110, 2150 2220, 2250, 2255, 2260, 2310, 2330, 2380, 2870, 2970
'reverse field'	lines 1030, 1040, 1045, 1100, 1700, 2000, 2100, 2200, 2300, 5310
'reverse field off'	lines 1030, 1040

Part A

```
100 PRINT"⊃     TT1-STAFF DEPLOYMENT ANALYSIS"
110 PRINT"        (CURRICULUM ANALYSIS)"
120 PRINT"         (C)KEITH JOHNSON 1979
220 PRINT"▓▓NO. OF PERIODS IN YOUR SCHOOL WEEK?"
240 INPUTW:U=W/9
300 PRINT"⊃NO. OF FULL-TIME-EQUIVALENT STAFF?
320 PRINT"(NOT INCLUDING THE HEAD;"
330 PRINT"BUT INCLUDING THE FULL-TIME"
340 PRINT"EQUIVALENT OF PART-TIME STAFF)"
350 INPUT T
360 PRINT"▓ENTER THE TOTAL NO. OF TEACHING"
370 PRINT"SPACES (NOT JUST ROOMS)
410 PRINT"OR JUST ENTER  0  (ZERO)"
420 INPUT R1
500 PRINT"⊃DO YOU HAVE A SIXTH FORM?(Y OR N)"
520 INPUTQ$
530 IFQ$="N"THENK1=5:GOTO600
540 IFQ$="Y"THENK1=6:GOTO560
550 GOTO 500
560 IFR1=0THEN600
```

TT1 - Staff deployment analysis

```
570 PRINT"XLOOKING AT YOUR TIMETABLE,HOW MANY
580 PRINT"TEACHING SPACES,ON AVERAGE,ARE NEEDED
585 PRINT"EACH PERIOD FOR YOUR 6TH FORM?"
590 INPUTR6
600 PRINT"XDO YOU WANT THE CU'S SHOWN:
605 PRINT"  1 AS WHOLE NUMBERS
610 PRINT"  2 TO ONE DECIMAL PLACE
615 INPUTM
620 IFM<1ORM>2THEN600
625 IFM=2THENM=10
640 R5=R1-R6
650 PRINT"3NOW CONSIDER HOW THE PUPILS ARE GROUPED"
655 PRINT"IN EACH YEAR-GROUP:"
660 PRINT"EG. ARE THEY GROUPED NATURALLY IN FORMS"
665 PRINT"OR IN BANDS (OR HALF-YEAR GROUPS)"
670 PRINT"XENTER A NO. EQUAL TO OR GREATER THAN"
675 PRINT"THE NO. OF THESE GROUPINGS IN ANY"
680 PRINT"  YEAR-GROUP.(MAX=12 FOR 8K PET)"
690 INPUT F:P=F:IFF<5THENP=5
695 DIMA$(F+1,K1),C(F+1,K1),D(F+1,K1),Y(P)
1000 FOR K=1TOK1
1010 NT=0:IFK=6THENGOSUB1700:GOTO1030
1020 PRINT"XXXNOW FOR THE 1ST GROUP IN YEAR "K"ENTER"
1030 PRINT"3GROUP NAME3 COMMA 3NUMBER OF PUPILS3 COMMA"
1040 PRINT"3NUMBER OF PERIODS3 (AND END WITH =)"
1045 PRINT"XBN.B. YOU MUST END WITH =
1050 PRINT"E.G. 1A,32,44=
1060 PRINT"E.G. 4X,94,18+16+12+4+4+12+3+2+1=
1065 PRINT"(SEE BOOK FOR DETAILS)
1070 FORI=1TOF
1080 INPUT Y$,N$,P$
1090 IF Y$="="THENI=F:GOTO1220
1095 L=LEN(P$):P=0:E=1
1100 IFRIGHT$(P$,1)<>"="THENPRINT"3REPEAT,END WITH =":GOTO1080
1110 FORJ=1TOL
1120 D$=MID$(P$,J,1)
1130 IF D$="+"OR D$="="THEND=J:P=P+VAL(MID$(P$,E,(D-E))):E=J+1
1140 NEXTJ
1150 X=P/U:P6=P6+P:B=X-(VAL(N$)/3)
1155 X=(INT((X*M)+.5))/M:B=(INT((B*M)+.5))/M:IFK=6THENI=F:GOTO1170
1160 PRINTY$,"N$" PUPILS,"P"PERIODS,"X"CU'S,    "B"BONUSES"
1170 A$(I,K)=Y$:C(I,K)=X:D(I,K)=B
1175 IFI=FTHEN1210
1180 PRINT"XXNOW ENTER THE NEXT GROUP IN YEAR "K
1190 PRINT"IF THERE ARE NO MORE GROUPS IN YEAR "K
1200 PRINT"THEN ENTER  =,=,=  ('RETURN')
1210 NT=NT+VAL(N$):XT=XT+X:BT=BT+B
1220 NEXTI
1230 A$(F+1,K)=STR$(NT):C(F+1,K)=(INT((XT*M)+.5))/M:N6=N6+NT
1240 D(F+1,K)=(INT((BT*M)+.5))/M:XT=0:BT=0
1250 NEXTK
1300 C=(INT((P6*1000)/(T*W)))/1000
1310 IF Q$="N"THENN5=N6:P5=P6:GOTO1340
1320 T6=(INT((P*10)/(C*W)))/10:P5=P6-P
1330 S6=(INT(NT*10/T6))/10:N5=N6-NT
1340 T5=(INT((T-T6)*10))/10:S5=(INT(N5*10/T5))/10
1350 X5=(INT((P5*M/U)+.5))/M:B5=(INT(((X5-(N5/3))*M)+.5))/M
1360 RB=(INT((B5*3000)/N5))/10
1370 IF R1=0THEN1390
1380 R=(INT(C*T5*100/R5))/100:J5=(INT(N5*10/R5))/10
1390 C1=(INT(40.7*S5))/1000:X1=INT(.3666*N5)
1395 C2=(INT(85*R5/T5))/100:X2=INT(7.65*R5)
1400 PRINT"3MENU"
1410 PRINT"————"
1420 PRINT"FOR MORE DETAILS,SEE KEITH JOHNSON'S"
1430 PRINT"BOOK:'TIMETABLING'(HUTCHINSON LTD)"
1440 PRINT"X1  CONTACT RATIO"
```

182 *Appendix 10*

```
1450 PRINT"2   RELATIVE BONUS"
1460 PRINT"3   ROOMING"
1470 PRINT"}04   STAFFING OF MAIN SCHOOL & SIXTH FORM"
1480 PRINT"5   PUPILS,PERIODS,STAFF FOR YEARS 1-5"
1490 PRINT"}06   BONUSES FOR YEARS 1-5 NUMERICALLY"
1500 PRINT"7   BONUSES FOR YEARS 1-5 GRAPHICALLY"
1510 PRINT"}08   BONUSES ACROSS ANY YEAR GROUP"
1515 PRINT"       (NUMERICALLY)"
1520 PRINT"9   BONUSES ACROSS ANY YEAR GROUP"
1525 PRINT"       (GRAPHICALLY)"
1530 PRINT"10 PRINT 1-9 ON A PRINTER"
1540 PRINT"}AFTER EACH SELECTION YOU WILL RETURN"
1545 PRINT"TO THE MENU"
1550 PRINT"TYPE THE NUMBER YOU WANT:"
1560 INPUT A:PRINT"]"
1570 ON A GOSUB 2000,2100,2200,2300,2500,2600,2700,3100,2800,4000
1580 GOTO1400
1600 PRINT"}PRESS ANY KEY TO CONTINUE"
1610 GETA$:IFA$=""THEN1610
1620 RETURN
1700 PRINT"}}}}}NOW FOR THE ENTIRE SIXTH FORM,ENTER:"
1720 RETURN
2000 PRINT"}CONTACT RATIO (C)
2010 PRINT"}C="C
2015 PRINT"(AVE. LOAD="(INT(C*W*10))/10"PERIODS/WEEK)"
2020 PRINT"}C(MIN) FOR B%=10% IS"C1
2030 IFR1>0THENPRINT"C(MAX) FOR R=0.85 IS"C2
2040 PRINT"}AT ANY TIME,THE AVERAGE NO. OF:"
2050 PRINT"   STAFF TEACHING,"
2060 PRINT"   CLASSES TIMETABLED,"
2070 PRINT"   ROOMS IN USE,IS:    "INT((P6/W)+.5)
2090 GOSUB1600
2095 RETURN
2100 PRINT"}RELATIVE BONUS(B%)"
2110 PRINT"}B%="RB"%"
2120 PRINT"B% SHOULD BE >10%"
2130 PRINT"IT IS RARELY >25%
2150 PRINT"}FOR THE MAIN SCHOOL:"
2160 PRINT"TOTAL NO. OF BONUSES="B5
2170 PRINT"TOTAL NO. OF CU'S="X5
2180 PRINT"MIN NO. OF CU'S(FOR B%>10%)="X1
2190 IFR1>0THENPRINT"MAX NO. OF CU'S(FOR R<0.85)="X2
2195 GOSUB1600
2197 RETURN
2200 PRINT"}ROOMING"
2210 IFR1=0THEN2280
2220 PRINT"}YOUR OVERALL ROOMING FRACTION (R)="R
2230 PRINT"IF R>0.85 THERE WILL BE A LOSS OF TIMETABLING FLEXIBILITY"
2250 PRINT"}YOUR VALUE OF (NO. OF PUPILS/NO. OF TEACHING SPACES)="J5
2255 IFJ5>21THENPRINT"}YOU HAVE LOST":GOTO2265
2260 PRINT"}IF THIS FIGURE RISES TO 21 YOU WILL"
2265 PRINT"LOSE CURRICULAR FLEXIBILITY (B>10%),OR"
2270 PRINT"TIMETABLING FLEXIBILITY(R>.85),OR BOTH!"
2280 GOSUB1600
2290 RETURN
2300 PRINT"}STAFFING"
2310 PRINT"}TOTAL FULL-TIME-EQUIVALENT (FTE) STAFF  IS"T
2320 IFQ$="N"THEN2410
2330 PRINT"}FTE STAFF FOR 6TH FORM="T6
2340 PRINT"STAFFING RATIO FOR THE 6TH FORM= 1:"S6
2350 PRINT"MOST LEA'S STAFF 6TH FORMS AT 1:11"
2360 IF S6<11THENPRINT"THIS PROBABLY MEANS THAT IT IS SUBSIDISED BY YRS
2370 IFS6>11.5THENPRINT"THIS MAY MEAN THAT IT IS SUBSIDISING YRS 1-5"
2380 PRINT"}FTE STAFF FOR YRS 1-5 ="T5
2410 PRINT"AVE STAFFING RATIO FOR YRS 1-5= 1:"S5
2420 GOSUB1600
2430 RETURN
```

TT1 - Staff deployment analysis

```
2500 PRINT"YEAR       NUMBER    NUMBER    NUMBER"
2510 PRINT"           OF        OF        OF FTE"
2520 PRINT"           PUPILS    PERIODS   STAFF"
2530 FORK=1TO5
2540 PRINTK,VAL(A$(F+1,K)),INT((C(F+1,K)*U)+.5),
     (INT((C(F+1,K)*10)/(9*C)))/10
2550 PRINT
2560 NEXTK
2570 PRINT"          ———       ———       ———"
2580 PRINT"TOTALS:",N5,P5,T5
2590 GOSUB1600
2595 RETURN
2600 PRINT"YEAR       CU'S     BONUSES    AVE SIZE"
2610 PRINT"          ———      ———         OF GROUP"
2620 FORK=1TO5
2630 PRINTK,C(F+1,K),D(F+1,K),(INT(((VAL(A$(F+1,K)))*90)/C(F+1,K)))/1
2640 PRINT
2650 NEXTK
2660 PRINT"          ———      ———"
2670 PRINT"TOTALS:",X5,B5
2680 GOSUB1600
2690 RETURN
2700 X=1:D=5
2710 FORI=1TOD
2720 Y(I)=D(F+1,I)
2730 IFY(I)>X*20THENX=Y(I)/20
2740 NEXTI
2750 GOSUB2900
2760 PRINT"YEAR:     1   2   3   4   5"
2770 PRINT"BONUSES:";:FORI=1TO5:D=(I*4)+5:PRINTTAB(D);D(F+1,I);:NEXTI
2780 PRINT:GOSUB1600
2790 RETURN
2800 X=1:D=F
2810 PRINT"WHICH YEAR?":INPUTK
2820 FORI=1TOD
2830 Y(I)=D(I,K)
2840 IFY(I)>X*20THENX=Y(I)/20
2850 NEXTI
2860 GOSUB2900
2870 PRINT"XGROUP:";:FORI=1TOF:D=(I*4)+6:PRINTTAB(D);A$(I,K);
     :NEXT:PRINT
2880 PRINT"BONUSES:";:FORI=1TOF:D=(I*4)+6:PRINTTAB(D);D(I,K);
     :NEXT:PRINT
2890 GOSUB1600
2895 RETURN
2900 FORI=1TOD
2910 Y(I)=INT((Y(I)/X)+.5)
2930 IFY(I)<0THEN2965
2940 FORJ=0TOY(I)
2950 POKE 33574-(J*40)+(I*4),102
2960 NEXTJ
2965 NEXTI
2970 PRINT"▓▓▓▓▓▓▓▓▓▓▓▓▓▓▓▓▓▓▓▓"
2980 FORI=1TOD
2990 IFY(I)>=0THEN3035
3000 FORJ=-1TOY(I)STEP-1
3010 Z=33534-(J*40)+(I*4):IFZ>33767THEN3030
3020 POKEZ,102
3030 NEXTJ
3035 NEXTI
3040 RETURN
3100 PRINT"WHICH YEAR?":INPUTK
3110 IFK<1ORK>5THEN3100
3120 PRINT"JGROUP       CU'S        BONUSES"
3130 FORI=1TOF
3140 PRINTA$(I,K),C(I,K),D(I,K)
```

Appendix 10

```
3150 PRINT
3160 NEXTI
3170 PRINT"                              "
3180 PRINT"TOTALS:",C(F+1,K),D(F+1,K)
3190 GOSUB1600
3195 RETURN
READY.
```

Part B

```
105 PRINT"                              "
130 PRINT"▒THIS PROGRAM WILL ANALYSE THE PRESENT"
140 PRINT"DEPLOYMENT OF THE STAFF OF YOUR SCHOOL."
150 PRINT"▒IT DOES NOT MAKE ANY DECISIONS FOR YOU,"
160 PRINT"MERELY HIGHLIGHTS YOUR PRESENT SITUATION"
170 PRINT"▒THE METHOD IS CONCERNED ONLY WITH THE"
180 PRINT"QUANTITY OF TEACHING TIME ALLOCATED TO"
190 PRINT"PUPILS (NOT THE QUALITY OF TEACHING)."
200 PRINT"▒FOR MORE DETAILS SEE KEITH JOHNSONS'S"
210 PRINT"BOOK 'TIMETABLING' (HUTCHINSON LTD)."
380 PRINT"INCLUDE THE FIELD AS 2 TEACHING SPACES"
390 PRINT"IF,ON AVERAGE,2 CLASSES ARE USING IT)."
400 PRINT"▒IF YOU WISH YOU MAY OMIT THIS"
410 PRINT"INFORMATION AND JUST ENTER  0  (ZERO)"
696 DIMB(F+1,K1),Z$(20,P)
700 PRINT"▒THE NEXT STEP IS TO ENTER INFORMATION"
710 PRINT"ABOUT EACH GROUP OF PUPILS (WHETHER A"
720 PRINT"FORM,BAND OR WHOLE YEAR-GROUP)."
730 PRINT"▒THREE ITEMS OF INFORMATION ARE NEEDED"
740 PRINT"FOR EACH GROUP OF PUPILS:"
750 PRINT"▒1-THE NAME OF THE GROUP"
760 PRINT"    E.G.  1A,  4U,  6L"
770 PRINT"▒2-THE NUMBER OF PUPILS IN THE GROUP"
780 PRINT"▒3-THE NO. OF TEACHER-PERIODS PROVIDED"
790 PRINT"   TO THE GROUP (INCLUDING PERIODS OF"
800 PRINT"   REMEDIAL WITHDRAWAL)."
810 PRINT"▒ THE NUMBER OF PERIODS MAY BE ENTERED"
820 PRINT"  AS ONE NUMBER FOLLOWED BY AN = SIGN"
830 PRINT"OR"
835 PRINT"  AS SEVERAL NUMBERS,WITH + SIGNS"
840 PRINT"  BETWEEN AND FINALLY ENDING WITH ="
860 GOSUB1600
880 PRINT"▒▒YOU WILL ENTER THE 3 ITEMS OF"
890 PRINT"INFORMATION,SEPARATED BY COMMAS,"
900 PRINT"FOR EACH GROUP.  FOR EXAMPLE:"
910 PRINT"E.G. 1A,32,44="
920 PRINT"E.G. 4X,94,18+16+12+4+4+12+3+2+1="
1172 B(I,K)=VAL(N$)

4000 PRINT "HAVE YOU GOT A PRINTER ATTACHED?"
4010 PRINT "(WITH AT LEAST 2 METRES OF PAPER LOADED)"
4020 PRINT "(PLEASE ANSWER Y OR N)"
4030 INPUT Q1$
4040 IF Q1$="N" THEN 1400
4050 PRINT"PLEASE ENTER A 1-LINE HEADING"
4052 PRINT"E.G.   DATE & NAME OF SCHOOL"
4053 INPUTQ1$
4100 OPEN 1,4
4110 GOSUB 6000
4190 OPEN 6,4,6
4199 PRINT#1,Q1$:PRINT#1:PRINT#1:PRINT#1
4200 PRINT#1,"    CONTACT RATIO   (C)"
4210 PRINT#1,"                           "
4220 PRINT#1,"C="C
4230 PRINT#1,"AVERAGE LOAD="(INT(C*W*10))/10" PERIODS/WEEK
```

TT1 - Staff deployment analysis

```
4240 PRINT#1
4250 PRINT#1,"C(MIN) FOR B% = 10% IS "C1
4260 IF R1=0 THEN 4280
4270 PRINT#1,"C(MAX) FOR R = 0.85 IS "C2
4280 PRINT#1
4290 PRINT#1,"AT ANY TIME:"
4300 PRINT#1,"     AVERAGE NO. OF STAFF TEACHING,"
4310 PRINT#1,"     AVERAGE NO. OF CLASSES TAUGHT,"
4320 PRINT#1,"     AVERAGE NO. OF ROOMS IN USE IS:" INT((P6/W)+.5)
4330 PRINT#1:PRINT#1:PRINT#1:PRINT#1
4340 PRINT#1,"    RELATIVE BONUS (B%)"
4350 PRINT#1,"                        "
4360 PRINT#1,"B%= "RB"%"
4370 PRINT#1
4380 PRINT#1,"ITS VALUE SHOULD BE > 10% FOR CURRICULAR FLEXIBILITY."
4390 PRINT#1,"IT IS RARELY > 25%"
4400 PRINT#1
4410 PRINT#1,"FOR THE MAIN SCHOOL:"
4420 PRINT#1,"TOTAL NO. OF BONUSES="B5
4430 PRINT#1
4440 PRINT#1,"TOTAL NO. OF CURRICULUM UNITS = "X5
4450 PRINT#1,"MIN. VALUE OF THIS (FOR B% > 10%) IS "X1
4460 IF R1=0 THEN 4480
4470 PRINT#1,"MAX. VALUE OF THIS (FOR R < 0.85) IS "X2
4480 PRINT#1:PRINT#1:PRINT#1:PRINT#1
4490 IF R1=0 THEN 4620
4500 PRINT#1,"    ROOMING"
4510 PRINT#1,"           "
4520 PRINT#1,"YOUR OVERALL ROOMING FRACTION (R) IS "R
4530 PRINT#1,"IF R RISES ABOVE 0.85 THERE WILL BE A LOSS OF
     TIMETABLING "
4535 PRINT#1,"FLEXIBILITY."
4540 PRINT#1
4550 PRINT#1,"YOUR VALUE OF : NO. OF PUPILS";CHR$(141);
4560 PRINT#1,"                _____"
4570 PRINT#1,"                NO. OF TEACHING SPACES    ="J5
4580 PRINT#1
4590 PRINT#1,"IF THIS FIGURE EXCEEDS 21 YOU WILL LOSE CURRICULAR
     FLEXIBILITY,"
4600 PRINT#1,"OR TIMETABLING FLEXIBILITY, OR BOTH!"
4605 PRINT#1,"ON THIS BASIS YOUR MAXIMUM CAPACITY (FOR THE MAIN SCHOOL)
4607 PRINT#1,"IS ABOUT"((INT(R5*2.08))*10)"PUPILS"
4610 PRINT#1:PRINT#1:PRINT#1:PRINT#1
4620 PRINT#1,"    STAFFING"
4630 PRINT#1,"            "
4640 PRINT#1,"TOTAL FULL-TIME-EQUIVALENT (FTE) STAFFING IS"T
4650 IF Q$="N" THEN 4740
4660 PRINT#1
4670 PRINT#1,"FULL-TIME-EQUIVALENT STAFF FOR SIXTH FORM="T6
4680 PRINT#1,"STAFFING RATIO FOR THE SIXTH FORM= 1:"S6
4690 PRINT#1,"MOST LEA'S STAFF SIXTH FORMS AT 1:11"
4700 IF S6<11 THEN PRINT#1,"THIS PROBABLY MEANS THAT YOUR SIXTH FORM IS"
4705 IFS6<11 THEN PRINT#1,"SUBSIDISED BY THE MAIN SCHOOL"
4710 IF S6>11.5 THEN PRINT#1,"THIS MAY MEAN THAT YOUR SIXTH FORM IS"
4715 IF S6>11.5 THEN PRINT#1,"SUBSIDISING THE MAIN SCHOOL"
4720 PRINT#1
4730 PRINT#1,"FULL-TIME-EQUIVALENT STAFF FOR THE MAIN SCHOOL IS"T5
4740 PRINT#1,"AVERAGE STAFFING RATIO FOR THE MAIN SCHOOL = 1:"S5
4750 PRINT#1:PRINT#1:PRINT#1:PRINT#1
4800 PRINT#1,"YEAR        NUMBER        NUMBER        NUMBER"
4810 PRINT#1,"____        OF            OF            OF FTE"
4820 PRINT#1,"            PUPILS        PERIODS       STAFF"
4830 FOR K=1 TO 5
4840 PRINT#2,K,VAL(A$(F+1,K)),INT((C(F+1,K)*U)+.5),
     (INT(C(F+1,K)/(.9*C)))/10
4850 PRINT#2:NEXTK
4860 PRINT#1,"TOTALS:     _____        _____        _____"
```

186 *Appendix 10*

```
4870 PRINT#2,(K-1),N5,P5,T5
4880 PRINT#1:PRINT#1:PRINT#1:PRIN
4890 GOSUB 6100:GOSUB 6200
4900 PRINT#1,"YEAR          CU'S
4910 PRINT#1,"────
4920 FOR K=1TO5
4930 PRINT#4,K,C(F+1,K),D(F+1,K),
     K))*90)/C(F+1,K)))/10
4940 PRINT#4:NEXTK
4950 PRINT#1,"TOTALS:       ────
4960 I=0:IF M=1 THEN I=.5
4965 PRINT#4,(K-1),(X5+I),(B5+I),
4970 PRINT#1:PRINT#1:PRINT#1:PRIN
4980 FORJ=1TO20:FORI=1TOF:Z$(J,I)
4990 PRINT#1,"GRAPHICALLY:"
5000 X=1:FOR K=1 TO 5
5010 IF D(F+1,K)>(X*20) THEN X=(D
5020 NEXTK
5030 FOR K=1TO5
5040 Y(K)=INT((D(F+1,K)/X)+.5)
5050 IF Y(K)<=0THEN5090
5060 FOR J=1 TO Y(K)
5070 Z$(J,K)="▓"
5080 NEXTJ
5090 NEXTK
5100 PRINT#6,CHR$(18)
5110 FOR J=20TO 1 STEP-1
5115 PRINT#1,"                ";
5120 FOR K=1TO5
5125 IF Z$(J,K)=""THEN PRINT#1,"
5130 PRINT#1,Z$(J,K);"  ";
5140 NEXTK
5150 PRINT#1:NEXTJ
5160 PRINT#1,"YEAR:      1  2  3
5165 PRINT#1
5170 PRINT#1,"BONUSES:";
5180 FOR K=1TO5:PRINT#1,(INT(D(F+
5190 PRINT#1:PRINT#1:PRINT#1:PRIN
5200 X=1:FOR K=1TO5
5210 FOR I=1TOF
5220 IF ABS(D(I,K))>X*10 THEN X=D
5230 NEXTI:NEXTK
5300 FOR K=1TO5
5310 PRINT#1:PRINT#1:PRINT#1,"▓ Y
5320 PRINT#1,"GROUP          CU'S
5330 PRINT#1,"
5340 FOR I=1 TO F
5350 IF A$(I,K)="" THEN 5390
5360 PRINT#1,A$(I,K)CHR$(141);
5370 PRINT#4,K,C(I,K),D(I,K),(INT
5380 PRINT#4
5390 NEXTI
5400 PRINT#1,"TOTALS:        ────
5405 J1=(INT(((VAL(A$(F+1,K)))*90
5410 PRINT#4,K,C(F+1,K),D(F+1,K),
5420 PRINT#1:PRINT#1
5490 FORJ=1TO20:FORI=1TOF:Z$(J,I)
5495 J1=11:J2=10
5500 FOR I=1 TO F
5510 Y(I)=INT((D(I,K)/X)+.5)
5520 IF Y(I)<=0 THEN 5550
5525 IF J1<(Y(I)+10) THEN J1=(Y(I
5530 FOR J=11 TO (10+Y(I))
5540 Z$(J,I)="▓":NEXTJ
5550 IFY(I)>=0THEN 5580
5560 IF J2>(Y(I)+10) THEN J2=(Y(I
5565 FOR J=10 TO (10+Y(I)) STEP-1
```

```
5570 Z$(J,I)="▓":NEXTJ
5580 NEXTI
5590 FORJ=J1 TO 11 STEP-1
5595 PRINT#1,"          ";
5600 FOR I=1 TO F
5605 IF Z$(J,I)=""THEN PRINT#1," ";
5610 PRINT#1,Z$(J,I);"  ";
5620 NEXTI:PRINT#1:NEXTJ
5630 PRINT#1,"         0";
5640 FORI=1TO(F*4):PRINT#1,"‾";:NEXTI:PRINT#1,"0";CHR$(141);
5650 FORJ=10 TO J2 STEP-1
5655 PRINT#1,"          ";
5660 FOR I=1 TO F
5670 PRINT#1,Z$(J,I);"  ";
5680 NEXTI:PRINT#1:NEXTJ
5690 PRINT#1:PRINT#1,"GROUP:    ";
5700 FORI=1TOF:PRINT#1,A$(I,K);"    ";:NEXTI:PRINT#1
5710 PRINT#1,"BONUSES:";
5720 FORI=1TOF:PRINT#1,D(I,K);" ";:NEXTI
5730 PRINT#1:PRINT#1:PRINT#1:PRINT#1:PRINT#1:PRINT#1
5740 NEXTK
5750 CLOSE1:CLOSE6
5755 GOSUB 6300
5760 GOTO1400
6000 OPEN 2,4,1
6010 OPEN 3,4,2:PRINT#3,"9","9999","9999","999.9"
6020 RETURN
6100 CLOSE2:CLOSE3:RETURN
6200 IF M=1 THEN 6240
6210 OPEN 4,4,1
6220 OPEN 5,4,2:PRINT#5,"9","9999.9","S9999.9","99.9"
6230 GOTO 6250
6240 OPEN 4,4,1
6245 OPEN 5,4,2:PRINT#5,"9","9999","S9999","99.9"
6250 RETURN
6300 CLOSE4:CLOSE5:RETURN
READY.
```

Appendix 11

TT2 — Combing Chart

Input

From the keyboard.

You will need

Your master Curriculum Plan showing the teacher teams for each large department

Sample output (see also sections 5.1 - 5.6)

```
COMBING CHART FOR THE MATHS DEPARTMENT

    1         10        20        30        40
    ├┬┬┬┬┬┼┬┬┬┬┼┬┬┬┬┼┬┬┬┬┼┬┬┬┬┼┬┬┬┬┼┬┬┬
    KJ555555WWWWW444444           6666
    JF▓▓▓▓▓▓▓WWWWW444444BBBBBB======*****
    AH5555553333331111  BBBBBB2222226666
    IH▓▓▓▓▓▓▓       11111      ======
    RR▓▓▓▓▓▓▓WWWWW444444      222222
    AJ555555333333                  *****
    ├┬┬┬┬┬┼┬┬┬┬┼┬┬┬┬┼┬┬┬┬┼┬┬┬┬┼┬┬┬┬┼┬┬┬
    1         10        20        30        40

    5=5A  W=5B  4=4A  ▓=4B  3=3A  B=3B  2=2A  ==2B
    1=1A  *=1B  6=6X
```

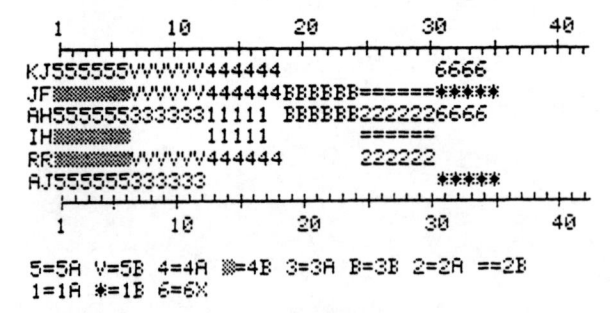

★ ★

Entering the information

This is explained in detail on the screen.

The symbols used to draw the chart can be chosen from any part of the keyboard (numbers, letters or graphics).

The chart is shown 37 periods wide on the screen; on the printer it is shown 42 periods wide. Vertically up to 15 teachers can be shown.

As the chart builds up it is easy to see which teacher is dominating the department by being in many teams and so filling the available timeframe.

The total number of periods filled horizontally should be less than or equal to the maximum teaching load of any member of the department (see section 5.5)

TT2 – Combing Chart

If you have a 16K or 32K PET and a printer then a chart could be drawn for more than 15 teachers by changing the 15s in line 100. This would allow you to enter the whole staff of the school if you wished.

The listing
The following special symbols appear:

'clear'	lines 10, 110, 200, 600
'cursor down'	lines 10, 30, 60, 80, 140, 170, 290, 310, 330, 345, 346, 365
'cursor up'	lines 770, 880
'reverse field'	line 345
'reverse field off'	line 345

```
10 PRINT"□□□          TT2-COMBING CHART"
15 PRINT"         ─────────────────────"
20 PRINT"        (C)1979 KEITH JOHNSON"
30 PRINT"□□□THIS PROGRAM WILL YOU SHOW THE TIME-"
40 PRINT"FRAME NEEDED BY THE TEACHER TEAMS IN"
50 PRINT"A DEPARTMENT OF UP TO 15 TEACHERS."
60 PRINT"□□□FOR MORE DETAILS,SEE THE BOOK"
70 PRINT"'TIMETABLING'  (HUTCHINSON LTD)"
80 PRINT"□□□HAVE YOU GOT A PRINTER CONNECTED?"
90 PRINT"PLEASE ENTER  YES OR NO"
95 INPUT Y$
96 IF Y$="YES" OR Y$="NO" THEN 100
97 GOTO 90
100 DIM A$(15,14),B$(15,14),C$(15,14),T$(15),Z(15),L$(25)
110 PRINT"□HOW MANY TEACHERS ARE THERE IN THIS"
120 PRINT"DEPARTMENT?       (MAXIMUM=15)"
130 INPUT T
140 PRINT"□□NOW,USING A 2-LETTER CODE,ENTER THE"
150 PRINT"MEMBERS OF THE DEPARTMENT ONE AT A"
160 PRINT"TIME,EACH FOLLOWED BY 'RETURN'"
170 PRINT"□E.G.      KJ    ('RETURN')"
180 FOR I=1 TO T
190 INPUT A$(I,0)
195 NEXT I
200 PRINT"□STARTING WITH THE LARGEST TEAM,"
220 PRINT"ENTER AS FOLLOWS:"
230 PRINT"-REAL NAME OF YEAR,BAND OR CLASS(COMMA)"
240 PRINT"-A SINGLE SYMBOL TO BE SHOWN ON THE"
250 PRINT" CHART    (COMMA)"
260 PRINT"-NUMBER OF PERIODS FOR THIS TEAM(COMMA)"
270 PRINT"-THE TEAM OF TEACHERS (2-LETTER CODE"
280 PRINT" WITH NO GAPS)    ('RETURN')"
290 PRINT"□E.G.     5A,A,4,IHAJRR"
300 PRINT"OR:     4B,*,6,RKCKMJBA"
310 PRINT"□□ALWAYS REFER TO THE SAME GROUP BY THE"
320 PRINT"SAME SINGLE SYMBOL"
330 PRINT"□TO GET A PRINTOUT ON A PRINTER,AT THE"
340 PRINT"VERY END,ENTER:  EOF (AND 4 'RETURN'S)"
345 PRINT"□▮PLEASE NOTE THESE POINTS▯-THEY WILL NOT"
346 PRINT"BE SHOWN AGAIN!□"
350 PRINT"START NOW:"
355 INPUT P$,Q$,R,S$
360 IF P$="EOF" AND Y$="YES" THEN 1100
365 PRINT"□PLEASE WAIT...."
```

190 Appendix 11

```
370 N=(LEN(S$))/2
380 FOR K=1 TO N
390 T$(K)=MID$(S$,((2*K)-1),2)
395 NEXT K
400 FOR J=1 TO 42
405 F=0
410 FOR I=1 TO T
420 Z(I)=1
430 IF J>28 THEN 470
440 IF J>14 THEN 460
450 IF A$(I,J)=Q$ THEN I=T:F=1:M=1:GOTO 550
455 GOTO 480
460 IF B$(I,(J-14))=Q$ THEN I=T:F=1:M=1:GOTO 550
465 GOTO 480
470 IF C$(I,(J-28))=Q$ THEN I=T:F=1:M=1:GOTO 550
480 FOR K=1 TO N
510 IF T$(K)=A$(I,0) THEN GOSUB 900
540 NEXT K
550 NEXT I
560 IF F=0 THEN GOSUB 1000
570 IF R=0 THEN J=42
580 NEXT J
600 PRINT"⊐  1         10        20        30"
610 PRINT"  ├┬┬┬┬┬┬┬┬┬┼┬┬┬┬┬┬┬┬┬┼┬┬┬┬┬┬┬┬┬┼┬┬┬┬┬┬┬"
700 FOR I=1 TO T
710 FOR J=37 TO 0 STEP -1
720 IF J>28 THEN 760
730 IF J>14 THEN 750
735 IF J=0 THEN PRINT A$(I,J):GOTO 770
740 PRINT TAB(J+1);A$(I,J):GOTO 770
750 IF B$(I,J-14)="" THEN 780
751 PRINT TAB(J+1);B$(I,J-14):GOTO 770
760 IF C$(I,J-28)="" THEN 780
761 PRINT TAB(J+1);C$(I,J-28)
770 PRINT"⊓"
780 NEXT J
785 PRINT
790 NEXT I
795 PRINT"  ├┬┬┬┬┬┬┬┬┬┼┬┬┬┬┬┬┬┬┬┼┬┬┬┬┬┬┬┬┬┼┬┬┬┬┬┬┬"
796 PRINT"   1         10        20        30"
800 IF M=0 THEN L=L+1:L$(L)=Q$+"="+P$
820 M=0:PRINT
830 FOR I=24 TO 1 STEP -1
840 IF L$(I)="" THEN 885
845 IF I>18 THEN J=I-19:GOTO 880
850 IF I>12 THEN J=I-13:GOTO 880
860 IF I>6 THEN J=I-7:GOTO 880
870 J=I-1
880 PRINT TAB(6*J);L$(I);"⊓"
882 IF I=7 THEN PRINT
883 IF I=13 THEN PRINT
884 IF I=19 THEN PRINT
885 NEXT I:PRINT
890 FOR K=1 TO N:T$(K)="":NEXT K
895 PRINT"NEXT ENTRY:":GOTO 355
900 IF J>28 THEN 940
910 IF J>14 THEN 930
920 IF A$(I,J)<>"" THEN F=1:K=N:I=T:RETURN
925 GOTO 950
930 IF B$(I,J-14)<>"" THEN F=1:K=N:I=T:RETURN
935 GOTO 950
940 IF C$(I,J-28)<>"" THEN F=1:K=N:I=T:RETURN
950 Z(I)=0:RETURN
1000 FOR I=1 TO T
1010 IF J>28 THEN 1050
```

```
1020 IF J>14 THEN 1040
1030 IF Z(I)=0 THEN A$(I,J)=Q$:GOTO 1060
1040 IF Z(I)=0 THEN B$(I,J-14)=Q$:GOTO 1060
1050 IF Z(I)=0 THEN C$(I,J-28)=Q$
1060 NEXT I
1070 R=R-1
1080 RETURN
1100 PRINT"PLEASE ENTER A LABEL"
1110 PRINT"E.G. NAME OF DEPARTMENT AND THE DATE"
1120 INPUT Y$
1130 OPEN 1,4
1135 PRINT#1,Y$:PRINT#1:PRINT#1
1140 PRINT#1,"    1         10        20        30        40"
1150 PRINT#1,"    ├┬┬┬┬┬┬┬┬┬┼┬┬┬┬┬┬┬┬┬┼┬┬┬┬┬┬┬┬┬┼┬┬┬┬┬┬┬┬┬┤"
1160 FOR I=1 TO T
1170 FOR J=0 TO 14
1180 IF A$(I,J)="" THEN PRINT#1," ";
1190 PRINT#1,A$(I,J);
1200 NEXT J
1210 FOR J=1 TO 14
1220 IF B$(I,J)="" THEN PRINT#1," ";
1230 PRINT#1,B$(I,J);
1240 NEXT J
1250 FOR J=1 TO 14
1260 IF C$(I,J)="" THEN PRINT#1," ";
1270 PRINT#1,C$(I,J);
1280 NEXT J
1290 PRINT#1
1300 NEXT I
1310 PRINT#1,"    ├┬┬┬┬┬┬┬┬┬┼┬┬┬┬┬┬┬┬┬┼┬┬┬┬┬┬┬┬┬┼┬┬┬┬┬┬┬┬┬┤"
1320 PRINT#1,"    1         10        20        30        40"
1325 PRINT#1
1330 FOR I=1 TO 24
1340 PRINT#1,L$(I)" ";
1350 IF I=8 OR I=16 THEN PRINT#1
1360 NEXT I
1370 PRINT#1:CLOSE1
1380 END
READY.
```

Appendix 12

TT3 — The Conflict Matrix

Input

From the keyboard. You will need your master Curriculum Plan showing the proposed teacher teams. (You may also need the proposed period-breakdown for each team, but this is optional). The program allows you to enter all the teams for two or more bands, half-year-groups or year-groups (up to 9 bands on an 8K PET) and then later you can choose for which pairs you wish to have the conflict matrices displayed or printed.

Sample output

```
4A      AGAINST    4B
        1     2     3     4     5     6     7     8     9
   1 |JWBH|*   |*   |    |    |    |    |* FH|*   |
        |JMPH|   |   |    |    |    |    |    |    |
   2 |*   |BJDS|*  |*   |*   |*   |*   |* DA|* DS|
        |    |DAJR|   |    |    |    |    |    |    |
   3 |*   |*   |LM  |*   |*   |*   |*   |*   |*   |
   4 |    |*   |*   |HBAK|    |HBMF|    |*   |*   |
   5 |    |*   |*   |    |    |    |    |*   |*   |
   6 |    |*   |*   |    |RC  |    |    |*   |*   |
   7 |    |*   |*   |HB  |    |HB  |    |*   |*   |
   8 |* FH|* DA|*   |*   |*   |*   |*   |FHDA|*   |
   9 |*   |*   |*   |*   |*   |*   |* MP|*   |    |
     * =DIFFERENT PERIOD-BREAKDOWN
```

Entering the information

The program asks for the number of bands, half-year-groups or year-groups that you intend to enter. The maximum is 9 in this 8K version. This will usually be enough (even if you have 3 bands in the 4th and 5th Years as well as an Upper Sixth, Lower Sixth and General Sixth). If you have a 16K or 32K PET this number can be increased (see changes detailed below).

The maximum number of teacher-teams (in any band) that can be displayed on the screen is 7. However if a printer is fitted, this number can be as large as 14.

TT3 – The Conflict Matrix

The maximum number of teachers in any one of these teacher-teams is limited by the available memory; it is calculated by the PET and shown on the screen; even an 8K PET should cope with all but the largest schools.

You can choose to enter:
   either (a) just the (initials of the) teachers in the teacher-teams;
     or (b) these teachers *and* the proposed period-breakdown for each team.

If method (a) is chosen, each cell of the matrix shows the initials of the teachers causing the clash (see the sample output and chapter 6). Up to 4 teachers may be shown in each cell.

If method (b) is chosen, each cell of the matrix will show an asterisk *if the period-breakdown is not identical.* (Up to 3 teachers may be shown in addition.)

Please note that an asterisk appears whenever the period-breakdown is not identical — it does not necessarily indicate a real clash. For example, if one team required three doubles (entered as DDD) and a team in another band required two doubles (entered as DD), then this would be shown by an asterisk (although they would not be incompatible in the same way that DD would be incompatible with SSSS). The sample output shows a large number of asterisks for this reason.

For these reasons it is usually preferable to enter only the basic period structure. e.g. enter only D if it is taught essentially in doubles; enter only S if it must be taught mainly in singles etc.

If you do enter the full period-breakdown, enter the code in descending order e.g. DDS, not SDD; TS, not ST.

When the program asks for the usual name of the year/band, a two-character code is usually sufficient, e.g. 4A, 6L, 6U.
When the program later asks for the names of the groups for which a matrix is to be drawn, you must be sure to use exactly these same names.

If you wish to include special equipment or rooms in the matrix (see section 6.5) then you must enter these when you enter the teachers' initials (by giving the equipment and rooms their own unique two-letter code).

If you have a 16K or 32K PET (or 8K with the new ROM-set) then the program can be simplified : remove all references to Z>5, Z>2, F>5, F>2, G>5, G>2, B$, C$; and change line 250: DIM A$ (X1, Y1, Z1). (Users of machines other than a PET should note that I have used the zeroth rows of the arrays and this may not be possible on your machine.)

The listing
The following special symbols are included:

'clear'   lines 10. 100. 270. 310. 350. 600. 800

194 *Appendix 12*

'cursor down'	lines 10, 40, 70, 150, 200, 280, 375, 380, 385, 460, 490 630, 650
'cursor left'	line 1100
'reverse field'	line 350

```
10 PRINT"◼◼◼          TT3-CONFLICT MATRIX"
20 PRINT"             ─────────────────"
30 PRINT"       (C)1979 KEITH JOHNSON"
40 PRINT"◼◼◼TO DISPLAY THE CLASHES BETWEEN"
50 PRINT"YOUR TEACHER TEAMS."
70 PRINT"◼◼◼DO YOU HAVE A PRINTER CONNECTED?"
80 PRINT"PLEASE ANSWER   YES OR   NO"
90 INPUT Q$
95 IF Q$="YES" OR Q$="NO" THEN 100
96 GOTO 80
100 PRINT"◼HOW MANY BANDS OR HALF-YEAR-GROUPS"
110 PRINT"OR YEAR-GROUPS DO YOU WISH TO ENTER?"
120 PRINT"(THE MAXIMUM IS 9 FOR THIS 8K VERSION)"
130 INPUT Z1
150 PRINT"◼◼WHAT IS THE MAXIMUM NUMBER OF"
160 PRINT"TEACHER TEAMS IN ANY OF THESE"
170 PRINT"BANDS OR YEAR-GROUPS?"
180 PRINT"(ON THIS SCREEN THE MAXIMUM IS 7)"
190 INPUT Y1
200 PRINT"◼◼WHAT IS THE MAXIMUM NUMBER OF"
210 PRINT"TEACHERS IN ANY OF YOUR TEACHER"
220 PRINT"TEAMS (THE MAXIMUM FOR AN 8K PET"
230 PRINT"IS "INT((85/Y1)-1)
240 INPUT X1
250 DIM A$(X1,Y1,2),B$(X1,Y1,2),P$(20),T$(Z1),X$(X1,Y1,1),Q$(20)
260 IF Z1>6 THEN DIM C$(X1,Y1,2)
270 PRINT"◼ARE YOU GOING TO ENTER:"
280 PRINT"◼ 1-TEACHERS' INITIALS AND THE"
285 PRINT "    PERIOD-BREAKDOWN OF THE SUBJECT,OR"
290 PRINT " 2-JUST THE TEACHERS' INITIALS"
295 INPUT M
296 IF M<1 OR M>2 THEN 270
300 FOR Z=0 TO Z1-1
310 PRINT"◼PLEASE GIVE THE USUAL NAME OF"
320 PRINT"THIS YEAR/BAND ("Z+1")"
330 INPUT T$(Z)
340 FOR Y=0 TO Y1-1
350 PRINT"◼◼FOR TEAM "Y+1" IN THIS YEAR/BAND "T$(Z)
355 IF M=2 THEN 385
360 PRINT"ENTER THE PERIOD-BREAKDOWN USING"
370 PRINT"CODE: Q T D S IN DESCENDING ORDER"
375 PRINT"◼E.G.   DDS"
380 PRINT"◼FOR MORE DETAILS,SEE KEITH JOHNSON'S"
381 PRINT"BOOK: 'TIMETABLING' (HUTCHINSON LTD)"
385 PRINT"◼IF THERE ARE NO MORE TEAMS IN "T$(Z)
390 PRINT"THEN PRESS     =   ('RETURN')"
392 IF M=2 THEN N$="S":GOTO 410
395 INPUT N$
400 IF N$="=" THEN Y=(Y1-1):GOTO 595
410 IF Z>5 THEN 450
420 IF Z>2 THEN 440
430 A$(0,Y,Z)=N$:GOTO 460
440 B$(0,Y,Z-3)=N$:GOTO 460
450 C$(0,Y,Z-6)=N$
```

TT3 - The Conflict Matrix

```
460 PRINT"XXNOW ENTER THE TEACHERS IN THIS TEAM"
470 PRINT"(TEAM "Y+1" IN "T$(Z)")"
480 PRINT"USING A 2-LETTER CODE"
490 PRINT"XE.G.   KJMJCKBA        ('RETURN')"
500 INPUT N$
510 IF N$="=" THEN Y=(Y1-1):GOTO595
520 N=(LEN(N$)/2)
530 FOR X=1 TO N
540 IF Z>5 THEN 580
550 IF Z>2 THEN 570
560 A$(X,Y,Z)=MID$(N$,((2*X)-1),2):GOTO 590
570 B$(X,Y,Z-3)=MID$(N$,((2*X)-1),2):GOTO 590
580 C$(X,Y,Z-6)=MID$(N$,((2*X)-1),2)
590 NEXT X
595 NEXT Y:NEXT Z
600 PRINT"JNOW THAT YOU HAVE ENTERED ALL YOUR"
610 PRINT"DATA YOU CAN CHOOSE TO DISPLAY THE"
620 PRINT"CONFLICT MATRIX BETWEEN ANY PAIR."
630 PRINT"XWHICH PAIR DO YOU WISH TO DISPLAY?"
640 PRINT"ENTER: YEAR/BAND  COMMA  YEAR/BAND"
650 PRINT"XE.G.    5A,4A    ('RETURN')"
660 INPUT F$,G$
670 FOR Z=0 TO Z1-1
680 IF T$(Z)=F$ THEN F=Z
690 IF T$(Z)=G$ THEN G=Z
695 NEXT Z
700 FOR Y=0 TO Y1-1
710 FOR X=0 TO X1
720 IF F>5 THEN 760
730 IF F>2 THEN 750
740 X$(X,Y,0)=A$(X,Y,F):GOTO 770
750 X$(X,Y,0)=B$(X,Y,F-3):GOTO 770
760 X$(X,Y,0)=C$(X,Y,F-6)
770 IF G>5 THEN 790
775 IF G>2 THEN 785
780 X$(X,Y,1)=A$(X,Y,G):GOTO 795
785 X$(X,Y,1)=B$(X,Y,G-3):GOTO 795
790 X$(X,Y,1)=C$(X,Y,G-6)
795 NEXT X:NEXT Y
800 PRINT"J"F$"        AGAINST       "G$
803 PRINT"         1    2    3    4    5    6    7"
805 PRINT"        ┌──────────────────────────────┐"
807 GOSUB1300
810 FOR J=0 TO Y1-1
815 GOSUB 1200
820 FOR Y=0 TO Y1-1
825 P=2*Y
830 FOR I=0 TO X1
840 FOR X=0 TO X1
850 IF I=0 AND X=0 THEN I=1:GOSUB 1000:GOTO 960
855 IF X$(I,J,0)="" THEN 960
860 IF X$(I,J,0)=X$(X,Y,1) THEN 910
900 GOTO 960
910 IF P>(2*Y)+3 THEN X=X1:GOTO960
920 IF P=(2*Y)+3 THEN Q$(P-2)=X$(I,J,0):GOTO 955
930 IF P=(2*Y)+2 THEN P$(P-1)=X$(I,J,0):GOTO 955
940 IF P=(2*Y)+1 THEN Q$(P-1)=X$(I,J,0):GOTO 955
950 P$(P)=X$(I,J,0)
955 P=P+1
960 NEXT X:NEXT I:NEXT Y
970 GOSUB 1100
975 GOSUB 1400
980 NEXT J
982 IF M=2 THEN 995
```

196 *Appendix* 12

```
984 M$="    * =DIF
985 PRINTM$
990 OPEN 1,4
991 PRINT#1:PRINT#
994 PRINT#1:PRINT#
995 PRINT"NEXT PAI
997 GOTO 660
1000 IF X$(0,J,0)=
1010 IF X$(0,J,0)<
1020 RETURN
1100 PRINT J+1"▊I"
1105 FOR P=0 TO 12
1110 PRINT P$(P);Q
1120 NEXT P
1123 PRINT
1125 PRINT "   I";
1130 FOR P=1 TO 13
1140 PRINT P$(P);Q
1150 NEXT P
1160 PRINT
1165 PRINT"    ┝───
1180 RETURN
1200 FOR P=0 TO 20
1210 P$(P)="    "
1220 Q$(P)="    "
1230 NEXT P
1240 RETURN
1300 IF Q$<>"YES"
1305 OPEN 1,4
1310 OPEN 2,4,6:PR
1312 PRINT#1:PRINT
1315 PRINT#1,F$"
1320 PRINT#1,"V
1330 PRINT#1,"
1340 PRINT#1,"      "
1350 CLOSE1:CLOSE2
1360 RETURN
1400 IF Q$<>"YES"
1410 OPEN 1,4
1415 OPEN 2,4,6:PR
1420 PRINT#1,(J+1)
1430 FOR P=0 TO ((
1440 PRINT#1,P$(P)
1450 NEXT P
1460 PRINT#1
1470 PRINT#1,"   I
1480 FOR P=1 TO ((
1490 PRINT#1,P$(P)
1500 NEXT P
1510 PRINT#1
1520 PRINT#1,"      "
1530 CLOSE1:CLOSE2
1540 RETURN
READY.
```

Appendix 13

TT4 — Zarraga's Rule

Input

From the keyboard. You will need your master Curriculum Plan showing the initials of the proposed teachers.

Output

The program finds the teachers who are in *parallel* in teacher teams and in *series* for pure class activities (see section 8.2) and lists them on the screen or on a printer. The timetabler can then consider what changes may be made to the staffing of the pure class activities in order to gain flexibility for the scheduling stage.

Sample output

```
THESE     ARE IN   SERIES  AND  PARALLEL
TEACHERS           IN           IN

KJBACKMJ           1A           4A TEAM 1
KJBACK             1A           4A TEAM 2
CKMJ               1B           4A TEAM 1
```

Entering the information

All the steps are explained clearly on the screen.

If any class is to be split or shared between two teachers in any way, both teachers' initials should be entered.

As explained on the screen an = sign can be entered if you want a quick exit. It can be used:
  (a) if, within any of the year/bands, you have entered all the parallel teams and wish to move on to the next year/band;
  or
  (b) if you have entered all the year/bands which have parallel teams and want to move on to part B;
  or
  (c) if you have entered all the teachers for all the pure class activities and you want the program to begin processing the data.

198   Appendix 13

If you do not have a printer and wish to copy the results from the screen then as it prints at the end: 'Press any key to repeat the display'. You can press 'RVS' to slow down the display. Alternatively, you can press 'stop' and later type CONT ('return').

The listing
The following special symbols are used:

'clear'	lines 10, 100, 400, 600, 725, 740
'cursor down'	lines 25, 40, 55, 60, 70, 140, 200, 310, 340, 440, 460, 500, 540, 596, 630, 650, 690, 970
'reverse field'	lines 30, 45, 400, 440, 510, 600, 630, 700
'reverse field off'	lines 510, 700

```
10 PRINT"◻          TT4-ZARRAGA'S RULE"
15 PRINT"          ̄ ̄ ̄ ̄ ̄ ̄ ̄ ̄ ̄ ̄ ̄ ̄ ̄ ̄ ̄ "
20 PRINT"         (C)1979 KEITH JOHNSON"
25 PRINT"▼THIS PROGRAM COMPARES THE TEAMS WHERE"
30 PRINT"YOUR TEACHERS ARE IN ▮PARALLEL"
35 PRINT"(E.G. IN OPTION POOLS),"
40 PRINT"▼WITH CLASSES WHERE YOUR TEACHERS"
45 PRINT"ARE IN ▮SERIES"
50 PRINT"(E.G. PURE CLASS ACTIVITIES IN LOWER    SCHOOL)"
55 PRINT"▼SO THAT YOU CAN FIND MORE FLEXIBILITY"
57 PRINT"BEFORE BEGINNING SCHEDULING."
60 PRINT"▼FOR MORE DETAILS,SEE KEITH JOHNSON'S"
65 PRINT"BOOK:   'TIMETABLING' (HUTCHINSON LTD)"
70 PRINT"▼HAVE YOU GOT A PRINTER CONNECTED?"
75 PRINT"PLEASE ANSWER  YES  OR  NO"
80 INPUT Q$
90 IF Q$="YES" OR Q$="NO"THEN 100
95 GOTO75
100 PRINT"◻THE STAFFING INFORMATION IS TO BE"
110 PRINT"ENTERED IN 2 PARTS:"
120 PRINT"PART A   FOR ENTERING THE NAMES OF"
125 PRINT"  ̄ ̄ ̄ ̄ ̄   THE TEACHERS IN THE PARALLEL"
127 PRINT"         TEACHER TEAMS (FOR OPTION"
130 PRINT"         POOLS,MATHS SETS ETC.)"
140 PRINT"▼ENTER A NUMBER EQUAL TO OR GREATER THAN"
150 PRINT"THE NUMBER OF BANDS,HALF-YEAR-GROUPS"
160 PRINT"OR YEAR-GROUPS WHICH HAVE TEAMS OF"
170 PRINT"TEACHERS IN PARALLEL"
180 INPUT K1
200 PRINT"▼NOW ENTER A NUMBER EQUAL TO OR GREATER"
210 PRINT"THAN THE NUMBER OF TEACHER-TEAMS IN"
220 PRINT"ANY ONE OF THESE BANDS OR YEAR-GROUPS"
230 INPUT J1
310 PRINT"▼PART B   FOR ENTERING THE NAMES OF THE"
320 PRINT"  ̄ ̄ ̄ ̄ ̄    TEACHERS IN THE PURE CLASS"
330 PRINT"         ACTIVITIES IN THE LOWER SCHOOL"
340 PRINT"▼ENTER A NUMBER EQUAL TO OR GREATER THAN"
350 PRINT"THE NUMBER OF CLASSES WHERE THIS APPLIES"
370 PRINT"E.G. CLASSES 1A,1B,1C COUNT AS 3"
380 INPUT Y1
390 DIM P$(K1,J1),S$(2,Y1)
400 PRINT"◻▮PART A"
410 PRINT"(ENTERING THE NAMES OF TEACHERS IN THE"
```

```
420 PRINT"TEAMS FOR OPTION POOLS,SETS ETC.)"
430 FOR K=1 TO K1
440 PRINT"XXFIRST ENTER THE NAME OF THE YEAR/BAND"
450 PRINT"E.G.     4A"
460 PRINT"X(IF YOU HAVE ENTERED ALL YOUR"
470 PRINT"YEAR/BANDS, ENTER  =  )"
480 INPUT P$(K,0)
490 IF P$(K,0)="=" THEN K=K1:GOTO 597
500 PRINT"XNOW FOR YEAR/BAND "P$(K,0)" ENTER"
510 PRINT"THE TEACHERS IN EACH TEAM USING A"
520 PRINT"2-LETTER CODE:"
530 PRINT"E.G.    KJMJCKBA      ('RETURN')"
540 PRINT"X(WHEN YOU HAVE ENTERED ALL THE TEAMS"
550 PRINT"FOR "P$(K,0)" ENTER   =  )"
560 FOR J=1 TO J1
570 PRINT"TEAM ";J
580 INPUT P$(K,J)
590 IF P$(K,J)="=" THEN J=J1
595 NEXT J
596 PRINT"XXXXFOR THE NEXT YEAR/BAND:"
597 NEXT K
600 PRINT"JPART B"
610 PRINT"ENTERING THE NAMES OF TEACHERS FOR"
615 PRINT"PURE CLASS ACTIVITIES"
620 FOR Y=1 TO Y1
630 PRINT"XXENTER THE NAME OF THE CLASS OR FORM"
640 PRINT"E.G.     1A"
650 PRINT"X(AFTER YOU HAVE ENTERED ALL YOUR"
660 PRINT"CLASSES, ENTER   =  )"
670 INPUT S$(1,Y)
680 IF S$(1,Y)="=" THEN Y=Y1:GOTO 730
690 PRINT"XNOW FOR FORM "S$(1,Y)" ENTER THE NAMES"
700 PRINT"OF THE TEACHERS,USING A 2-LETTER CODE:"
710 PRINT"E.G.    KJCKBAMJ      ('RETURN')"
720 INPUT S$(2,Y)
725 PRINT"JFOR THE NEXT CLASS:"
730 NEXT Y
740 PRINT"JTHESE     ARE IN    SERIES AND PARALLEL"
750 PRINT"TEACHERS            IN      IN"
760 IF Q$<>"YES" THEN 800
770 OPEN 1,4
780 PRINT#1,"THESE    ARE IN    SERIES  AND  PARALLEL"
790 PRINT#1,"TEACHERS          IN           IN"
795 PRINT#1:CLOSE 1
800 FOR Y=1 TO Y1
810 S=LEN(S$(2,Y))
820 FOR K=1 TO K1
830 FOR J=1 TO J1
835 T=1
840 P=LEN(P$(K,J))
850 FOR X=1 TO S STEP 2
860 N$=MID$(S$(2,Y),X,2)
870 FOR I=1 TO P STEP 2
880 IF MID$(P$(K,J),I,2)=N$ THEN T$(T)=N$:T=T+1:I=P
890 NEXT I
900 NEXT X
910 IF T>2 THEN GOSUB 1000
920 FOR I=1 TO T:T$(I)="":NEXT I
940 NEXT J:NEXT K:NEXT Y
970 PRINT"XPRESS ANY KEY TO REPEAT THE DISPLAY"
980 GET A$:IF A$="" THEN 980
990 GOTO 740
1000 FOR I=1 TO T
1010 PRINT T$(I);
1020 NEXT I
1030 PRINT"     ",S$(1,Y),P$(K,0);"TEAM";J
```

```
1040 IF Q$<>"YES" THEN 1150
1100 OPEN 1,4
1110 FOR I=1 TO T
1120 PRINT#1,T$(I);
1130 NEXT I
1135 PRINT#1,CHR$(141);
1140 PRINT#1,TAB(19)S$(1,Y),P$(K,0);" TEAM";J
1150 CLOSE 1
1160 RETURN
READY.
```

Appendix 14

TT5 — Timetable memory

This program is for use while you are scheduling. If you are trying to fit a team of several teachers and wish to find the times of the week when they are all free, this program will tell you those times.

Entering the information

As it stands, the program will work with either a 35-period week or a 40-period week. It can be used as it stands with other timeframes but the output will not be as tidy.

For each teacher in turn (in the team that you are trying to fit) scan down your partly-completed timetable and enter the times when he or she is already scheduled to teach:
e.g. enter   14 for Monday period 4
                 15 for Monday period 5
                 25 for Tuesday period 5
                 234 for Tuesday periods 3 and 4
                 546 for Friday periods 4 and 6
Up to two periods at a time may be entered as shown in these examples.

On pressing = ('return') the screen shows only those periods (if any) when all the members of the team are free.

Then pressing any key allows you to add more data if you wish.
This is useful if you know or suspect that there are no periods when they are all free, but you wish to find those periods when almost all of the teachers are free so that you can begin to try to free the remainder. In this case enter the data in stages:
either (a)   one teacher at a time, the most essential person first;
    or (b)   one class at a time, the most immovable class first.
By pressing = ('return') after each entry you can see how the available periods diminish, and which periods offer you the most hope for clearing by the musical chairs moves shown in chapter 9.

The listing
The following special symbols are used:

'clear'   lines 10, 2000

'cursor down'   lines 20, 50, 70, 75, 80, 100, 2300

```
10 PRINT"]        TT5-TIMETABLE MEMORY"
15 PRINT"                                "
18 PRINT"       (C)KEITH JOHNSON 1979"
20 PRINT"XX   THIS PROGRAM WILL HELP YOU TO"
30 PRINT"    FIND THE PERIODS WHEN ALL THE"
40 PRINT"    MEMBERS OF A TEAM ARE FREE."
50 PRINT"X   FOR EACH TEACHER TIMETABLED,ENTER "
60 PRINT"    THE DAY AND UP TO 2 PERIODS,"
65 PRINT"    AS FOLLOWS:"
70 PRINT"X   13 FOR MONDAY,PERIOD 3"
71 PRINT"    23 FOR TUESDAY,PERIOD 3"
72 PRINT"    256 FOR TUESDAY,PERIODS 5 & 6"
75 PRINT"XX   ENTER '=' TO PROCESS THE DATA"
80 PRINT"XXIS YOUR SCHOOL WEEK?"
82 PRINT"    1 =35 PERIODS"
84 PRINT"    2 =40 PERIODS"
86 INPUT A:IF A<1 OR A>2 THEN 80
90 DIM N$(44)
100 PRINT"XXENTER DAY+PERIOD(S)"
110 INPUT A$
200 D$=LEFT$(A$,1)
210 P$=MID$(A$,2,1)
220 Q$=MID$(A$,3,1)
250 IF A=2 THEN 300
260 FOR X=1 TO 5:N$((9*X)-1)="1":NEXT X
300 IF D$="1"THEN D$="MON":P=VAL(P$):Q=VAL(Q$):GOTO 1000
310 IF D$="2"THEN D$="TUES":P=9+VAL(P$):Q=9+VAL(Q$):GOTO 1000
320 IF D$="3"THEN D$="WED":P=18+VAL(P$):Q=18+VAL(Q$):GOTO 1000
330 IF D$="4"THEN D$="THURS":P=27+VAL(P$):Q=27+VAL(Q$):GOTO 1000
340 IF D$="5"THEN D$="FRI":P=36+VAL(P$):Q=36+VAL(Q$):GOTO 1000
345 IF D$="="GOTO 2000
350 PRINT"INCORRECT ENTRY":GOTO100
1000 PRINTTAB(20);D$;" ";P$;Q$
1100 N$(P)="1":N$(Q)="1"
1200 GOTO 100
2000 PRINT"]ALL THE MEMBERS OF THE TEAM ARE"
2001 PRINT"FREE AS FOLLOWS:"
2005 FOR I=1 TO 44
2010 IF N$(I)="" THEN GOSUB 3010
2020 NEXT I
2300 PRINT"XPRESS ANY KEY TO ADD MORE DATA"
2305 PRINT"(PRESS 'STOP' TO END)"
2310 GET G$:IF G$="" GOTO 2310
2320 GOTO 100
3010 IF I<9 THEN PRINT"MON "I
3020 IF I>9 AND I<18 THEN PRINT"TUES "I-9
3030 IF I>18 AND I<27 THEN PRINT"WED "I-18
3040 IF I>27 AND I<36 THEN PRINT"THURS "I-27
3050 IF I>36 THEN PRINT"FRI "I-36
3100 RETURN
READY.
```

Appendix 15

TT6 — Printing individual timetables

Input

From the keyboard. You will need your completed timetable. This program is too large to run on an 8K PET.

Output

The program prints out (on a printer) timetables for
(a) each class
(b) each teacher
(c) each room that you specify (this need not be all the rooms)

For each of these you are asked to specify the number of copies that you want printed.

In addition, two lists are printed. These show, for each period in the week,
(d) the names of 'free' staff (this list is needed for covering for staff absence)
(e) the numbers of the rooms that are empty (this list is useful when rearranging rooms for external examinations, etc.)

Sample output

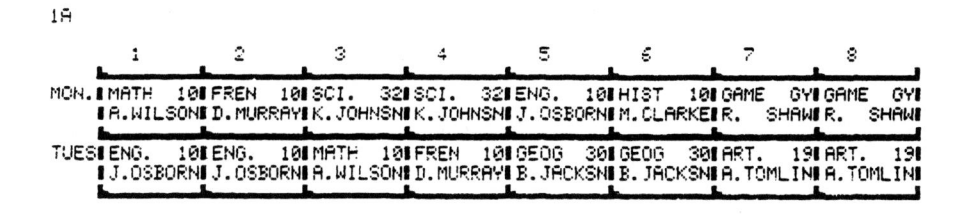

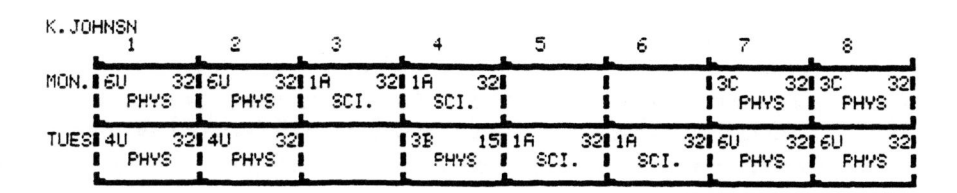

```
1A
          1         2         3         4         5         6         7         8
MON.  MATH   10 FREN  10 SCI.  32 SCI.  32 ENG.  10 HIST  10 GAME  GY GAME  GY
      A.WILSON D.MURRAY K.JOHNSN K.JOHNSN J.OSBORN M.CLARKE R.  SHAW  R.  SHAW

TUES  ENG.   10 ENG.  10 MATH  10 FREN  10 GEOG  30 GEOG  30 ART.  19 ART.  19
      J.OSBORN J.OSBORN A.WILSON D.MURRAY B.JACKSN B.JACKSN A.TOMLIN A.TOMLIN


K.JOHNSN
          1         2         3         4         5         6         7         8
MON.  6U    32 6U    32 1A    32 1A    32            3C    32 3C    32
      PHYS     PHYS     SCI.    SCI.                 PHYS     PHYS

TUES  4U    32 4U    32       3B    15 1A    32 1A    32 6U    32 6U    32
      PHYS     PHYS          PHYS    SCI.    SCI.    PHYS     PHYS
```

204 *Appendix 15*

```
▮STAFF▮ROOM▮TEACHING▮
▮MONDAY▮
PERIOD 1
DM.JO.BJ.AT.
PERIOD 2
AW.KJ.JO.RS.
PERIOD 3
AW.DM.RS.BJ.AT.
```

```
ROOM 10
          1       2       3       4       5       6       7       8
MON. ▮A.WILSON▮D.MURRAY▮J.OSBORN▮J.OSBORN▮J.OSBORN▮M.CLARKE▮M.CLARKE▮M.CLARKE▮
     ▮1A  MATH▮1A  FREN▮3A   ENG▮3A   ENG▮1A   ENG▮1A  HIST▮3A  HIST▮3A  HIST▮
TUES ▮J.OSBORN▮J.OSBORN▮A.WILSON▮D.MURRAY▮J.OSBORN▮J.OSBORN▮        ▮        ▮
     ▮1A   ENG▮1A   ENG▮1A  MATH▮1A  FREN▮2D   ENG▮2D   ENG▮        ▮        ▮
```

```
▮FREE▮ROOMS▮
▮MONDAY▮
PERIOD 1
05.30.
PERIOD 2
32.24.
PERIOD 3
05.30.24.
```

Time required

Perhaps 3 hours to type in the data if you have a helper to read it out. Printing can take a long time so it is wise to begin early in the day.

Disadvantage

Unfortunately, at present, this program is not as useful as it might seem. This is because of the large amount of memory required to store the data. Even a 32K machine is too small for most comprehensive schools. There are ways of overcoming this (they are detailed below) but this program will not be really useful until the larger machines arrive.

* *

Entering the information

The printout can be chosen to be:
    1. *continuous,* with only four-line gaps between timetables;
or 2. *partly-paged,* so that the printer moves to a new page whenever it has printed a timetable needing more than half a page. (This allows many class-timetables and all teacher- and room-timetables to be printed two to a page);

TT6 – Printing individual timetables

or 3. *paged,* so that the printer starts a new page for each timetable. (This requires much more paper.)

If you choose 2 or 3, set the printing head near the top of a page on the continuous roll of paper.

The number of copies you request for (a) class-timetables, (b) teacher-timetables, or (c) room-timetables, can in each case be any number from zero upwards, but it is advisable not to overwork your printer. (You could take one copy and photocopy others.) For class timetables will two be enough (for the Form Tutor and form noticeboard)? For Staff Timetables, who else will need a copy besides the teacher, the Head, the Deputies, the School Office?

For room timetables will one copy be sufficient?

When you are asked for the number of rooms, this should be the number of rooms:
  (i) for which you want a room timetable *and*
  (ii) which will be included in the list of free rooms.
(These two categories are identical.)

You need not include all your rooms unless you wish to.

You have the choice of
  1. a standard 40-period week (5 days × 8 periods); or
  2. a standard 35-period week (5 days × 7 periods); or
  3. any other arrangement. If you choose this last alternative you will be asked the number of days in your school week and then have to name them, using *four* characters for each. For example, you can type DAY1 or MON. (Note that it must be MON. or MON- not just MON). You will then be asked the number of periods in your school day. If you have a system where the number of periods per day varies, enter the largest number.

You have to enter the name of each class, using a *two*-character code
  e.g. 1A ('return')   or   6U ('return')

The order of entry here determines the order of printing later.

You have to enter: a two-character code for each teacher, comma, with the name to be printed limited to exactly *eight* characters (including full stops). If the name is short then you can pad it out with blanks provided these do not come at the beginning or the end. A grid is printed on the screen as a guide to length.
  e.g.   KJ,K.JOHNSN   ('return')
  e.g.   JT,JTOMLNSN   ('return')
  e.g.   MD,M.   DODD   ('return')

The order of entry here determines the order of printing later.

It asks for the actual numbers or names of the rooms that you wish to be considered by the program. These must be entered as two characters, e.g. 02 ('return'). You can use any two characters, e.g. L3 ('return').

It asks for a one-character code for each subject, comma, with the name to be

printed limited to exactly *four characters* (including full stops or hyphens).
e.g. P,PHYS   ('return')
e.g. N,N-WK   ('return')

Then the program asks you to enter the details of your timetable.

The screen specifies which period, on which day and for which class.

Each entry consists of: a one-character subject code,
                          a two-character teacher code,
                          a two character room code,   in that order.

e.g. PKJ32 ('return')

Note 1
If there is a team of teachers then the entry is made as a multiple of five. e.g. PKJ32CRW33BGW35 ('return')
The number of characters must be 5 or a multiple of 5 (see the grid on the screen). The maximum number of characters is 75 (corresponding to a team of 15 teachers).

Note 2
If for any period the entry is to be the same as for the last period (e.g. because it is a double period or a triple period) then simply enter: + ('return')

Note 3
If a team of teachers entered as in Note 1 is to teach two (or more) classes (in parallel) then the entry for the second class (or further classes) can be made quickly by entering = and the name of the first class. e.g. if the full entry of the teacher team has already been made for class 4A, and class 4B is to share the same teacher team for this period, then for 4B simply enter: =4A ('return') (with no space).

When all the periods have been entered, the program pauses and then starts printing (make sure your printer was switched on earlier!).

After all the printing, the program allows you to print extra copies if you wish (while the data is still stored in the memory). If you only want an extra list of the 'free' staff and free rooms then enter zero when asked for the number of class, staff and room timetables.

Copying with an inadequate size of memory

Until you get a machine which is large enough there are two ways of using the program:
1. Printing the timetables in *sections of time*. For example, printing two days of the week at a time. That is, you enter only two days of the timetable on each run and get a printout of just two days. This means you would have to add the sections of the timetables together at the end. (Scissors and a photocopier are a help.)

TT6 – Printing individual timetables

2. Printing the timetables in *sections of the school*. For example, entering and printing only the lower school timetable on your first run. In this case each class timetable would be complete but the staff and room timetable would have to be added together (and scissors and a photocopier would not be of much use this time).

An alternative would be to modify the program to write all the timetable data on a long tape (see lines 1000-1400 in OPT1). Then at each pass of the data tape the program could extract a few timetables (see lines 710-795 of OPT4). With a long data tape this sounds a tedious business — a floppy disc system would be much better.

The listing

The following special symbols appear:

'clear'	lines 500, 610, 700, 800, 970, 1100, 1150, 1270, 1380, 1530, 1760.
'cursor down'	lines 200, 250, 500, 530, 555, 570, 590, 610, 700, 710, 730, 750, 800, 805, 830, 860, 940, 980, 990, 1000, 1110, 1160, 1280, 1390, 1560, 1620, 1640, 1660, 1690, 1770, 1780.
'reverse field'	lines 25, 245, 410, 805, 830, 860, 880, 940, 1100, 1144, 1150, 1170, 1250, 1270, 1360, 1380, 1410, 1470, 1530, 1620, 1640, 1660, 1740, 2440, 2860.
'reverse field off'	lines 25, 860, 1170, 1410, 1530, 1620, 1640, 1660.

```
1 GOTO500
10 FORX=0TOP
11 IFX=0THEN15
12 IFLEN(Q$(X))<8THENQ$(X)=Q$(X)+" ":GOTO12
15 PRINT#1,Q$(X);"▌";:NEXTX:PRINT#1:F=F+1:RETURN
20 PRINT#1,V$;
25 FORX=1TOP:PRINT#1,"▌━━━━━━";:NEXTX:PRINT#1,"▌":F=F+1:RETURN
30 FORX=1TOP:PRINT#1,"        ";X;:NEXTX:PRINT#1:F=F+2
40 GOSUB20:RETURN
60 IFA=1THEN90
65 IFA=2ANDF<28THEN90
70 FORX=FTO(((INT(F/65))+1)*65)STEP2
80 PRINT#1,CHR$(13)
85 NEXTX:F=0
90 RETURN
110 DATA"MON ","TUES","WED ","THUR","FRI "
120 FORI=1TO5:READD$(I):NEXT:RETURN
150 P$(N,2)=C$(K):GOSUB370:GOSUB160:RETURN
160 FORX=1TOT
170 IFMID$(A$(N,K),((J*5)-3),2)=T$(1,X)THENP$(N,V)=P$(N,V)+T$(2,X):X=T
180 NEXTX:RETURN
200 PRINT"◖HOW MANY DAYS IN YOUR SCHOOL WEEK?
210 INPUTD:DIMD$(D)
220 PRINT"NOW ENTER THE NAMES OF THESE DAYS
225 PRINT"N.B. THEY MUST BE 4-CHARACTERS EACH!"
```

208 Appendix 15

```
230 PRINT"E.G.   DAY1  ('RETURN')
235 PRINT"E.G.   MON.  ('RETURN') (SEE BC
240 FORI=1TOD
242 INPUTD$(I)
245 IFLEN(D$(I))<>4THENPRINT"ERROR,REPE
247 NEXTI
250 PRINT"XHOW MANY PERIODS IN EACH DAY?
255 PRINT"(MAXIMUM=8)
260 INPUTP:RETURN
300 Q$=RIGHT$(A$(X,K),2)
310 FORY=1TOC:IFC$(Y)=Q$THENN=Y:Y=C
320 NEXTY
330 A$(X,K)=A$(X,N):RETURN
350 P$(N,1)=C$(K)
360 P$(N,2)=MID$(A$(N,K),((J*5)-1),2)
370 FORX=1TOS
380 IFMID$(A$(N,K),((J*5)-4),1)=S$(1,X)T
390 NEXTX:RETURN
400 FORI=1TOD
410 PRINT#1," "D$(I)"DAY"
420 FORX=1TOP
430 PRINT#1,"PERIOD"X
440 N=((I-1)*P)+X:M=LEN(P$(N,4)):IFM<2TH
450 FORY=1TO(M-1)STEP2
460 PRINT#1,MID$(P$(N,4),Y,2)".";
470 IFY=25THENPRINT#1
480 NEXTY:PRINT#1
490 NEXTX:PRINT#1:PRINT#1
495 NEXTI:F=F+(D*((P*2)+3))+1:GOSUB60:RE
500 PRINT"     TT6-PRINTING INDIVIDUAL 1
510 PRINT"
520 PRINT"       (C)KEITH JOHNSON 1979
530 PRINT"XXXFROM YOUR FULL TIMETABLE,TH
540 PRINT"WILL EXTRACT INDIVIDUAL TIMETA
550 PRINT"FOR CLASSES/STAFF/ROOMS AND TH
552 PRINT"LIST FREE STAFF AND ROOMS.
555 PRINT"XXXFOR MORE DETAILS,SEE THE BC
556 PRINT"'TIMETABLING' (HUTCHINSON LTD)
570 PRINT"XXXHAVE YOU GOT A PRINTER CONI
580 PRINT"WITH AMPLE PAPER LOADED?
590 PRINT"XPLEASE ENTER  YES  WHEN READY
600 INPUTQ$:IFQ$<>"YES"THEN590
610 PRINT"XDO YOU WANT YOUR PRINTOUT:"
620 PRINT"  1) CONTINUOUS (IGNORING FOLI
630 PRINT"  2) PARTLY PAGED (SEE THE BOC
635 PRINT"  3) PAGED (NEEDS MUCH MORE PA
640 INPUTA
650 IFA=2ORA=3THENPRINT"SET PRINTER HEAL
700 PRINT"XHOW MANY COPIES WILL YOU NEE
710 PRINT"X-OF THE CLASS TIMETABLES?
720 INPUTZ1
730 PRINT"X-OF THE TEACHER TIMETABLES?
740 INPUTZ2
750 PRINT"X-OF THE ROOM TIMETABLES?
760 INPUTZ3
770 IFV=5THEN1800
800 PRINT"XPLEASE ENTER:"
805 PRINT"X-THE TOTAL NUMBER OF CLASSE
810 PRINT" E.G.  1A,1B,4U,4L,6X,6L,6U =
820 INPUTC
830 PRINT"X-THE TOTAL NUMBER OF TEACHE
840 PRINT" (THE TOTAL NO. OF PEOPLE ON
850 INPUTT
860 PRINT"X-THE NUMBER OF ROOMS FOR W
870 PRINT" A) YOU NEED A ROOM TIMETABLE
```

TT6 – Printing individual timetable

```
880 PRINT"      RAND"
890 PRINT" B) YOU NEED INCLUDED ON THE LIST OF"
900 PRINT"    FREE ROOMS  (SEE THE BOOK)
910 PRINT" (YOU NEED NOT INCLUDE ALL YOUR ROOMS)"
930 INPUTR
940 PRINT"N-THE TOTAL NUMBER OF SUBJECTS"
950 PRINT" (THAT ARE MENTIONED ON THIS TIMETABLE)"
960 INPUTS
970 PRINT"PLEASE CHOOSE:"
980 PRINT"N 1 -STANDARD 40-PERIOD WEEK (5DY X 8PD)"
990 PRINT"N 2 -STANDARD 35-PERIOD WEEK (5DY X 7PD)"
1000 PRINT"N 3 -SOME OTHER SCHOOL WEEK"
1030 INPUTI
1040 IFI<1ORI>3THEN970
1050 IFI=1THEND=5:P=8:GOSUB110
1040 IFI<1ORI>3THEN970
1050 IFI=1THEND=5:P=8:GOSUB110
1060 IFI=2THEND=5:P=7:GOSUB110
1070 IFI=3THENGOSUB200
1080 DIMA$((P*D),C),T$(2,T),C$(C),R$(R),S$(2,S),P$((P*D),4)
1100 PRINT"NOW FOR THE"C" CLASSES:"
1110 PRINT"FOR EACH CLASS IN TURN,ENTER A"
1120 PRINT"2-CHARACTER NAME FOR EACH CLASS.
1130 PRINT"E.G.   1A   ('RETURN')"
1140 FORI=1TOC
1142 INPUTC$(I)
1144 IFLEN(C$(I))<>2THENPRINT"ERROR,REPEAT":GOTO1142
1146 NEXTI
1150 PRINT"NOW FOR THE"T" TEACHERS:"
1160 PRINT"FOR EACH TEACHER IN TURN,ENTER A"
1170 PRINT"2-CHARACTER CODE,COMMA, EIGHT-CHARACTER"
1180 PRINT"NAME TO BE PRINTED ON THE TIMETABLE"
1190 PRINT"(MORE DETAILS IN THE BOOK)
1200 PRINT"E.G.
1210 PRINT"   KJ,KJOHNSON    ('RETURN')
1212 PRINT"   KJ,K.JOHNSN    ('RETURN')
1214 PRINT"   MT,M. TODD     ('RETURN')
1220 FORI=1TOT
1230 PRINT"   ⊓,⊓⊓⊓⊓⊓⊓ ←GUIDE
1240 INPUTT$(1,I),T$(2,I)
1250 IFLEN(T$(2,I))<>8THENPRINT"REPEAT,8":GOTO1230
1260 NEXT
1270 PRINT"NOW FOR THE"R" ROOMS:"
1280 PRINT"ENTER A 2-CHARACTER NAME FOR"
1290 PRINT"EACH ROOM THAT YOU WISH TO BE"
1300 PRINT"CONSIDERED.
1310 PRINT"E.G.   02    ('RETURN')
1320 PRINT"E.G.   L1    ('RETURN')
1340 FORI=1TOR
1350 INPUTR$(I)
1360 IFLEN(R$(I))<>2THENPRINT"REPEAT,2":GOTO1350
1370 NEXT
1380 PRINT"NOW FOR THE"S" SUBJECTS:"
1390 PRINT"FOR EACH SUBJECT MENTIONED IN THE"
1400 PRINT"TIMETABLE,ENTER:"
1410 PRINT"ONE-CHARACTER CODE,COMMA, FOUR-CHARACTER"
1420 PRINT"NAME TO BE PRINTED"
1430 PRINT"E.G."
1435 PRINT"   P,PHYS"
1440 PRINT"   N,N-WK"
1445 PRINT"   &,ENG1"
1450 FORI=1TOS
1455 PRINT"   ⊓,⊓⊓⊓⊓ ←GUIDE
1460 INPUTS$(1,I),S$(2,I)
1470 IFLEN(S$(2,I))<>4THENPRINT"REPEAT,2,4":GOTO1460
```

```
1480 NEXT
1500 FORI=1TOD
1510 FORJ=1TOP
1520 FORK=1TOC
1530 PRINT"◻FOR ▮PERIOD"J"▮ON ▮"D$(I)"▮ FOR ▮CLASS"C$(K)
1540 IFI>1THEN1620
1550 IFI>2THEN1690
1560 PRINT"▮ENTER:"
1565 PRINT"        1-CHARACTER SUBJECT
1570 PRINT"        2-CHARACTER TEACHER
1580 PRINT"        2-CHARACTER ROOM.
1590 PRINT"E.G.
1600 PRINT"PKJ32            ('RETURN')
1610 PRINT"PKJ32PJS36       ('RETURN')
1620 PRINT"▮▮NOTE1:▮MUST BE 5-CHARACTER GROUP FOR"
1630 PRINT"EACH TEACHER  (MAX=15 TEACHERS)
1640 PRINT"▮▮NOTE2:▮USE +    ('RETURN') TO MAKE"
1650 PRINT"DOUBLES,TRIPLES ETC.  (SEE BOOK)
1660 PRINT"▮▮NOTE3:▮USE  =4A  ('RETURN') IF THIS"
1670 PRINT"CLASS,IN PARALLEL,HAS SAME STAFF AS 4A"
1690 PRINT"▮CHECK EACH ENTRY AGAINST THE GRID:"
1695 PRINT"  ⌐   ⌐   ⌐   ⌐   ⌐   ⌐   ⌐   ⌐   ⌐ "
1700 X=((I-1)*P)+J
1710 INPUTA$(X,K)
1720 IFA$(X,K)="+"THENA$(X,K)=A$(X-1,K):GOTO1750
1730 IFLEFT$(A$(X,K),1)="="THENGOSUB300:GOTO1750
1740 IF(INT((LEN(A$(X,K)))/5))*5<>LEN(A$(X,K))THENPRINT"▮NO-REPEAT":GOTO
1750 NEXTK:NEXTJ:NEXTI
1760 PRINT"◻ENTRY OF DATA IS NOW COMPLETE"
1770 PRINT"▮PRINTING WILL BEGIN SOON"
1780 PRINT"▮PLEASE BE PATIENT............"
1800 OPEN1,4
1810 V$="     "
1820 IFZ1=0THEN2200
1830 FORK=1TOC
1840 FORN=1TO(P*D)
1850 FORX=1TO4:P$(N,X)="":NEXTX
1860 M=((LEN(A$(N,K)))/5):V=2
1870 FORJ=1TOM
1880 FORX=1TOS
1890 IFMID$(A$(N,K),((J*5)-4),1)=S$(1,X)THENP$(N,1)=P$(N,1)+S$(2,X):X=S
1900 NEXTX
1910 IFJ>9THENV=3
1920 GOSUB160
1950 P$(N,4)=P$(N,4)+MID$(A$(N,K),((J*5)-1),2)
1960 NEXTJ:NEXTN
1970 FORZ=1TOZ1
1990 PRINT#1,C$(K):GOSUB30
2000 FORI=1TOD:V=2:M=0
2010 FORX=1TOP
2020 N=((LEN(P$(((I-1)*P)+X,1)))/4)
2030 IFM<NTHENM=N
2040 NEXTX
2050 Q$(0)=D$(I)
2060 FORY=1TOM:J=Y
2070 FORX=1TOP:N=((I-1)*P)+X
2080 Q$(X)=MID$(P$(N,1),((J*4)-3),4)+"  "+MID$(P$(N,4),((J*2)-1),2)
2090 NEXTX:GOSUB10
2100 Q$(0)=V$
2110 IFJ>9THENV=3:J=Y-9
2120 FORX=1TOP:N=((I-1)*P)+X
2130 Q$(X)=MID$(P$(N,V),((J*8)-7),8)
2140 NEXTX:GOSUB10
2145 IFM>1ANDY<MTHENFORX=1TOP:Q$(X)=V$+V$:NEXTX:GOSUB10
2150 NEXTY:GOSUB20:NEXTI:PRINT#1:PRINT#1:F=F+2:GOSUB60:NEXTZ:PRINT#1:PRI
2160 F=F+2:NEXTK
```

TT6 – Printing individual timetables

```
2190 FORX=1TO(P*D):P$(X,4)="":NEXTX
2200 FORY=1TOT
2210 FORN=1TO(P*D)
2220 FORX=1TO3:P$(N,X)="":NEXTX:V=0
2230 FORK=1TOC
2240 M=((LEN(A$(N,K)))/5)
2250 FORJ=1TOM
2260 IFMID$(A$(N,K),((J*5)-3),2)=T$(1,Y)THENGOSUB350:V=1:J=M:K=C
2270 NEXTJ:NEXTK
2280 IFV=0THENP$(N,4)=P$(N,4)+T$(1,Y)
2290 NEXTN
2300 IFZ2=0THEN2430
2310 FORZ=1TOZ2
2330 PRINT#1,T$(2,Y)
2340 GOSUB30
2350 FORI=1TOD:Q$(0)=D$(I)
2360 FORX=1TOP:N=((I-1)*P)+X
2370 Q$(X)=P$(N,1)+V$+P$(N,2)
2380 NEXTX:GOSUB10:Q$(0)=V$
2390 FORX=1TOP
2400 Q$(X)="  "+P$(((I-1)*P)+X,3)+"  "
2410 NEXTX:GOSUB10:GOSUB20
2420 NEXTI:PRINT#1:PRINT#1:F=F+2
2425 GOSUB60:NEXTZ:PRINT#1:PRINT#1:F=F+2
2430 NEXTY
2440 PRINT#1,"█ STAFF NOT TEACHING:"
2450 GOSUB400
2600 FORX=1TO(P*D):P$(X,4)="":NEXTX
2610 FORY=1TOR
2620 FORN=1TO(P*D)
2630 FORX=1TO3:P$(N,X)="":NEXTX:V=0
2640 FORK=1TOC
2650 M=((LEN(A$(N,K)))/5)
2660 FORJ=1TOM
2670 IFMID$(A$(N,K),((J*5)-1),2)=R$(Y)THENV=1:GOSUB150:J=M:K=C
2680 NEXTJ:NEXTK
2690 IFV=0THENP$(N,4)=P$(N,4)+R$(Y)
2700 NEXTN
2710 IFZ3=0THEN2840
2720 FORZ=1TOZ3
2740 PRINT#1,"ROOM "R$(Y)
2750 GOSUB30
2760 FORI=1TOD:Q$(0)=D$(I)
2770 FORX=1TOP:N=((I-1)*P)+X
2780 Q$(X)=P$(N,1)
2790 NEXTX:GOSUB10:Q$(0)=V$
2800 FORX=1TOP:N=((I-1)*P)+X
2810 Q$(X)=P$(N,2)+"  "+P$(N,3)
2820 NEXTX:GOSUB10:GOSUB20
2830 NEXTI:PRINT#1:PRINT#1:F=F+2:GOSUB60:NEXTZ:PRINT#1:PRINT#1:F=F+:
2840 NEXTY
2860 PRINT#1,"█ FREE ROOMS:"
2870 GOSUB400
2900 PRINT"DO YOU WISH TO PRINT ANY FURTHER"
2910 PRINT"COPIES WHILE THE DATA IS STILL STORED?
2920 PRINT"(YES OR NO)
2930 CLOSE1:INPUTQ$
2940 IFQ$="YES"THENV=5:GOTO700
2950 IFQ$="NO"THEN END
2960 GOTO2920
READY.
```

Bibliography

Brookes, J.E., Dixon, C., and Zarraga, M.N., *The Mechanics of School Timetabling,* School Timetabling Applications Group 1975
A short, straightforward introduction to the principle of compatibility, conflict matrices and schematic diagrams.

Brookes, J.E., *Management in Education, Unit 9 - School Timetabling,* Open University 1976
Includes part of the previous book, a comparison of the thinking behind different computer systems, a closer look at the Nor-Data system and a case study analysis.

Brookes, J.E., *Timetable Planning,* Heinemann 1980
Includes detailed descriptions of conflict matrices, schematic diagrams, schematic matrices and solution space diagrams.

Davies, T.I., *School Organisation,* Pergamon 1969
The original statement on the methods of staff deployment analysis, but very difficult to read; definitely not recommended.

Delacour, A.W. *Logical Timetabling,* Pulin Publishing 1971
A wordy book, covers the timetabling process but never quite gets down to details.

Gray, H.L., Chapter 2.9 in Dobson, Gear and Westoby (eds.), *Management in Education, reader 2 - some techniques and systems,* Open University 1975
A look at block timetabling.

Local Authorities Management Services and Computer Committee, *Computer Assisted School Timetabling - project report,* LAMSAC 1978
Compares the three main computer systems and includes details of various option sorting programs. Available from LAMSAC, 3 Buckingham Gate, London SW1; price £3.50.

Lawrie, N., and Veitch, H., *Timetabling and Organisation in Secondary Schools*, NFER 1975

Includes examples of Scottish option pools, a survey of the sequences in which timetablers tackle the problem and an interesting review of computer timetabling.

Lewis, C.R., *The School Timetable*, Cambridge University Press 1961

A short, readable book, but based on simple grammar school curricula.

Reid, M.I., Barnett, B.R., and Rosenberg, H.A. *A Matter of Choice – a study of guidance and subject options*, NFER 1974

Includes the results of research into how pupils choose their options, and gives some examples of option pools.

Salt, F.B., *Timetabling Models for Secondary Schools*, NFER 1978

If you are prepared to allocate the same number of periods to each department or faculty, this may be the book for you.

Walton, J. (ed.), *The Secondary School Timetable*, Ward Lock 1972

Desultory treatment of timetabling; contains one good chapter on block timetabling.

Index

assessing the timetable, 132

balancing departments, 50-1
block timetabling, 133-4
bonus, 38 ff., 45, 48
   relative 43, 45, 46, 48, 91, 92, 144, 175
booklet
   curriculum, 51-3, 55, 97, 103
   options, 13, 22, 23

Clash Table, 26 ff., 98
class-combinations, 73-4
Combing Chart, 54, 60ff.
compatibility, principle of, 62-3, 115
   and classes, 73-4
   and rooms, 75, 90, 115
   and teachers, 62 ff., 115
   and time, 72-3
compromises, 58-9
computer programs, 24, 25, 27, 31, 32, 33, 48, 67, 84, 97, 98, 132, 135, 148 ff.
Conflict Matrix, 77 ff., 103, 192
contact ratio, 42, 44, 48, 91, 144, 175
'courses' option pools, 18
curriculum analysis, *see* staff deployment analysis
Curriculum Booklet, 51-3, 55, 97, 103
Curriculum Equation, 43, 46, 144
Curriculum formulae, 43, 46, 48, 93, 144, ff.
Curriculum Plan, 11, 13, 51-3, 97, 103, 127
curriculum unit, 37, 42, 90, 144

distributing the timetable, 131-2

'faculty' option pools, 17 ff.
flexibility, 18, 62, 63, 67, 70, 72, 73, 80, 82, 84, 87, 92, 95, 96, 98, 100, 106, 110 114, 117-18, 130
flow chart
   complete, 140 ff.
   outline, 10

Form-Tutors, 16, 55, 56, 57
formulae, 43, 46, 48, 93, 144 ff.
'free choice' option pools, 15 ff., 134

heterogeneous pools, 15 ff., 134
homogeneous pools, 17 ff.

Johnson's rule, 46, 92, 93, 129, 147

minority subjects, 99–100
models of timetabling, 106 ff., 136

nomogram
   staff, 45–7
   rooms, 46–7, 91–2
Nor-Data system, 137–8

OPT1 program, 24, 27, 31, 32, 33, 98, 148 ff.
OPT2 program, 31, 32, 33, 148–9, 155 ff.
OPT3 program, 32, 148–9, 161 ff.
OPT4 program, 33, 148–9, 165 ff.
OPT5 program, 33, 148–9, 169 ff.
OPT6 program, 148–9, 172 ff.
option group lists, 33, 148–9, 165 ff.
option pools, 13, 14 ff. 97–9
Options Booklet, 13, 22, 23
Options Form, 13, 24
options, Sixth Year, 33, 97–100
Oxford system, 139

part-time teachers, 54, 55, 84, 102
period-breakdown, 29, 51, 52, 58, 65, 70, 72, 80, 81–4, 100, 127, 128
principle of compatibility, 62–3, 115
   and classes, 73–4
   and rooms, 75, 90, 115
   and teachers, 62 ff., 115
   and time, 72–3
priorities, 76, 80, 81, 89, 101 ff., 114, 115

quality, 125, 128–9, 132

relative bonus, 43, 45, 46, 48, 91, 92, 144
room-combinations, 75, 90
rooming, 84, 104, 129–30
rooming equation, 46, 90, 145

216 Index

rooming fraction, 46, 86–90, 92, 94, 104, 144, 175
rules for timetabling, 112–13, 114 ff.

scheduling, 13, 58, 76, 84, 105, ff.
Schematic Diagram, 71–2, 73, 82–4, 99, 100
Sixth Form, 33, 41, 45, 90, 97–100
SPL system, 138
split-site schools, 55, 56, 103, 147
staff deployment analysis, 11, 35 ff., 144 ff., 175 ff
Staff Loading Chart, 13, 55–7, 103
staff loading factor, 43
staffing equation, 43, 144
Staffing Forms, 13, 53–5, 59, 73
staffing ratio, 41, 42, 45, 48, 146

teacher-teams, 59, 103
timetable
  assessing, 132
  booklet, 131
  cards, 109–12
  checking, 130–1
  cycles, 72, 73, 88, 128, 133
  distributing, 131–2
  homework, 131
  models, 106 ff., 136
  of timetabling, 13
timetabling
  block, 133–4
  computer, 135 ff.
TT1 program, 48, 175 ff.
TT2 program, 67, 188 ff.
TT3 program, 84, 192 ff.
TT4 program, 97, 197 ff.
TT5 program, 201 ff.
TT6 program, 132, 203 ff.

Zarraga's rule, 96–7, 118, 126, 197 ff.

```
       OPT2 IMPROVMENT #1
      EQUALIZES GROUP SIZES IF
      THE OPTION POOLS ARE CYCLIC

200 IF R(I1,J1)>R(I2,J2) THEN I1=I2:J1=J2
205 S$(I1)=P$(I1,J1)


       OPT2 IMPROVEMENT #2
      FOR SPEED   20% FASTER

792 FOR X=1 TO P:F=0
793 FOR I=1 TO P:FOR J=1 TO Q
794 IF Y$(I)=Q$(X,J) THEN F=F+1:J1=J:K=I:J=Q
795 NEXT J:NEXT I
796 IF F=1 THEN I1=X:GOSUB 205
797 NEXT X
799 K=0:F=0
```

```
       OPT4 IMPROVEMENT
       SHELL-METZNER SORT
       6 TIMES FASTER FOR 100 NAMES
      12 TIMES FASTER FOR 200 NAMES

800 M=B
810 M=INT(M/2):IF M=0 THEN 900
820 K=B-M:J=1
830 I=J
840 F=I+M:IF B$(I)>B$(F) THEN 860
850 GOTO 890
860 PRINT".";:T$=B$(I):B$(I)=B$(F):B$(F)=T$
870 I=I-M:IF I<1 THEN 890
880 GOTO 840
890 J=J+1:IF J>K THEN 810
895 GOTO 830
900 IF G=0 THEN 1000
905 M=G
910 M=INT(M/2):IF M=0 THEN 1000
920 K=G-M:J=1
930 I=J
940 F=I+M:IF G$(I)>G$(F) THEN 960
950 GOTO 990
960 PRINT".";:T$=G$(I):G$(I)=G$(F):G$(F)=T$
970 I=I-M
980 IF I<1 THEN 990
985 GOTO 940
990 J=J+1:IF J>K THEN 910
995 GOTO 930
```